INDEX MUTUAL FUNDS

PROFITING FROM AN INVESTMENT REVOLUTION

W. SCOTT SIMON

NAMBORN PUBLISHING CO.
CAMARILLO, CALIFORNIA

Namborn Publishing Co.
P.O. Box 3131
Camarillo, California 93011-3131

Typeface: 11/13 Times Roman

Printer: Publishers Press

Printed in the United States of America

Publisher's Cataloging-in-Publication
(Provided by Quality Books, Inc.)

Simon, W. Scott
  Index mutual funds : profiting from an investment revolution / by W. Scott Simon. -- 1st ed.
  p. cm.
  Includes index

  1. Mutual funds.   I. Title.
HG4530.S56 1998   332.63'27
                                          QBI97-41220
  ISBN 0-9661172-7-1

Library of Congress Catalog Card Number: 97-92705

To My Mother And Father For All That They Have Done For Me

FOREWORD

The simple case for index funds is part theory, part practice, and part arithmetic. Theory says that since (a) gross returns earned by investors as a group must equal the gross returns earned by the total stock market, (b) net returns - after advisory fees and other investment expenses - earned by investors as a group must fall short of the returns of the market by the amount of those costs.

Practice confirms the theory. Returns earned by the average equity mutual fund in the past have typically fallen short of the returns on appropriate stock market indexes by an amount approximately equal to the operating expenses and transaction costs incurred by the funds. Over the past 25 years, the average fund has earned annual returns averaging 11.6% compared to a return of 13.1% for the Standard & Poor's 500 Stock Index, a shortfall of 1.5 percentage points per year. In fact, only 32% of actively managed equity funds have outpaced this unmanaged index, and no one has ever suggested a methodology by which those few winners could have been selected in advance.

And simple arithmetic makes it clear that this difference is critically important. Over 25 years, a $10,000 investment in the Index would have risen in value to $217,100, compared to $155,500 in the average fund. This shortfall - $61,600 - is clearly enormous. For over time, the miracle of compounding changes a difference *in degree* in annual return to a difference *in kind* in capital accumulation. *Costs matter.* That sums up the simple case for index funds.

Intelligent investors, however, will want more information about index funds, and you deserve it. Here is where W. Scott Simon's book enters the picture. *Index Mutual Funds: Profiting from an Investment Revolution* presents the complex case for index funds, an assiduous analysis of mutual fund past performance and a careful articulation of how index funds work, followed by a discussion of the role of index funds in an asset allocation program and their special cost, risk, and tax characteristics. I commend his fine book to you, for I believe index funds have a vital role to play in enhancing the long-term returns of your investment program.

I think it is fair to place myself in the first wave of believers in the merits of market indexing. Indeed, within a year after I founded The Vanguard Group in 1974, we formed the first index mutual fund. It began operations in 1976 with just $11 million in assets. The going was slow at first, for the idea was rife that "Index funds are un-American" and represented an acceptance of mediocrity. Vanguard's "First Index Investment Trust" (now known as the 500 Portfolio of Vanguard Index Trust) was described as "Bogle's folly" more times than I care to count.

Competitors simply didn't believe - or didn't want to believe - that indexing made consummate sense and, given its low costs, was predictably capable of providing superior economic value to shareholders. In this industry where rapid copying of marketable ideas is a way of life, something much better - a sound new idea - wasn't copied for a decade, and acceptance proceeded at a truly glacial pace.

But our index fund grew over the years, as it fulfilled its performance promise. By early 1992, when its assets had gradually increased to $4.3 billion, it was the 7th largest U.S. equity fund. Encouraged by the past and optimistic about the future, I publicly predicted that "market indexing will come into its own as a major force . . . and that by the turn of the twentieth century, our index fund will be the largest equity fund in the world."

By 1995, we had grown ever bolder, publishing a booklet entitled "The Triumph of Indexing." I noted the remarkable success of index investment strategies over the long term, even as I disavowed the notion that the then-recent performance of the Standard & Poor's 500 Index - it had outpaced 85% of all managed equity funds over the previous three years - was either sustainable or repeatable.

As it happened, I was wrong. The Index record soared to even higher levels, outpacing more than 90% of all funds since then. As a result, index funds became the "industry darling," according to *The Wall Street Journal*. Some 200 index funds have been formed to capitalize on the boom led by our pioneering index fund. Investor interest in index funds soared.

Investors, I fear, are making the right decision, but for the wrong reasons. Indexing owes much of its recent popularity, not to a recognition of the case for index funds as a sound long-term investment - based on the theory, practice, and arithmetic I postulated at the outset - but to a desire to own a top-performing fund based on a truly remarkable short-term record. The recent record of superiority of funds modeled to match the returns of the Standard & Poor's 500 Index, I would warrant, will not long continue, and may well disappoint for a time, even as its long-term superiority should prevail.

In short, as the saying goes, "having survived defeat, a good idea can also survive victory." And index funds of all types - those based on the total stock market, or various stock market segments, or for that matter the bond market, as well as those based on the S&P 500 Index - will continue to flourish for investors with patience, perspective, and conviction. And with the assets of the 500 Portfolio of Vanguard Index Trust now at $45 billion - second largest in the industry and rapidly closing on the leader - my rash prediction that it will be the largest equity fund by the turn of the century, now barely two years away, may not seem so far fetched after all.

John C. Bogle
Chairman
The Vanguard Group of Investment Companies
July 29, 1997

ACKNOWLEDGMENTS

No one can write a book alone. I wish to thank my colleagues at Silver Oak Advisory Group, especially Bruce J. Temkin and Deborah L. Thomas, for their tremendous help and support. Bruce truly is a teacher in the best sense of the word. He challenges many of the assumptions underlying some of the most commonly accepted ideas in the investment arena. As a result of our numerous discussions, I have gained a deeper understanding of the complexities of the investment process and have attempted to impart an understanding of some of them in this book. Deborah has been most helpful in providing her unique insights about many of the investment and financial issues that confront investors today.

I would also like to thank the following people for reading all or parts of the manuscript and offering thoughtful suggestions about ways to improve it: George U. Sauter at the Vanguard Group of Investment Companies, Rex A. Sinquefield, Weston J. Wellington and Arthur H.F. Barlow at Dimensional Fund Advisors Inc., Campbell R. Harvey at Duke University's Fuqua School of Business, John B. Shoven, Charles Schwab Professor of Economics at Stanford University's Graduate School of Business, Robert D. Arnott at First Quadrant Corporation, Harry M. Markowitz, Nobel Laureate in Economic Science and Edward C. Halbach, Jr., Reporter, *Restatement (Third) of Trusts* and Professor of Law, Boalt Hall, University of California.

Others who were of immense help to me were Jeffrey C. Mayhew, Douglas A. Tooth, Maron Moses, Theodore K. Rich, Mary Markarian Trimarco and Richard J. Simon. David A. Schaechtel provided extensive technical assistance in producing this book. Scott J. Blackburn at Lipper Analytical Services, Inc. most kindly furnished certain investment data. A special thanks is due Rose Marie Suarez for her endless word processing of the manuscript.

I am particularly grateful to John C. Bogle, founder and Chairman of the Vanguard Group of Investment Companies, for his willingness to write the foreword to this book. He has done more than any other individual to further the cause of index funds and the interests of the investing public in general. Many American investors as well as those in other parts of the world owe him an enormous debt of gratitude.

Last, but certainly not least, I want to acknowledge Campbell, who was with me every step of the way.

While I have tried to minimize the errors in this book, it is certain that some remain. It is also certain that I alone am responsible for them.

W.S.S.

PREFACE

This book is a complete departure from investment books which purport to teach investors how to "beat the market." Instead, it explains why relatively few long term investors are able to achieve this goal. A multitude of academic studies over the last 30 years that has examined the stock picking and market timing records of mutual fund and pension fund managers confirms this. In fact, these studies prove conclusively that a heavy majority of actively-managed funds *underperform* the market.

But haven't superstar mutual fund managers such as Peter Lynch, John Templeton and John Neff and other stock pickers such as Warren Buffett been able to beat the market? Of course they have, yet the inescapable fact is that these tiny few investment wizards can only be identified years later *after* they have run the race. Years *before* at the beginning of the race, they could have never been separated out from the others who had all assembled with them on the starting line.

The same maddening logic also applies to efforts made today to pick out the future Lynches, Templetons, Neffs and Buffetts. These efforts are even more futile now because there are so many more professional stock pickers to select from compared to when these legends started their investment careers.

However, none of this should distress an investor because there is a solution. That solution is to create a properly diversified portfolio of index mutual funds and invest in it for life. At first this may be surprising since indexing is often derided as a "mediocre" investment approach that only achieves the average market return. But the ironic fact is that an investor who is well educated about indexing and remains committed to it over the long run is likely to secure investment performance superior to that earned by most investors who pick stocks (and mutual funds) and time markets.

The reason for this is that an indexer's portfolio bears low costs and taxes. Thus, its net performance virtually matches the market return. In contrast, the typical investor who picks stocks and/or times markets holds an investment portfolio that generates high costs and taxes. Its net performance therefore falls below the market return.

This is why a committed indexer is likely to outperform, over the long run, most active investors, whether professional or amateur, even though he 'only' earns the average market return. As a result, an indexer can be a *superior* investor without needing to beat the market.

W. Scott Simon

ABOUT THE AUTHOR

W. Scott Simon is a principal with Silver Oak Advisory Group. Silver Oak is a fee only investment advisory and financial consulting firm with offices in Encino, California, Sacramento, California and Portland, Oregon. Its clients include individuals, corporations, pension and profit sharing plans and private trusts.

Silver Oak specializes in creating, implementing and managing portfolios of index mutual funds. The firm's philosophy is grounded in the belief that its clients should be thoroughly educated about the realities of the investment process before they invest their money.

Prior to joining Silver Oak, Mr. Simon was an investment advisor and developed numerous educational programs on investing with special emphasis on investment and portfolio theory. He also previously practiced business, corporate and tax law. It is Mr. Simon's investment expertise combined with his legal experience that uniquely qualifies him to help investors meet their investment goals.

AN IMPORTANT NOTE

In writing this book it was infinitely easier and less cumbersome to use single personal pronouns. For this reason, only "he" and "him" appear in the text. In every other respect these pronouns should be regarded as interchangeable with "she" and "her." As such, no difference should be read into the investment expertise (or lack thereof) between men and women for the simple reason that there is none.

TABLE OF CONTENTS

INTRODUCTION

SECTION I

WHY THE INDEXING REVOLUTION WAS NECESSARY

THEME OF THE SECTION:

THE SHORTCOMINGS OF THE TRADITIONAL SYSTEM OF INVESTING

xvi

SECTION II

INDEX MUTUAL FUNDS: A REVOLUTIONARY CALL TO ARMS

THEME OF THE SECTION:

*INDEX MUTUAL FUNDS ARE THE BEST INVESTMENT CHOICE
FOR MOST INVESTORS*

UNDERSTANDING THE BASICS

THE SPECIFIC ADVANTAGES OF INDEX MUTUAL FUNDS

SECTION III

JOINING THE INDEXING REVOLUTION

THEME OF THE SECTION:

*A SUMMARY OF WHY INVESTORS SHOULD INVEST IN
INDEX MUTUAL FUNDS*

SIMON SAYS INDEX

INTRODUCTION

ONE

THE SECOND WAVE OF AN INVESTMENT REVOLUTION

[Most investors would] be better off in an index mutual fund.[1]
- Peter Lynch (1943-   )

Overview

Investors who invest in index mutual funds are participating in the beginning of the second wave of an investment revolution. Although indexing is only starting to catch on with individual investors, their past behavior has shown that they inevitably follow the investment practices of major institutional investors. Since American institutional investors index about 35% of all money that they invest in stocks and individual investors index only about 6%, individual investors can be expected to invest an increasingly greater percentage of money in index funds in the future.

The Genesis Of An Investment Revolution

It is July 1971. Samsonite, the luggage manufacturer, has withdrawn $6 million from its corporate pension plan and contributed it to an institutional index fund set up by Wells Fargo Bank. This is the first investment in the world's first index fund and it is the genesis of an investment revolution.[2]

Flash forward a quarter century. Approximately *one trillion dollars* is invested in index funds in this country and elsewhere in the world.[3] Why did this revolution in the investment and management of money occur? What are the advantages of index funds and how can individual investors profit from them? This book will provide the answers to these and other important questions.

What Is An "Index Mutual Fund?"

Before proceeding any further, it is necessary to first briefly define the subject of this book. An "index mutual fund" attempts to *provide the investment performance of its underlying index* by holding all (or a sample) of the individual stocks or bonds that are represented in the index. (This is how an "index" fund gets its name.) For example, the Vanguard S&P 500 index fund seeks to provide the investment performance of the stocks in the S&P 500 stock index by holding them in the same proportionate amounts as they are represented in the index.

How well an index fund meets the goal of providing the performance of the fund's underlying index is determined by how closely its manager *matches* the composition of the stocks or bonds held by the fund to the composition of the stocks or bonds represented in the index. (Chapter Nine fully explores the nuts and bolts of an index fund.)

The goal of an index fund is *not* to "beat the market." In this way, an index fund radically differs from an "actively-managed" mutual fund. That kind of mutual fund employs a manager who attempts to beat the market by "picking stocks." (These attempts may also involve "market timing" which is separately discussed in Chapter Seven). The vast majority of mutual fund investors invest in actively-managed (or "active") funds.

Attempts to beat the market with smart stock picking involve a process whose goal is to identify (1) undervalued stocks and purchase them and (2) overvalued stocks and sell them (or not buy them in the first place and avoid them altogether). (Chapter Two discusses how stock pickers identify "undervalued" and "overvalued" stocks.) In this process, an active mutual fund manager (or any other active money manager[4] or amateur or professional investor) usually employs some particular "investment style." This involves a certain approach to selecting individual stocks such as "growth" stocks or "value" stocks.

SIMON SAYS: *First Things First*

It is important to understand at the outset that one of the main contentions of this book is that there is no difference among the abilities of individual investors, professional investment advisors, mutual fund managers or any others to beat the market. Each of these groups is in the same boat in terms of its potential to beat the market: none can be expected to do it and none is any more likely than the other in expecting to do it.

In addition, this book makes no distinction between "picking stocks" and "picking mutual funds." Hence, the term "picking stocks" includes the term "picking mutual funds" (and vice versa). So any reference to "an investor picking stocks" includes individual investors, professional investment advisors, mutual fund managers and any others picking stocks and mutual funds.

Institutional Investors: The First Wave Of The Indexing Revolution

Revolutions arise in order to change the way that things have been done and to do away with the old order. The first wave of the indexing revolution began to sweep through the world of institutional investing a quarter century ago. ("Institutional investors" are entities such as public and corporate pension plans, educational endowment funds, charitable trusts and foundations, insurance companies and banks who invest their own assets or those held in trust for others.)

The way that things had been done prior to the indexing revolution involved attempts by those who managed money for institutional investors to beat the market with smart stock picking and artful market timing. Indeed, these managers who represented the old order were all convinced that they could consistently beat the market. The only issue in doubt from year to year was the number of percentage points by which they would achieve this goal.

However, the agonizingly painful and lengthy 21-month down market of 1973-1974 wiped out as much as one-half the value of many institutional investment portfolios. These losses were so devastating that some institutional investors completely fled the stock market. Yet this investment bloodbath only confirmed what some at these institutions had already learned from academic studies that had been appearing for almost a decade. These studies quite clearly found that the average money manager who picked stocks and timed markets not only failed to beat the market but often significantly underperformed it. The money managers who made up this average came from the ranks of those employed by institutional investors.

Some of those responsible for overseeing institutional investment portfolios realized that the way that things had been done - trying to beat the market by picking stocks and timing markets - wasn't working very well anymore. They understood that the institutions that employed them were getting less in investment performance from their money managers and paying them more in investment fees. These individuals knew that there was a better way to manage money. Things had to change. The old order had to be swept away. As a result, this small group became the revolutionary vanguard that spearheaded the indexing revolution.

What made this movement so revolutionary was that its leaders were the first to envision the enormously significant implications of certain investment theories such as the Efficient Market Theory and Modern Portfolio Theory.[5] This revolutionary clique could see that index funds were the most efficient and effective way to put these exciting theories into practice in order to enhance investment return and/or decrease risk. At the time these individuals initially mounted the ramparts a quarter century ago, the investment portfolios that they supervised became the first to invest in index funds. When this happened, a revolution was launched in the way that money would be managed throughout the world.

After Samsonite made the inaugural investment in the world's first index fund, the original index fund created for use by an investment advisor's own clients was introduced by American National Bank of Chicago in 1973.[6] Two years later, the New York Telephone Co. placed $40 million of its pension assets in an S&P 500 index fund, the earliest major retirement plan sponsor to make this kind of investment. In 1976, Vanguard created the world's first index mutual fund for individual investors.

These were the first shots fired in the indexing revolution. Initially, they didn't have much of an impact because indexing was greeted with open skepticism by many parts of the institutional investment community. As recently as 1973, only $50 million was invested in index funds. But since then, institutional investors, which are among the largest and most sophisticated in the world, have widely adopted indexing investment strategies. Indeed, indexing has become the very foundation of many institutional investment portfolios in America.

The great bulk of indexed money is held by institutional investors.[7] (It should be noted, however, that a majority of institutional money is still managed by those who pick stocks and time markets.) This is concrete evidence that the battle over the acceptance of indexing as a viable and even clearly superior investment strategy has already been fought and won by the institutional advocates of indexing.

Institutional Investors That Are Taking Part In The Investment Revolution

Indexing continues to spread among institutional investors. More and more of them are opting out of high cost actively-managed funds in favor of index funds. For example, Intel, the manufacturer of computer chips, fired its army of investment advisors and became another large corporation that has switched to indexing. An Intel spokesman explained:[8] "Our goal had been to try to outperform the index fund and over the last five years we have failed to meet that goal. So we decided to change our goal to staying with the equity [index] fund." The outside advisors who picked stocks for

Intel's $1 billion retirement plans were replaced by Intel's own corporate in-house money managers who invest in index funds.

Index fund managers are able to keep investment expenses low because they do not make costly "bets" on individual stocks or specific industry sectors in attempts to beat the market. Kimberly-Clark estimates that, by avoiding these bets and indexing its pension assets, it will save about $100 million in expenses over the coming decade. This company currently indexes 90% of its $2 billion pension plan.[9] When companies such as Intel and Kimberly-Clark invest in index funds and thereby sharply reduce costs, they can actually increase investment performance without needing to beat the market.

Some of the institutional investors that index their investments are shown in Illustration 1 on page 8. One investor on this list is the Teachers Insurance and Annuity Association and College Retirement Equities Fund (TIAA-CREF). TIAA-CREF is a nationwide pension system for employees of colleges, universities, teaching hospitals, museums and other non-profit educational organizations. It has more than 5,500 institutional and 1.8 million individual participants. All told, TIAA-CREF manages nearly $200 billion. TIAA is the portion of the pension plan that holds the fixed-income portfolio and CREF is the portion that holds the stock portfolio. 65% of CREF's $81 billion stock portfolio is indexed to the Russell 3000 index.[10]

Another institutional investor listed in Illustration 1 is the California Public Employees' Retirement System (CALPERS). CALPERS manages a total of $100.7 billion[11] on behalf of 1.1 million current and retired California public employees. 85% of the $41.3 billion invested in domestic stocks by CALPERS is indexed to the Wilshire 2500 stock index.

50% of the state of Connecticut's $14.6 billion pension fund is invested in index funds.[11] One advantage that this offers is a vast savings in money management costs. For example, the expense of managing Connecticut's S&P 500 index fund runs about one-third the amount that would be charged by active money managers.

The Los Angeles County Employees Retirement Association (LACERA) currently invests $20.2 billion.[13] Approximately 30% of this total is indexed to the S&P 500, the Russell 2000 Value, EAFE and the Lehman Brothers Aggregate Bond indexes. By indexing a significant portion of its pension fund assets, LACERA can markedly cut costs and improve the bottom line return for its many investors who are current and retired public employees.[14]

Illustration 1

Some Institutional Investors Invested In Index Funds

Alabama Employees' Retirement System	Kysor Industrial Corporation
Alabama Teachers' Retirement System	Maryland State Retirement Systems
American Cyanamid	Michigan Department of Treasury
Amoco Corporation	State of Mississippi
Associated Benefits Corporation	University of Nevada
AT&T Corporation	New York State Common Retirement Fund
Atlantic Mutual Insurance Companies	New York State Teachers Retirement System
Baptist General Conference	
BellSouth Corporation	Northern Illinois Gas Company
Blue Cross of California	NYNEX Corporation
Boise Cascade Corporation	Owens-Corning Fiberglass
British Telecom Staff Superannuation Scheme	Owens-Illinois, Inc.
California Public Employees' Retirement System	Pacific Telesis
	Pennsylvania Teachers Retirement Fund
Ceco Corporation	Peoples Energy Corporation
College Retirement Equities Fund	PepsiCo, Inc.
Colorado Public Employees Retirement System	Post Office Staff Superannuation Scheme
	The Rand Corporation
Continental Corporation	Rolls Royce Ltd. Works and Staff Pension Fund
Credit Union National Association	
Charles A. Dana Foundation	Sandia Corporation
Decision Focus Inc.	Sara Lee Corporation
Deere & Company	City of Seattle
Florida State Board of Administration	City of Sioux Falls
GE Investment	Southern California Edison
General Motors Corporation	The Spencer Foundation
Gerber Products Company	St. Louis Public Schools Retirement System
W.W. Grainger, Inc.	
W.R. Grace & Co.	Stanford University
Gulf States Paper Corporation	State Farm Insurance Companies
Health Care Service Corporation	Sunkist Growers Inc.
IBM Corporation	Sutter Health
Illinois Municipal Retirement Fund	Tektronix, Inc.
INCO United States, Inc.	The Timken Company
Interco	Tribune Company
International Brotherhood of Teamsters	United Mine Workers of America
James S. McDonnell Foundation	United Telecommunications, Inc.
City of Kalamazoo	Unocal
County of Kalamazoo	The Upjohn Company
K Mart Corporation	Utah State Retirement System
Kentucky Teachers' Retirement System	Washington University

Source: Dimensional Fund Advisors Inc., Standard & Poor's and Teachers Insurance and Annuity Association and College Retirement Equities Fund (TIAA-CREF).

Individual Investors: The Second Wave Of The Indexing Revolution

The second wave of the indexing revolution has been led by individual investors who invest in index mutual funds. Despite the fact that index mutual funds have exploded in popularity over the past several years, individual investors index only about 7% of the money that they invest in stocks and bonds.[15]

Yet even though indexing is only starting to catch on with individual investors, index funds will eventually be the investment choice for many of them. The reason why is that individual investors inevitably follow the investment practices of major institutional investors.[16] Since American institutional investors now index about 35% of all money that they invest in stocks,[17] we can expect individual investors to invest an increasingly greater percentage of money in index funds in the future.

The second wave of the indexing revolution will gather momentum as more and more investors are exposed to the many advantages of indexing, they gain a fuller understanding of the typically large difference between pre-tax and after-tax investment returns and indexing penetrates into more and more kinds of investments.

SIMON SAYS: *There Are Indexers And Then There Are Those Who Invest In Index Funds*

The term "indexer" as used in this book only includes those investors who have a thorough understanding of the reasons why they invest in index funds. These are investors who are well educated about the whys and wherefores of indexing and as a result will remain committed to it over the long run.

This term does *not* include investors who have little understanding of why they are invested in index funds. These investors invest in index funds simply because they are a current investment fad and/or because they are chasing after high returns. Since such investors have no real commitment to indexing, many of them will flee index funds at the first sign of a market downturn.

Is The Case For Index Mutual Funds Overstated?

Don Phillips, president of Morningstar, believes that the case for indexing "is overstated."[18] For example, when advocates of index fund investing present their evidence to investors, they usually make a statement such as this: "Over the long run, an index fund mimicking the performance of the S&P 500 stock index will beat 65% [or 75% or 80%] of all actively-managed mutual funds that pick stocks and/or time markets." (This leads many investors to falsely believe that it is the *same* 35% (or 25% or 20%) of actively-managed mutual funds that outperform an S&P 500 index fund. However, while on average a certain percentage of these funds will beat such an index fund every year, the individual winners making up the percentage *change* from year to year.[19])

Many critics of indexing point out that over the last ten years the large company stocks of the S&P 500 (and thus S&P 500 index funds) have turned in abnormally strong performances. Since many actively-managed mutual funds invest in at least some small company stocks, it is no wonder, these critics explain, why high percentages of active funds during this period have underperformed the large company stocks that comprise the S&P 500. For example, over the decade ending in mid-1995, the S&P 500 beat 83% of all general stock mutual funds.[20] Once taxes are factored in, this figure rises to about 90%.[21]

But indexing critics are quick to remind investors that once small company stocks again outperform large company stocks, many active funds that invest in small stocks will outperform the S&P 500. Indeed, in most of the years during the second half of the 1970s and the early 1980s a majority of active mutual funds did outperform the S&P 500. (In spite of this, the S&P 500 still managed to outperform about 65% of all active funds over the 25-year period of 1971-1995.[22])

But whether the stated percentage of active funds that underperform the market over a given time period is high or low, the *actual percentage will always be higher*. This is true for the following three reasons.

First, mutual fund data upon which the stated percentages are based does not measure the enormous effect that taxes and, to a lesser extent, commission loads have on an investor's fund performance.

Second, this data does not take into consideration how the "negative compounding effect" of taxes, annual operating expenses, trading costs and commission loads (examined in Chapter Twelve) against accumulating wealth in a mutual fund impacts its performance. This impact, which is present in any mutual fund, is generally more severe in active funds and becomes increasingly so the longer a person remains invested in such funds. It is yet another factor increasing the actual percentage of active funds that underperform the market.

Third, this percentage is further increased by taking into account the "survivorship bias" (examined in Chapter Eight) that is inherent in mutual fund ratings.

After allowing for these three factors, it is very likely that the actual percentages of active funds underperforming the market are too low even when the stated percentages are 65%, 75%, 80% or more. Thus, the case for indexing as it is usually presented to the investing public is not over-stated but may well be *understated!*

Will Active Mutual Funds Continue To Underperform The Market In The Future?

One of the themes of this book is that attempts to predict the future are not very profitable expenditures of time or money. But there are a number of reasons why it can be expected that a large majority of actively-man-aged mutual funds will continue to underperform the market in the future. (This is true whether "the market" is defined as the U.S. stock market whose performance is measured by the S&P 500 index or the Wilshire 5000 index,[23] the U.S. bond market whose performance is measured by The Lehman Brothers Aggregate Bond Index or the Salomon Brothers Broad Investment Grade Bond Index or even portions of these markets or other markets whose performances are measured by other more special-ized indexes.)

First, as we will see in Chapter Three, any financial market is a zero sum game. This means that, after costs and taxes, the average actively-managed dollar will always underperform the average indexed dollar (and therefore the markets in which all these dollars are invested). *This is a simple law of arithmetic that will not go away in the future.*

Second, the investment costs associated with actively-managed mutual funds have generally trended upward over the last decade.[24] This has oc-curred despite the fact that investors have poured huge amounts of money into active funds over this period. The resulting economies of scale would seem to dictate that these funds should pass on the cost savings to their investor-shareholders. This has not happened. At the same time, the costs of investing in index funds have trended downward as they have become more popular with investors.

Naturally, there is always the possibility that the costs of active mutual funds will decrease in the future, thereby narrowing the cost gap with index funds. But all evidence to date has shown just the opposite trend - the costs of active funds continue to go up and the costs of index funds continue to go down.

Third, actively-managed mutual funds typically generate relatively large amounts of taxes while index funds generate relatively small amounts. Some of the resulting gap in performance caused by taxes would seemingly be narrowed if the federal government were to lower tax rates. Congress did this at the end of July 1997 when it reduced the maximum long term capital gains tax rate from 28% on investments held more than *one year* to 20% on investments held *18 months* or longer.[25] The tax bill provides that in the year 2001 this rate will be reduced to 18% for investments held *five years* or longer.

Even though the lowering of tax rates on long term capital gains is good news for actively-managed mutual funds, it may be even better news for index funds. The new tax law clearly encourages investors to hold on to their investments for longer periods of time. Thus, it favors indexers tax-wise because they typically do not buy and sell their mutual fund shares as often as active investors.

It is problematic that the future direction of tax rates will be a downward one since the federal government continues to face a myriad of deep-rooted fiscal and budgetary problems.[26] So active investors who may be counting on Congress to help them narrow the gap in after-tax performance with indexers may be in for a long wait.

Fourth, a trend characterizing financial markets the world over is that they are getting more efficient (the meaning of an "efficient market" is fully explored in Chapter Three). Thus, it isn't getting any easier for active money managers to outperform such markets - rather, it is increasingly difficult. Even many prominent active money managers admit this. One such manager is Ken Gregory who observes:[27] "The markets are getting more and more efficient. There's so much more data available more quickly."

While many active money managers will admit that it is getting more difficult to outperform efficient markets, they quickly add that there are plenty of opportunities to beat "inefficient markets," especially those in many foreign countries. However, as we will see in Chapter Three, the laws of arithmetic that govern the zero sum game of efficient financial markets also apply to inefficient markets. In *both* kinds of markets, the average actively-managed dollar will underperform the average indexed dollar, after costs and taxes. This is why the high costs and taxes that are usually present in inefficient financial markets such as many foreign markets often adversely impact investment performance *more* than the margin by which a money manager is able to beat such markets.

For these reasons, *it is likely that in the future a given index fund will generate net long term performance superior to most similarly invested actively-managed mutual funds.*[28] This is true for both stock and bond index funds. For example, a Wilshire 5000 index fund will likely outperform most actively-managed stock mutual funds over the long run. It is even likelier that a bond index fund that tracks the performance of a total market bond index such as the Lehman Brothers Aggregate Bond Index will outperform most active bond funds. Furthermore, index funds invested in more specialized asset classes such as foreign stocks will likely beat most active funds that invest in foreign stocks.

Testimonials To Indexing From Leading Investment Experts

John C. Bogle is one of the most respected leaders in the mutual fund industry and is Chairman of the Vanguard Group of Investment Companies, the second largest mutual fund family in the world. Bogle was the driving force in the creation of the world's first index mutual fund for individual investors in 1976. Bogle notes:[29] "Vanguard is the sole apostle of indexing" among all mutual fund companies. Approximately $85 billion is indexed by Vanguard for individual and institutional investors.

Bogle explains why indexing is such a logically compelling method of investing:[30] "In the world of investing, there are very, very few sure things. But the closest thing to a sure thing is that the Wilshire 5000 index will outperform actively-managed funds by 1.5 to 2 percentage points a year over a sustained period. The logic behind this startling fact is as follows. All mutual fund managers *together* provide *average* investment performance (those who do well are offset by those who do not do so well). But in fact, investing in an index fund that matches the average market return can be your best chance of getting an *above average* return compared to other non-indexing investors.

"There are three reasons for this: superior diversification, lower annual operating expenses and lower taxes. That's why indexers recognize that the advantages of indexing lie, not in impressive short 'sprints' of strong investment performance such as in 1995, 1996 and 1997, but with the steady, cumulative power of broad diversification and lower expenses and taxes."

Rex A. Sinquefield is Co-Chairman of Dimensional Fund Advisors Inc. Over twenty years ago, Sinquefield and Roger G. Ibbotson were the first to compile and present in an organized way historical investment data which has come to be widely used in the investment world. DFA is a worldwide leader in the practical application of academic theories to the management of asset class index funds. DFA manages more than \$20 billion for over one hundred institutional investors.

Sinquefield describes the strong theoretical support for indexing:[31] "A large volume of academic studies examining the performances of mutual funds under actual market conditions establishes very convincingly that the 'beat the market' efforts of investors who pick stocks and time markets are impressively and overwhelmingly negative. In contrast, indexing stands on solid theoretical grounds, has enormous empirical support and works very well for investors. The message of indexing is therefore unmistakably obvious: the only consistent superior performer is the market itself and the only way to capture that superior consistency is to invest in a properly diversified portfolio of index funds."

Paul A. Samuelson became the first American to win the Nobel Prize in Economic Science in 1970 and is one of the most influential economists of the twentieth century. He concisely summarizes the case for indexing:[32] "The most efficient way to diversify a stock portfolio is with a low fee index fund. Statistically, a broadly based stock index fund will outperform most actively-managed equity portfolios. Hardly ten of one thousand [money managers who pick stocks and time markets] perform in a way that convinces a jury of experts that a long term edge over indexing is likely."

Jane Bryant Quinn is the *Newsweek* financial affairs columnist and best-selling author of *Making The Most of Your Money*. She describes the problems faced by investors when they attempt to pick active mutual fund winners and how investing in index funds can avoid these problems:[33] "Indexing is for winners only. Let's see why this is true. Every month in the personal finance magazines you are seduced by the promise of Funds To Buy Now! The truth about funds on the Top Ten lists is that most of them will not do as well as the major market indexes such as the S&P 500.

"Their highly paid managers face two almost insuperable tasks. They have to pick stocks that go up in price by more than other investors expect - which usually is not possible in a world where so many players know so much. They also have to cover their costs: say, 1.5 per cent in annual expenses and for some funds, sales loads. On the other hand, index mutual funds are easy, inexpensive, save taxes and help investors diversify. In this light, it's not hard to understand that some of the most successful investments such as index funds often are the simple ones."

Burton G. Malkiel is the author of the best-selling investment guide, *A Random Walk Down Wall Street*, and a professor of economics at Princeton University. Malkiel observes:[34] "Index funds allow investors an opportunity to buy securities of all different types and are a sensible, serviceable method of obtaining the benefits of equity (as well as bond) investing with no effort, minimal expense and considerable tax savings."

Douglas Dial is portfolio manager of the CREF Stock Account Fund which is part of the Teachers Insurance and Annuity Association and College Retirement Equities Fund (TIAA-CREF). CREF is *the largest single pool of money invested in stocks in the world*. Although Dial was formerly a stock picking money manager, he has seen the light and become a strong proponent of indexing:[35] "Indexing is a marvelous technique. I wasn't a true believer. I was just an ignoramus. Now I am a convert. Indexing is an extraordinarily sophisticated thing to do."

Dial warns investors that the stock picking and market timing activities of active money managers aren't prudent because they "will produce greater deviations from market returns." "Given that these are retirement assets, avoiding the terrible downer is worth the price of missing the moon-shot years. If people want excitement, they should go to the race track or play the lottery."

The investment goal of many long term investors is the *maximum accumulation of wealth after expenses, costs, commissions and taxes with a minimum amount of stress*. These testimonials from leading investment experts attest to the fact that the most efficient and effective way to achieve this goal is to participate in the indexing investment revolution.

Index Funds Are Increasing Their Market Share

Although individual investors are generally unaware of their many advantages, index funds are taking additional market share from actively-managed mutual funds employing managers who pick stocks and time markets. In mid-1997, the amount of money being invested in index funds was growing at a rate *eighteen* times greater than the mutual fund industry as a whole.[36]

SIMON SAYS: *Don't Invest In Index Funds For The Wrong Reason*

A good part of the reason why index funds have surged in popularity over the last decade (particularly since 1995) is due to the strong performance of the large company stocks that are represented in the S&P 500 index. The market environment has generally favored large company stocks at the expense of small company stocks during this period. This has directly contributed to the growth in the number and size of S&P 500 index funds.

While it is good news that investors are investing an increasing amount of money in S&P 500 index funds, it is also cause for concern. The concern stems from the fact that too many investors have invested in S&P 500 index funds simply because they have recently outperformed most actively-managed mutual funds. This is a problem because it largely represents merely a *reaction* to a streak of outstanding performance achieved by a particular sector of the market - the large company stocks of the S&P 500.

But chasing after high returns is the *wrong* reason to invest in an S&P 500 index fund (or any other kind of index fund). After all, the stocks of the S&P 500 (or any other stock or bond asset class) will inevitably have some (or possibly many) bad years in the future. When this happens, many if not most actively-managed mutual funds will outperform the S&P 500 and S&P 500 index funds. But that won't mean that indexing will stop being a viable investment strategy. The only thing that it would mean is that large company stocks failed to outperform small company stocks during that particular time period.

In fact, investors should invest in index funds for the *right* reason - to carry out with minimal stress well conceived investment strategies that are likely to generate net performance superior to most active funds over the long run.

The tremendous performance of index funds in 1995, 1996 and 1997 has hastened this trend. For example, index funds tracking the S&P 500 index beat more than 85% of domestic stock mutual funds in 1995.[37] By the end of that year, the Vanguard Index Trust 500 Portfolio held assets of $17.4 billion and leaped from being the tenth largest mutual fund in America to the fourth largest by growing 86%.[38] By late 1997, the Vanguard Index Trust 500 Portfolio was the second largest mutual fund in America holding $45 billion in assets.

In addition, index funds accounted for about 10% of the cash flows to stock mutual funds in 1995.[39] 401(k) retirement plan investors are also helping to fuel the growth of indexing.[40] Currently, about 45% of 401(k) plans offer stock index funds and this figure increases to 60% when such plans contain more than $200 million in assets. Indexed investments represent about 6% of the assets of 401(k) retirement plans.[41]

SIMON SAYS: *Indexing Is Not Just Investing In The Stocks Of The S&P 500*

Too many investors equate indexing with index funds that only invest in the stocks of the S&P 500. But indexing is much more than this. In fact, there is a wide variety of stock index funds that invests in many different asset classes such as large company, small company and medium company stocks. There are even index funds that seek to provide the performance of certain stock investment styles such as "growth" and "value." Investors can also invest in bond index funds tracking bond indexes that represent corporate bonds, Treasury bonds and combinations of them.

The Spread Of The Indexing Revolution To Other Parts Of The World

The indexing revolution has spread to other parts of the world including Japan, Great Britain, Europe and Australia. In the mid-1980s, Japanese investment managers began to invest heavily in index funds once they were introduced to the new ideas that had been pioneered by American academics and index mutual fund managers.[42] It is estimated that the Japanese index 30% of their pension funds and 25% of the money invested in mutual funds. As Mamoru Aoyama, a professor of finance at Yokohama University explains:[43] "Even in Japan, academic researchers and consulting firms have provided consistent evidence that the majority of actively-managed funds fail to earn as good a rate of return as the index fund."

Great Britain has a longer history of indexing investments than Japan. Since British money managers have a good familiarity with indexing, it was no surprise that London-based Barclays Bank PLC spent $443 million at the end of 1995 to buy San Francisco-based Wells Fargo/Nikko Investment Advisors, a firm that indexes vast amounts of money. Since Wells Fargo was one of the pioneers of indexing in the United States, Barclays wanted to tap into its expertise to more effectively bring the advantages of indexing to its clients all over the world.[44] Australia, with the fifth largest pool of retirement money in the world, has taken to indexing enthusiastically.

Of course, the reason why indexing strategies have been successful in other parts of the world is the same reason why they are successful in this country: superior investment performance. In Great Britain over the ten-year period to the end of 1995, only 2 of 79 growth and income mutual funds outperformed the market.[45] This means that *less than 3%* of these funds that employ money managers who "take themselves seriously and pay themselves accordingly"[46] were able to achieve what their managers were paid to do: beat the market.

What's worse, they couldn't even achieve what indexing's detractors regard as a "no brainer:" match the market's performance! These figures do not take into consideration the effect of taxation, so it could well be that *none* of these funds beat the market on a tax-adjusted basis over this period.

The inferior investment returns registered by active mutual funds as well as the fact that foreign stocks alone represent a market value of $10 trillion[47] are why indexing investment strategies continue to make great inroads not only in this country but elsewhere in the world.

Your Guide To The Indexing Revolution

This book is your guide to the indexing revolution. You can join this revolution by investing in a portfolio of index mutual funds. But *only a thorough understanding of why you are investing in index funds will allow you to maintain a long term commitment to the revolution.* This book should provide that understanding, thus allowing you to maximize your investment performance with a minimum amount of stress.

Section I of this book is an analysis of the shortcomings of the traditional system of investing in which investors attempt to beat the market by picking individual stocks, bonds and/or mutual funds. It describes why this system forces most active investors to underperform the market (and indexing investors). The introduction to Section II provides a basic understanding of index funds. The remainder of that section presents their many advantages and why this makes them the better investment choice for most investors in comparison to actively-managed mutual funds or individual stocks and bonds. Section III is a brief summary of why investors should invest in index mutual funds.

Before we can fully appreciate why index funds are the best investment choice for most investors, it is necessary to first understand some of the shortcomings of the traditional system of investing and why they do not let active investors reach their full investment potential. The first chapter of Section I explores the basic shortcoming - the impossibility of being able to accurately predict the future behavior of investments which largely negates efforts made to beat the market over the long run.

Chapter Notes

[1] "Is There Life After Babe Ruth?", *Barron's*, April 2, 1990, page 15. *See Bogle on Mutual Funds* by John C. Bogle (Burr Ridge, Illinois: Irwin Professional Publishing, 1994), page 173. *See also John Bogle and the Vanguard Experiment* by Robert Slater (Chicago, Illinois: Irwin Professional Publishing, 1997), page 166.

[2] *Capital Ideas* by Peter L. Bernstein (New York: Free Press, 1992), page 249.

[3] Rex A. Sinquefield in "Active or Passive: The Debate about Investment Management Styles," a speech at the International Association for Financial Planning Success Forum, Boston, Massachusetts, September 12, 1994.

[4] Any person seeking the services of an investment advisor to manage his money must endure a sales pitch that will include a review of the self-proclaimed 'excellence' of the advisor's track record.

[5] The intellectual roots for the ideas that led to the indexing revolution and the creation of index funds can be traced back over 200 years to the collected works of Adam Smith, the famed Scottish classical economist. His principal work, *The Wealth of Nations*, was published in 1776. It is one of the most influential books on economics ever written and is the linchpin of the economic theory of capitalism. This book describes how rational self-interest in a free market economy leads to widespread economic well-being. *See An Inquiry into the Nature and Causes of the Wealth of Nations* by Adam Smith (Chicago: The University of Chicago Press, 1976), Volume One, Book IV, Chapter II, page 477. *See also The Fatal Conceit: The Errors of Socialism* by F. A. Hayek (Chicago: The University of Chicago Press, 1991), page 14. Hayek is a co-recipient of the 1974 Nobel Prize in Economic Science. Rex A. Sinquefield summarizes the legacy of Adam Smith: "Smith observed that the market system effectively and efficiently coordinates human economic cooperation. Smith used the metaphor of an 'invisible hand' guiding the market in ways that exceed our knowledge or perception. The competitive market order gathers knowledge through the pricing system - an ever-changing pattern of freely-floating prices for all goods and services, financial and otherwise. In this way, the market generates knowledge of the value of a good or service far better than any person or group of persons - whether such persons are investment managers or political central planners attempting to create such a system." Sinquefield adds: "More recently, the general idea that free and competitive markets work has been specifically applied to the financial markets of stocks, bonds and other investments." Rex A. Sinquefield in "Active or Passive: The Debate about Investment Management Styles," a speech at the International Association for Financial Planning Success Forum, Boston, Massachusetts, September 12, 1994. A scholarly body of work published by a group of economists over the last forty years has explored this "general idea" as it applies to financial markets. These economists include Harry M. Markowitz, William F. Sharpe, Paul A. Samuelson and Eugene F. Fama - all recipients (except Fama) of the Nobel Prize in Economic Science.

Much of the research conducted by these eminent scholars has profoundly changed the way in which institutional and individual investors have managed money over the last 25 years. It is directly responsible for the introduction of index investing to institutional pension plan investors in 1971 and to individual investors by way of the world's first index mutual fund in 1976. Collectively, their theories led to the conclusion that a properly diversified portfolio of index funds is the best investment strategy for most investors.

[6] "Indexing: Still a Good Investment Approach?" by Weston J. Wellington, *Personal Financial Planning*, November/December 1995, pages 21-25.

[7] A trade publication for institutional investors reported that as of May 1997 U.S. institutional tax-exempt indexed assets totaled about $920 billion. Of this total, approximately $632 billion was invested in U.S. stock index funds and another $288 billion in bond and international index funds. "Non-U.S. Indexing Gains Most in Survey" by Sabine Schramm, *Pensions & Investments*, August 18, 1997, pages 3 and 34. An earlier estimate by this publication indicated that as of January 1, 1994, there was $452 billion invested in index funds in the United States and Canada. But neither this survey nor the 1997 estimate took into consideration the significant amount of money invested in index funds in Great Britain, Europe, Australia and Japan.

[8] "Intel Fires Active Money Managers in Switch to Indexing" by John R. Dorfman, *The Wall Street Journal*, August 24, 1995, page C1.

[9] "The Stampede To Index Funds" by Jeffrey M. Laderman, *Business Week*, April 1, 1996, page 78.

[10] According to TIAA-CREF as of December 31, 1996.

[11] According to CALPERS as of June 30, 1996.

[12] According to the State of Connecticut, Office of the Treasurer as of November 30, 1996. The state treasurer runs various index funds that track the S&P 500, the Russell 2500, EAFE and the Lehman Brothers Aggregate Bond indexes.

[13] According to the Los Angeles County Employees Retirement Association (LACERA) as of June 30, 1996.

[14] In 1993 institutional investors such as public and private pension plans paid about $6 billion a year to professional stock pickers and market timers to manage about $3 trillion. Close to half that fee was pure profit. *See* "The Coming Investor Revolt" by Jaclyn Fierman, *Fortune*, October 31, 1994, page 66.

[15] According to John C. Bogle, stock index funds account for about 6% of the money invested in all stock mutual funds in the United States, while bond index funds account for about 1% of the assets of all taxable bond funds.

[16] "Indexing: Still a Good Investment Approach?" by Weston J. Wellington, *Personal Financial Planning*, November/December 1995, pages 21-25.

[17] Rex A. Sinquefield in "Active or Passive: The Debate about Investment Management Styles," a speech at the International Association for Financial Planning Success Forum, Boston, Massachusetts, September 12, 1994. John C. Bogle esti-

mates that indexed money represents about 25% of the assets of corporate pension plans. John C. Bogle in "Be Not the First, Nor Yet the Last," a speech at the annual conference of the Association for Investment Management and Research, Atlanta, Georgia, May 8, 1996.

[18] "Debate: Active vs. Passive Investing," *Financial Planning*, December 1996, page 22.

[19] Robert Stovall, a well known money manager, appeared on ABC News' 20/20 on November 27, 1992 and stated: "It's just not true that you can't beat the market. Every year about one-third of the fund managers do it. Of course, each year it is a different group."

[20] *Money*, August 1995, page 9.

[21] "Happily Average" by Andrew Bary, *Barron's*, April 10, 1995, page F13.

[22] John C. Bogle in "Be Not the First, Nor Yet the Last," a speech at the annual conference of the Association for Investment Management and Research, Atlanta, Georgia, May 8, 1996.

[23] The Wilshire 5000 stock index is a more accurate barometer of "the market" than the S&P 500 index. The S&P 500 represents only about 70-75% of the total market value of publicly traded stocks in America while the Wilshire 5000 represents virtually 100%. This includes all the stocks listed on the New York Stock Exchange, the American Stock Exchange and the NASDAQ Over-The-Counter Market. Moreover, since its inception, the Wilshire 5000 has shown a significantly higher correlation of performance (.90) to the average general stock fund than the S&P 500 (.79). *Ibid.* In spite of this, the S&P 500 continues to be the most widely recognized barometer of the market.

[24] *See* "Mutual Funds' Rivalry Doesn't Include Giving Buyers a Break on Fees" by Vanessa O'Connell and Ellen E. Schultz, *The Wall Street Journal*, November 28, 1995, page A1.

[25] The maximum tax rate on ordinary income and short term capital gains remained at 39.6%.

[26] It should be noted that in the 1980s and late into the 1990s Congress failed to keep tax rates stable. For example, from 1981 through 1996, Congress changed the ordinary income tax rate five times (or, on average, once every three years). The most recent change *raised* this rate. It is also worth noting that as this book went to print in late 1997, the news from Washington was all rosy - a sharply lower budget deficit as well as low unemployment and inflation. However, the narrowing of the deficit has been accomplished primarily because of the recent strength of the economy and the resultant increased amount of taxes that have poured into the Treasury. But this can only temporarily mask the enormous spending demands - such as Social Security and Medicare - that will be placed on the national budget over the next several generations. While these problems can be solved, it will take more than a few years of a booming economy to do it. In fact, programs such as Social Security and Medicare must be genuinely reformed because otherwise the

unrelenting arithmetic of the problem will simply swamp American taxpayers.

[27] "Faceless Hero" by Eric J. Savitz, *Barron's*, January 8, 1996, pages 15-16. Peter L. Bernstein also notes: "If [stock prices are] more random than ever, information must be moving faster, prices must be holder closer to intrinsic values, and out-guessing the market must be growing increasingly difficult." *Capital Ideas* by Peter L. Bernstein (New York: Free Press, 1992), page 304.

[28] This is not to say that an investor in a bond index fund will be likely to achieve better long term performance than an investor in an actively-managed stock fund.

[29] John C. Bogle in "Be Not the First, Nor Yet the Last," a speech at the annual conference of the Association for Investment Management and Research, Atlanta, Georgia, May 8, 1996.

[30] This quotation has been assembled from some of Bogle's published writings and has been used with his permission.

[31] Rex A. Sinquefield in "Active or Passive: The Debate about Investment Management Styles," a speech at the International Association for Financial Planning Success Forum, Boston, Massachusetts, September 12, 1994. This quotation has been slightly edited and condensed.

[32] Foreword to *Bogle on Mutual Funds* by John C. Bogle (Burr Ridge, Illinois: Irwin Professional Publishing, 1994).

[33] "Indexing: For Winners Only" by Jane Bryant Quinn, *Newsweek*, April 17, 1995, page 62. This quotation has been slightly rearranged and condensed.

[34] "Not So Random" by Burton G. Malkiel, *Barron's*, April 22, 1996, page 55.

[35] "Caution Guides Manager of Huge Fund" by Jonathan Clements, *The Wall Street Journal,* April 4, 1995, page C1. Some of the quotations have been condensed in this paragraph. Clements is editor of the "Getting Going" column in *The Wall Street Journal*. He appears to think that indexing is a good idea: "Index funds are brilliant, top-performing, tax-efficient investments that should play a major role in the stock-fund portfolio of every rational investor." "Index-Fund Investing Demands a Plan Of Attack, Not Just a Blindfolded Shot" by Jonathan Clements, *The Wall Street Journal*, June 11, 1996, page C1.

[36] According to HD Brous & Co., a consulting firm. Of course, the overwhelming majority of mutual funds available to the investing public consists of active funds.

[37] "It's Strange! It's Pricey! It's a Winner!" by Robert McGough, *The Wall Street Journal*, January 5, 1996, page R4.

[38] According to Lipper Analytical Services, Inc., as of December 31, 1995.

[39] According to Strategic Insight, Inc., a mutual fund consulting firm.

[40] According to Access Research, Inc., a consulting firm specializing in 401(k) plans.

[41] John C. Bogle in "Be Not the First, Nor Yet the Last," a speech at the annual conference of the Association for Investment Management and Research, Atlanta, Georgia, May 8, 1996.

[42] "Is MPT Applicable to Japan?" by Mamoru Aoyama, *The Journal of Portfolio*

Management, Fall 1994, pages 103-110.

[43] *Ibid.*

[44] The new investment firm that took over, Barclays Global Investors, now manages more money - over $100 billion - that tracks the performance of the S&P 500 index than any other money manager in the world. In total, it managed $285 billion of indexed investments as of mid-1997.

[45] "Fund Managers As Fruit Flies" by Catherine Barron, *Investors Chronicle*, March 22, 1996, pages 16-18.

[46] *Ibid.*

[47] John C. Bogle in "Be Not the First, Nor Yet the Last," a speech at the annual conference of the Association for Investment Management and Research, Atlanta, Georgia, May 8, 1996.

SECTION I

WHY THE INDEXING REVOLUTION
WAS NECESSARY

THEME OF THE SECTION:

*THE SHORTCOMINGS OF THE TRADITIONAL
SYSTEM OF INVESTING*

TWO

IS IT POSSIBLE TO
PREDICT THE FUTURE?

The future is unpredictable; we are not gods.
 - Andrei Sakharov (1921-1989)
   Russian nuclear physicist, human rights advocate and recipient of the
   1975 Nobel Peace Prize

The ability to foresee that some things cannot be foreseen is a very necessary quality.
 - Jean Jacques Rousseau (1712-1778)
   French philosopher and writer

Overview

The ability to beat the market first requires that an investor accurately predict the future investment behavior of stocks and bonds. It is essentially impossible to do this over the long run because no one investor, whether professional or amateur, can know the infinite number of factors that influence the prices of stocks and bonds, much less accurately predict which stocks and bonds will be profitable.

Can Investors Accurately Predict The Future In A Consistent Way?

Investors who pick stocks and time markets are usually considered successful only if they can beat the market. Yet there are probably a good number of investors who consider themselves successful even if they underperform the market. (Actually, these investors make ideal recruits for the indexing revolution because they are paying too much in investment costs and taxes for the privilege of earning inferior investment returns.[1])

When all is said and done, though, most individuals believe that it is only those investors who outperform the market that are successful. But few stop to think that the indispensable prerequisite for beating the market is the ability to accurately predict, in a consistent way, *future* price movements of individual stocks or bonds, mutual funds or entire asset classes. Of course, this depends on the ability to correctly assess the infinite number of factors that influence the prices of these investments. An investor who cannot do this on his own must *also identify today* an investment advisor (or a mutual fund manager or managers) who has the ability to make consistently profitable stock picking and market timing decisions.

Naturally, stock pickers and market timers maintain that it is possible to accurately predict the future in a consistent enough way to beat the market over the long run. After all, it doesn't seem all that difficult since following the completion of any market transaction in which a stock or bond is traded, sooner or later one of the two sides will *always* be right in predicting the future. This is true whether it is the side whose purchased investment went up in value or the one whose sold investment went down in value.

A good example of this is what happened when the stock market "crashed" on October 19, 1987. On that day, a large number of investors bailed out of the market because they predicted that, in the future, the value of their stocks or mutual fund shares would be worth *less* than they were prior to that traumatic day. Yet for every share that was sold, a corresponding purchase of the same share[2] was made because the buyer predicted that, in the future, that share would be worth *more*. 50% of these predictions were therefore accurate. (As French mathematician Louis Bachelier stated nearly a century ago:[3] "Contradictory opinions concerning these changes [in stock prices] diverge so much that at the same instant, buyers believe in a price increase and sellers in a price decrease."[4])

SIMON SAYS: *Contradictory Investment Predictions From The Same Source*

Sometimes contradictory investment predictions come from the same active money management firm. In August 1994, the media carried stories that the chief stock strategist for Lehman Brothers predicted in a report issued by the firm that all scenarios pointed to a flat or declining stock market. This firm published another report on the same day by its director of sector analysis that predicted the stock market might be going up.

These are obviously entirely different predictions. But it would still be possible for Lehman Brothers to come out of this situation smelling like a rose. How? Because later on, depending on which direction the market went - up, down or sideways - Lehman could point to either one of its analysts and say that he made a brilliant market call, thus creating another investment guru![5] No one would care about, or even remember, the analyst who guessed wrong - except those who were financially hurt by their reliance on that wrong prediction.

But is it good enough for active investors to simply invest their money and hope, on a random flip of the coin basis, that their stock picks and market timing moves will pay off in market-beating performance? Absolutely not. In fact, active investors must *consistently* predict the future in a way that will allow them to beat the market over the long run. (For example, we will see in Chapter Seven that market timers must be right in their predictions a minimum of 70% of the time. No known market timer has yet accomplished this over a long period.)

One way to see whether investors can generally predict the future is to examine the behavior of Fidelity Magellan shareholders during the time (1979 and 1980) when Peter Lynch was at his zenith as manager of that mutual fund. Those few who were invested in Magellan during these years (many of whom were Fidelity employees) were in an ideal position to take advantage of its outstanding performance over the ensuing decade. This is a particularly good example because if there was ever a group of investors who shouldn't have left a mutual fund during a particular period, it was Magellan investors in 1979 and 1980.

In both years Magellan was closed to new investors,[6] so obviously there was no increase in their numbers. But surprisingly, from year-end 1978 through year-end 1980, the number of Magellan shareholder accounts *declined* over 20%.[7] Lynch himself isn't sure of the reason for this.[8] He guesses that the investors from Essex (a Fidelity fund that merged with Magellan in 1976) who were involuntarily thrown into Magellan got out once Magellan's tremendous gains enabled them to recover the losses that they suffered while invested in Essex.

It is also probable that investors pulled out of Magellan during this period because they feared that the terrible state of the economy in those years (a prime rate of 21% and 13% inflation) would catch up with Magellan's fabulous returns. Another factor may have been that after two outstanding years in a row investors may have figured that it was tempting fate to stay around much longer.[9]

Whatever the explanation for their actions, the fact that a significant percentage of investors left Magellan during its best years clearly demonstrates that they could not predict the future. If they had been able to do so, they would have never departed the fund since Lynch still had some good years left in him.[10]

SIMON SAYS: *Many Investors Use The Crutch Of Stock Market Forecasting*

Stock market forecasters expend enormous amounts of money and resources in efforts to accurately forecast the future of financial markets. But the precision required to actually achieve this continues to elude them. There are two reasons why.

First, the statistical market forecasting models that they use assume that the world is a rational and orderly place. In fact, the world is very uncertain. This is what makes the stock market so unpredictable - it reflects the uncertainty of the world at large. Second, the assumptions used by these models are based on what has happened in the past. Since we cannot know over any particular period of time in what meaningful ways the future will ever repeat the past, many assumptions from the past have little relevance to the future.

Many investors rely to some degree on stock market forecasting as a crutch to guide their buying and selling investment decisions. They seem to feel better if there *appears* to be a rational process underlying these decisions. This is why investors retain an insatiable appetite for stock market forecasts even though they are not helpful in assisting them to accurately predict the future.

This example indicates that it is highly problematic that either amateur or professional investors have the ability to accurately predict the future in a way that will allow them to beat the market over a long period of time. After all, investors make millions of buying and selling decisions every day in the world's financial markets, which affect, and are affected by, constant unpredictably changing stock and bond prices. How, then, is it possible to even be aware of the infinite number of factors that influence the prices of these investments, much less accurately predict which of them will be profitable?

John Maynard Keynes recognized this kind of uncertainty and observed:[11] "The sense in which I am using the term ["uncertain knowledge"] is that in which the prospect of a European war is uncertain, or the price of copper and the rate of interest twenty years hence, or the obsolescence of a new invention . . . About these matters, there is no scientific basis on which to form any calculable probability whatsoever. *We simply do not know!*"

Yet many active mutual fund managers and investment advisors are able to convince a good number of investors that they *do* know. Their efforts to prove that they possess such unique powers of prophecy are aided by the use of slick advertising and the presentation of an overwhelming amount of confusing investment data. No doubt many investors think that these soothsayers (or even themselves) have the ability to predict the future in a profitable way over the next year or two. Although this is very unlikely, it is entirely beyond reason for such investors to think that anyone can do it consistently for twenty or thirty years.

SIMON SAYS: *The Poor Forecasting Turned In By Experts*

Investors shouldn't put faith in the ability of anyone, especially professional forecasters, to accurately predict the future. Two examples of poor professional forecasting are found in *Business Week*. This well respected magazine publishes a year-end double issue which provides the consensus forecast of the nation's top economists for the upcoming year. In the 1973 *Business Week* year-end issue, 31 of 32 economists predicted that the Gross National Product (GNP) would be positive in 1974. At the time of this prediction, the country was already in the third month of its worst recession since the Great Depression. So all these leading economists except 1 out of 32 got the predicted *direction* of the GNP wrong!

The 1982 recession was the second worst recession since the Great Depression. (The 1990 recession was quite mild in comparison.) The year-end 1981 issue of *Business Week* featured predictions from 39 of 41 economists that there would be no recession in 1982, which proved to be entirely wrong as the economy went into a tailspin in 1982.

More recently, in 1994 it was revealed that the top economic advisors to President Clinton decided that interest rates wouldn't be rising, so many refinanced their homes with adjustable rate mortgages. Interest rates then promptly increased so that they ended up paying almost twice the amount of their previous mortgage payments. Again, this shows that experts often can't even correctly predict the future direction of financial markets, much less the magnitude of the movements of those markets.

In reality, any successful predictions of the future made by self-styled investment oracles are usually lucky rolls of the dice. (The word "usually" in the preceding sentence implies that there are those who sometimes do successfully predict the future. While these individuals do exist, they (1) are few and far between, (2) can only be identified after the fact and (3) need to have a long track record so that we can be sure that their successful predictions were based on skill and not just luck.)

SIMON SAYS: *Why Pass The Word On?*

It is said that Peter Lynch made $3-5 million a year picking stocks (he didn't time markets) for Fidelity Magellan.[12] That's appropriate compensation for the hundreds of millions that he brought in for Fidelity in the form of commission loads and annual mutual fund expenses.[13] Yet Lynch (or for that matter, any other active money manager, including nearly 7,000 mutual fund managers) never knew when he assembled with others on the starting line of the investment racetrack each year whether he would actually end up beating the market for that year.

If an active money manager could *really tell* that he would be a winner every year, there would be no incentive to hand over to his clients any profitable returns that he already knew were coming to him. These profits would represent far more wealth than a trivial few million dollars a year that he would earn for running a mutual fund. As Alfred Cowles III recognized many years ago:[14] "Market advice for a fee is a paradox. Anybody who really knew just wouldn't share his knowledge. Why should he? In five years, he could be the richest man in the world. Why pass the word on?"

Fundamental Analysis And Technical Analysis: The Tools Used By Active Investors In Attempting To Predict The Future

Active investors, whether professional or amateur, rely either directly or indirectly on one or both tools of stock analysis - fundamental analysis and technical analysis - to help them in their attempts to accurately predict the future.

The fundamental analysis of an individual company's stock involves not only the study of the company's earnings and balance sheet but can encompass many other factors. These factors include the quality of the company's management, plans for expansion, physical plant such as buildings and other properties, market position against competitors and even the caliber of its method of accounting. The accuracy of much of this analysis is conditioned on how the overall economy's interest rates, inflation, unemployment rate, industrial production and other crucial variables impact the company.

A manager of an actively-managed mutual fund uses this quantitative data about the company's past to make predictions about the amount and likelihood of its future earnings. Based on this, he estimates a value for the stock which is compared to its current market price.

If the manager buys a stock, he believes that the market has "undervalued" it. That is, he regards the current market price of the stock to be too low in comparison to its true investment value. The manager thinks that he is the only one who knows the real value of the stock so he believes, unconsciously or not, that he is smarter than the market. According to his thinking, when the market finally realizes that the stock is mispriced it will correct its 'mistake' and bid up the stock's price to that which he had identified as the correct one. When this happens, he can sell the stock and make a profit.

Conversely, when an active fund manager sells a stock, he believes that the market has "overvalued" it. That is, he regards the current market price of the stock to be too high in comparison to its true investment value. His thinking is that if he can sell the stock prior to its decrease in price (before the rest of the market also realizes that the market price is higher than its true value), he will avoid a loss. In the situation where he thinks that he has identified an overvalued stock that isn't held in the mutual fund, an active fund manager won't buy it.[15]

Although the fundamental analysis of a stock may appear to be exact, this process is highly dependent on fallible human predictions and forecasts that are simply *crude estimates* of what might happen in the future. Because of this, fundamental analysis isn't a very useful tool in helping investors accurately predict the future.

Technical analysis is another tool used by investors in their attempts to accurately predict the future. Technical analysts (also known as "chartists") care nothing about a stock's price/earnings ratio or its dividend policy - factors that excite a fundamental analyst. Instead, they study charts that detail past changes in the prices of individual stocks. Technical analysts examine these pricing "patterns" from the past and compare them to any patterns that may appear in the current prices of the same stocks to see if there is a "fit." (They even have a stylized jargon for the patterns that they see in their beloved charts: "heads and shoulders," "triple tops," "double bottoms," "wedges" and "channels.") If there is a fit, chartists fervently believe that they can make profitable forecasts about future changes in the prices of these stocks.

However, any patterns that may appear in past changes in stock prices are entirely meaningless for the purpose of predicting future changes in stock prices. This was shown in a revealing experiment carried out by a professor at the University of Chicago Graduate School of Business in the early 1960s.[16] He programmed a computer to generate a series of random numbers (which produced patterns virtually identical to those found in the charts used by technical analysts), plotted them on different charts and labeled each chart with the name of a stock.

The professor then took the charts to the leading technical analysts of the day and asked them for investment advice. The fact that the patterns plotted on the graphs were only created from randomly generated numbers with no objective meaning didn't stop these 'experts' from having strong opinions about the best way to profit from the 'information' contained in them.

If so-called experts can be fooled by this experiment, then it shouldn't be surprising that ordinary investors could be led to believe that random numerical patterns actually contain useful investment information. After all, it stands to reason that if investors 'see' patterns in a mass of investment data then they can 'understand' them better. This understanding makes them think that the patterns are not random at all and that they actually contain objective meaning such as signaling changes in stock pricing trends.

But the sad fact (sad because investors pay good money for the services of technical analysts), overwhelmingly confirmed by a large volume of academic studies and long market experience, is that the only meaning that these patterns have is found in the fertile minds of chartists. Thus, technical analysis is a tool rather less accurate than reading tea leaves. This is why it cannot help investors accurately predict the future.

———————

The discussion in this chapter has shown that investors are unable to accurately predict the future behavior of investments. The next chapter explains why no particular investor who we can point to today can be expected to beat the market.

Chapter Notes

[1] By switching to properly diversified portfolios of index funds, underperforming active investors will likely *improve* their chances of accumulating enough wealth to meet their financial goals.

[2] Except shares bought by "market makers" to maintain the liquidity of financial markets. ("Liquidity" provides investors with the ability to easily and conveniently trade stocks at current market prices.) Market makers "make" a market in certain stocks and bonds by purchasing and selling these investments for their own accounts. Since they take no commissions, they expect to profit from the bid-ask spreads (explained in Chapter Twelve) on stock and bond trades. Obviously, there are always fluctuations in the market prices of the investments that market makers hold in their inventory. So if a market maker accumulates too much inventory at too high a price or disposes of inventory at too low a price, he can easily go out of business. Market makers play a critical role in the maintenance of fair and orderly markets.

[3] "Theory of Speculation" by Louis Bachelier in *The Random Character of Stock Prices* edited by Paul H. Cootner (Cambridge, Massachusetts: The MIT Press, 1964), page 17. Bachelier also found that past changes in stock prices are of no help in predicting future changes. As we will see, this discovery has been validated by countless studies and actual market experience that both indicate technical analysis is of no use to investors attempting to profitably predict the future.

[4] This means that an investor who sells a stock thinks that the buyer is purchasing a loser that will go down in value while the buyer thinks that the seller is letting go of a bargain that will go up in value. Thus, an investor who wants to buy low and sell high assumes that the investor on the other side of the trade will *sell low and buy high*.

[5] "Lehman Brothers is Bullish, or Is It Bearish? Or Both?" by Warren Getler and William Power, *The Wall Street Journal*, August 31, 1994, page C1. *See* "Learning to Live With Bear Markets," Trinity Investment Management Corporation, Boston, Massachusetts, October 1994, page 1, "Some Research Reports Tout and Pan the Same Stock" by William Power, *The Wall Street Journal*, March 21, 1995, page C1 and "Wien vs. Biggs: Clashing Views on the Market" by Dave Kansas, *The Wall Street Journal*, September 18, 1995, page C1.

[6] As of the end of September 1997, Fidelity Magellan was again closed to new investors.

[7] *See* page 102 for more discussion of this point.

[8] *Beating the Street* by Peter Lynch with John Rothchild (New York: Fireside/ Simon & Schuster, 1993), page 99.

[9] This example suggests that investors can get into trouble when they rely on investment track records to predict the future - whether their psychological orientation to the future is based on fear *or* optimism. (Chapter Four fully explores "track

record investing.") As the main text explains, some of the early Magellan investors who focused on its great investment track record were *fearful* that the good times would soon end. Thus, they prematurely departed from what turned out to be a spectacularly winning mutual fund. But most investors who focus on an impressive track record are *optimistic* and believe that it will continue into the future. Yet Chapter Six will show that as the past performance of even an outstanding mutual fund "regresses to the mean" (statistical language for "becomes average"), it is likely that many of its investors will turn pessimistic. Even greater disappointment and frustration await investors when such a fund regresses to *less than* the mean as Magellan did in 1995, 1996 and 1997.

[10] It is understandable that active investors would challenge the conclusions drawn from this example. First, they could argue that nearly 80% of the *existing* Magellan investors *did* remain invested in the fund during these two years, thus demonstrating their ability to predict the future. But of this small number (fewer than 7,000 were left by the beginning of 1981), how many actually remained invested in Magellan during Lynch's golden years in the 1980s? Page 29 and the immediately preceding Chapter Note 9 describe how difficult it can be for many investors to stay put even in an active fund that is wildly successful. This is the "it's too good to last" disease and it infects many active investors. Second, active investors could argue that *new* investors were able, in effect, to predict the future because they flocked to Magellan. Over the decade of 1982-1991, Magellan grew in size from $107 million to $19.2 billion. $18.3 billion of the $19.2 billion (or more than 95% of the total) was new money poured in by investors. However, most of the excess performance turned in by Lynch was *already* achieved by the time the vast majority of this money made its move to Magellan. If the new Magellan investors could have really predicted the future, they would have invested *before* this outperformance. In fact, they couldn't predict the future which is why relatively few investors are ever invested early enough to benefit from the entire span of an outstanding investment performance. *See* pages 102 and 108, Chapter Note 9 for additional discussion of this point as it relates to Magellan. Third, active investors could also argue that this example is an aberration because Magellan was closed to new investors until June 1981. *See* page 108, Chapter Note 9 for an answer to this argument. Fourth, a final argument advanced by active investors concerns the relevance of this example since the events that it describes took place nearly 20 years ago. Today, investors can much more quickly identify and thus invest in a winning mutual fund than was possible a generation ago. While true, this still begs the real question: can investors reliably predict the future behavior of investments so as to consistently profit from such predictions? All available evidence points to an emphatic negative for both yesterday's investors who presumably were privy to less information and acted on it with less speed and today's investors who can obtain much more information at much greater speed. Again, if amateur or professional investors could reliably predict the future, they would *already* be invested in soon-

to-be-spectacular mutual funds (or individual stocks and bonds) waiting to profit from their market-beating returns.

[11] "The General Theory" by John Maynard Keynes, *Quarterly Journal of Economics*, Volume LI, February 1937, pages 209-233. Italics added.

[12] *Fortune*, April 23, 1990, page 200.

[13] For the fiscal year ending in March 1995, Fidelity Investments was paid $268 million in management fees alone as the investment advisor to Fidelity Magellan. "Magellan Falls Below S&P's 3-Year Return" by Robert McGough, *The Wall Street Journal*, May 2, 1996, page C1. Edward C. ("Ned") Johnson III, Chairman of Fidelity Investments, is not a multibillionaire for nothing.

[14] *Capital Ideas* by Peter L. Bernstein (New York: The Free Press, 1992), pages 35-36. During the depths of the Great Depression in the early 1930s, Cowles founded the Cowles Commission, an organization devoted to, among other things, the study of investment performance. Virtually every recipient of the Nobel Prize in Economic Science has been associated in some way with this organization.

[15] An active fund manager may also determine that the market has "correctly" priced a stock, making it neither undervalued nor overvalued.

[16] The results of this experiment are described in "Stock Market 'Patterns' and Financial Analysis: Methodological Suggestions" by Harry V. Roberts, *The Journal of Finance*, Volume 14, No. 1, March 1959, pages 1-10. A scholar at Stanford University carried out a similar test a quarter century earlier with the same results. *See* "A Random Difference Series For Use In The Analysis Of Time Series" by Holbrook Working, *Journal of the American Statistical Association*, Volume 29, March 1934, pages 11-24.

THREE

CAN AN INVESTOR BE EXPECTED TO BEAT THE MARKET?

One can resist the invasion of armies, but not the invasion of ideas.
- Victor Hugo (1802-1885)
  French poet, dramatist, novelist, essayist and critic

Overview

No particular investor who we can point to today can be expected to beat the market. The principal reason for this is the high costs and taxes that typify active investment strategies. This results in most actively-managed mutual funds not only failing to outperform the market but underperforming it as well. This is true regardless of whether these funds are invested in efficient or inefficient markets.

Can An Investor Be Expected To Beat The Market?

Many investors, either on their own or with the help of their investment advisors, beat the market over short periods of time. There is even a small minority of investors that manages to beat the market over extended periods of time. In fact, there will always be some investors who beat the market over any period of time, whether by skill or with luck.

SIMON SAYS: *How Many Studies Does It Take To Beat The Market?*

A landmark study of mutual fund performance which is often cited by investment experts was conducted in 1968 by Michael C. Jensen who was then at the University of Chicago.[1] He found that (1) mutual funds, on average, underperform the market and (2) individual performances by mutual funds are no better than that predicted by random chance. More than 200 published studies since Jensen first examined this issue 30 years ago confirm the validity of his conclusions. One of the most recent of these studies found that a person investing in actively-managed mutual funds cannot fashion a dependable strategy to consistently achieve market-beating returns over long periods of time.[2]

However, we cannot point to any *particular* investor today (whether the most skillful professional money manager or the luckiest amateur) and *expect* him to automatically outperform the market for any given time period.[3] This is not to say that there are not many investors who make money by picking stocks and timing markets. Nevertheless, the fact remains that no particular investor can be expected to beat the market.[4]

High Costs And Taxes: The Factors Ultimately Responsible For Underperformance Of The Market

The high costs and taxes that typify actively-managed mutual funds usually outweigh the margin by which an investor, whether amateur or professional, can outperform the market. In fact, their cumulative impact is so great that, over the long run, most active funds *underperform* the market.

While different managers of active funds can overcome the hurdles of high costs and taxes over relatively short time periods, it is incredibly difficult for any one manager to do consistently over the long run. As a result, most active funds are likely to underperform financial markets (and index funds which fully invest in them). It is important to understand that this is true whether the market in question is a zero sum *efficient* market or a zero sum *inefficient* market. In both markets, the story is the same: high costs and taxes are the factors ultimately responsible for the inferiority of most actively-managed mutual funds.

Financial Markets Are A Zero Sum Game

In a very fundamental way, any financial market is a kind of "game." "Game theory" (which is a branch of mathematics) posits that there are three kinds of games: "positive sum" games where everybody wins, "negative sum" games where everybody loses and "zero sum" games where some win and some lose.[5] The stock market in the United States (as well as all other financial markets elsewhere in the world) is a zero sum game.

The players who compete in the zero sum game of a given financial market are investors who believe that they can outperform it by picking stocks (or bonds) and timing markets. These players consist of two groups of investors - those who underperform the market (losers) and those who outperform the market (winners).

In a financial market, the sum of all investment gains and losses registered by all active investors must total up to the market return (i.e., the zero sum). This means that, relative to a particular market trade, whatever is won by one investor must be lost by another. So even though two investors on the opposite sides of a trade can make money in an up market, one of the two will outperform the market relative to that trade and one will underperform it.

The active investors who comprise a financial market must engage in a costly trading game among themselves that requires a loser (or losers) for every winner (or winners). In effect, the losing active investors who underperform a market are "sacrificial lambs" for the winning active investors who outperform it. For example, any extra return on top of the market return earned by a well known mutual fund manager such as Mario Gabelli can only be extracted from other active investors who will suffer commensurate losses that will result in earning less than the market return.

There is also a "neutral" group of players - indexers - in the zero sum game of any financial market. Their neutrality arises from the fact that they do not compete with the two groups of active investors - winners and losers - who play in such games. The result is that indexers will never be winners or losers in terms of outperforming or underperforming a financial market. However, each will always earn the market return (i.e., the zero sum) in a given market because they hold the market portfolio.[6] Thus, indexers are never sacrificial lambs who lose to winning active investors.

So in the zero sum game of any financial market (1) the aggregate investment return of all active investors will always sum up to the market return and (2) indexers will always earn the market return. This is illustrated by the following example. In 1995, the market return of the stock market (as measured by the S&P 500 index) was 37.6%. Suppose that the investors in a stock picking mutual fund obtained a 50% return for that year. This group outperformed the market by 12.4 percentage points so it is obvious that they were winners. The active investors who were on the other side of the stock trades that led to this market-beating performance collectively underperformed the market by 12.4 percentage points (earning 25.2%) and thus were losers. Investors who followed a simple indexing strategy by holding an S&P 500 index fund earned the 37.6% market return.

The following is a summary description of the zero sum game which characterizes all financial markets.

1. All investors, both active investors and indexers, who invest in a particular financial market collectively own all the investments in that market.

2. All investors therefore collectively hold the market portfolio and, as a group, can earn no more and no less than the market return (i.e., the zero sum).

SIMON SAYS: *The Basic Arithmetic Of Investing*[7]

It is a matter of basic arithmetic that, in the aggregate, active investors will always underperform the market and indexers who hold the market portfolio. Yet the media, mutual fund ratings and even academic studies sometimes show that the "average" active money manager or mutual fund beats the market (usually defined as the S&P 500) or a particular index (and index funds tracking the index). Since this is a mathematical impossibility, how is it that an average can show this? There are three reasons.

First, the average does not represent the performance of the average actively-managed *dollar*. To measure this performance, the return earned by every active manager should be *proportionately* weighted for the amount of dollars managed by each at the start of the period in question. Instead, an *equally* weighted average such as a "simple" or "median" average is commonly used to compare average investment performance to an index or the market. This means that the investment performance of a manager who manages, say, ten times the amount of money as another manager counts the *same* as the other manager in calculating an average.

Obviously, this creates misleading averages. For example, there are a greater number of active mutual fund managers who invest in small company stocks than in large company stocks. Thus, an equally weighted average of active manager performances will show a bias toward small company stocks in comparison to the market as a whole. The result (particularly over the past ten years) is that the average active manager is widely beaten by the market (the S&P 500) when large company stocks (which make up the S&P 500) outperform small company stocks. But when small company stocks excel, the average active manager soundly outperforms the market. In both situations, investors fail to understand that the average actively-managed dollar *still* underperforms the market after costs and taxes.

Second, the average does not represent the performances of all active *investors* that invest in the market in question.[8] For example, the average performance of stock mutual fund managers excludes those of individual investors invested in stocks. Of course, it is always possible that either one of these groups can outperform the other or that the average investor in one group can outperform the average investor in the other group. But either result is feasible only if all other active investors investing in the market in question collectively underperform it by a commensurate amount.

Third, the average represents the performance of *investments* that are not part of the market in question. For example, the average performance of stock mutual funds that hold cash is often compared to the performance of an all-stock market index or a cashless stock index fund. Predictably, the averages show that most active funds are beaten in up markets by the market index and index fund while the opposite occurs in down markets.

Thus, any media stories, mutual fund ratings or academic studies that show the average active mutual fund or money manager outperforming the market or a particular index are simply *wrong*. They mismeasure the performances of active funds, their managers and the markets in which they invest money.

3. *Before* costs and taxes, the investment performance of the average actively-managed dollar invested in this market will be the *same* as that of the average indexed dollar.

4. But *after* costs and taxes, the investment performance of the average actively-managed dollar invested in this market will be *less* than that of the average indexed dollar.

5. Therefore, *in the aggregate*, active investors have in the past, now in the present and will in the future *always* underperform any market (and indexers who hold the market portfolio).[9]

There is no getting around this mathematical certainty. The only rejoinder that active investors can make is to say that they aren't really concerned about the performance of active investors in the aggregate. Instead, they stress the importance of superior *individual* investment performances. But as we will now see, the Efficient Market Theory holds that even on an individual basis most active investors underperform the market and indexers who hold the market portfolio.

The Efficient Market Theory

The Efficient Market Theory was first set forth in 1965 by economist Eugene F. Fama to explain the workings of free and efficient financial markets.[10] (Although the principles of this theory apply to *all* organized and well established financial markets - markets that are remarkably efficient in processing vastly dispersed information and incorporating it into a constantly changing set of new prices - we will focus on the stock market.)

According to this theory, (1) information about stocks is widely and cheaply available to all investors, (2) all known and available information is already reflected in current stock prices, (3) the current price of a stock agreed on by a buyer and a seller in the market is the best estimate, however good or bad, of the investment value of the stock and (4) stock prices will almost instantaneously change as new information about them appears in the market.

This pricing efficiency which characterizes any organized and well established financial market is created by the efforts of those very people who do not believe that markets are efficient - stock pickers and market timers! Their competitive and costly efforts (both successful and unsuccessful) to beat the market collectively make an efficient market - a market which only a minority of investors are likely to outperform over the long run. This remarkable irony can be explained as follows.

Every day in the jungle of the stock market, highly skilled and aggressive stock pickers engage in a savagely competitive struggle to beat each other and the market. This extremely competitive process in which stock pickers attempt to find undervalued and overvalued stocks largely entails the use of fundamental analysis.[11]

Although the basic tools used in fundamental analysis may be the same, stock pickers look at stocks in uniquely different ways. For example, some stock pickers may decide that the stock of Varccek Industries is undervalued and decide to buy it. Other stock pickers may conclude after scrutinizing this stock that it is correctly priced, while still others may judge that it is overvalued by the market. Yet even the stock pickers who came to a same conclusion - whether the stock should be bought, sold or held - likely based their assessments on different factors. It is apparent, then, that there is nothing clear-cut about the value of a stock - the value is in the eye of the beholder. Yet even though stock pickers attach a wide range of estimated values to a given stock at any point in time, it can only have *one* current market *price*.

The sum total of these estimates collectively creates a market price for a stock that is virtually the *same* as its value.[12] Because of this process, it is relatively rare to find and profit from a mismatch between a stock's price and its value (i.e., to identify an undervalued or overvalued stock). This unintentionally creates an efficient market hard to beat where most stock prices accurately reflect their true underlying investment values. As a result, the immense collective talent of the stock picking herd that roams the market every day *cancels out* for all but a minority of stock pickers (none of whom are identifiable until after the fact) the ability on a cost efficient basis to outperform the market over the long run.

One way to understand the pricing efficiency of a market is to see what happens after a widely followed financial analyst releases his report on a stock.[13] The report's conclusion may be that the stock is undervalued relative to its market price (i.e., the current market price of the stock is too low). If the market collectively 'believes' that the analyst is wrong in this assessment, the stock's market price will probably remain the same. If the market believes that he is correct, then this new information about the stock is nearly instantaneously incorporated into its market price which then immediately rises towards the analyst's estimated price. Only a relatively few stock pickers will be able to "beat the market to the punch" and profit by purchasing the stock at its original lower price.

SIMON SAYS: *The "Market Failure Theory" - The Dissenting View From The Efficient Market Theory*

Indexers believe that the market is efficient so that most efforts to beat it with stock picking or market timing are likely to fail over the long run. This is decidedly a *minority* position in the investment world. The majority position, relentlessly promoted by the professional money management industry and the investment media, is that it is entirely possible to beat the market. This means that even though the market is efficient, most investors follow investment strategies that presume the market to be inefficient.

According to Rex A. Sinquefield, these investors believe in the "Market Failure Theory:"[14] "This theory rejects the Efficient Market Theory's assessment that stock prices are fair and reflective of all available information in the market which will enable no investor, whether professional or amateur, to expect to systematically beat the market. Instead, the Market Failure Theory views the market as inefficient where stock prices react to changes in information slowly enough to allow some investors, presumably professionals, to beat the market and most other investors."

A professor at The London School of Economics offers the following analogy to help explain the pricing efficiency of a market:[15] "Imagine you have a thousand fruit flies milling about in the kitchen. Now and again someone spills a drop of jam on the floor. But the instant one clever fly gets to it, the rest do. None of the flies get any benefit from it - except the first. Your chances of being the first fruit fly are one in a thousand. Your chances of being the first fruit fly twice are infinitesimal. In the analogy, the jam is a piece of price-sensitive news. By the time you're phoning your stockbroker to place your order, the share price in question will have moved. Just one buyer - the first - has the dead certainty of an extra profit. That's an efficient market."

The ultimate test of market efficiency is whether (apart from luck) an active investor can beat the market over the long run. The nearly instantaneous adjustment of stock prices in reaction to new information and the absence of long term profitable stock picking and market timing strategies are potent evidence that only a minority of investors are likely to achieve this goal. The vast remainder will end up as "victims of market efficiency."[16]

SIMON SAYS: *Human Nature Guarantees The Efficiency Of Organized And Well Established Financial Markets*

Human nature guarantees the continuing efficiency of organized and well established financial markets. How can we be sure of this? Because it is human nature that drives most active investors to believe that they (or someone they hire) can beat the market and other active investors. It is precisely this impulse that also creates efficient financial markets. Since most investors by nature will continue to believe that they can beat the market, we can therefore be confident that organized and well established financial markets will remain efficient for the minority of investors who are indexers and that indexing strategies will never go out of date.

Some Implications Arising From The Creation Of Efficient Financial Markets

Some surprising implications arise from the competitive struggle waged among stock pickers who unintentionally create efficient financial markets.

First, the fact that most stock pickers do not beat a given financial market isn't because they are stupid, without skill or lazy. Rather, it is precisely *because* they are so intelligent, skillful and diligent in attempting to beat the market that most of them are likely to underperform it. Consequently, while the *individual* effort of each stock picker is usually wasted for the purpose of trying to *beat the market*, the *collective* efforts made by all stock pickers in their attempts to beat the market are important for the purpose of *creating and maintaining an efficient market*. This is why indexers are glad to see more stock pickers enter the money management profession every year.[17] Their added attempts to beat financial markets help make them more efficient by ensuring that stock prices stay in line with their underlying investment values.

Second, indexers get to "piggyback" on the costly efforts made by stock pickers to beat the market. Since indexers don't try to beat the market, they need not incur the high stock picking fees and trading costs that stock pickers have to pay in their search for undervalued and overvalued stocks that will (hopefully) beat the market.

> **SIMON SAYS: *Cover Your Bets***
>
> The vast majority of investors invest in active mutual funds because they believe that they (or someone they hire) can beat the market. However, if these investors are wrong they run the risk of significantly underperforming the market. On the other hand, if investors acknowledge that they cannot beat the market and thus invest in index funds the worst that they can do if they are wrong is to earn the market return. Which bet should an intelligent investor make?[18]

The Rationality Of An Efficient Market

Indexers presume that an efficient market accurately values and thus "rationally" (i.e., correctly) sets the prices of stocks; this makes them neither undervalued nor overvalued. After all, if the market didn't collectively 'think' that the current price of a stock was the correct one, it would not be there and it would set a different higher or lower price.[19]

However, even in an efficient market some stocks are priced "irrationally" (i.e., incorrectly); this makes them either undervalued or overvalued. This can happen, for example, when investors as a group become wildly optimistic or pessimistic and the psychology of the crowd takes over the market. Although an efficient market may irrationally set the prices of some stocks, the costs of trying to find these stocks are usually greater than any potential profit to be derived from knowing their correct prices. Even if this process was costless, it would still be impossible to know *in advance which* stocks, out of a vast number, would be those relatively few mispriced by an efficient market. As if these hurdles were not high enough for active investors to overcome, they also have no way to predict *who* will be the skillful (or lucky) ones that uncover these rarities.

SIMON SAYS: *Taking A Random Walk*

The origins of the Efficient Market Theory lie in the Random Walk Theory.[20] This theory describes the process in which stock prices unexpectedly change as a result of unpredictable new information that appears in the market. This "random walk" of changing prices has created a popular misconception among investors that stock prices change randomly for no apparent reason. For example, most investors believe that it makes no sense that a stock worth $25 yesterday is worth only $15 today.

While it is easy to agree with this, it is important to remember that in an unpredictable world, unexpected events can happen that may completely change our lives in a moment. These events can be exhilarating such as winning the lottery or devastating such as experiencing the death of a loved one. Because our personal lives can sometimes be turned upside down overnight by such random and unpredictable (yet rational) events, it may be more understandable that the overnight change in a stock's price from $25 to $15 can be *rational* even though it is caused by *random* and unpredictable events.

Thus, in an efficient market (1) stock *prices* are *rationally* set *at* any particular point in time although (2) *changes* in stock prices are *random* with no predictability *over* any particular time period. This is why random and unpredictable changes in stock prices must always be part of a rational and efficient stock pricing system.

So sit back, relax and don't be surprised when there are random movements in stock prices. These unpredictable (yet usually rational) changes in prices only reflect the uncertainty of new and unexpected information in an ever changing world.[21]

Active investors believe that the prices of many stocks do not accurately reflect their true underlying investment values. Hence, these prices are set irrationally by the market. Yet active investors have no way of 'proving' the irrationality of a stock's price (and profiting from it) until the market has 'recognized' that irrationality and 'agreed' to change its price. *Only then* can stock picking Monday Morning Quarterbacks confidently say with 20/20 hindsight that any fool should have known that the previous price of the stock was irrational.[22]

The "January Effect:" 'Proof' Of Market Inefficiency?

Investors who search for undervalued and overvalued stocks believe (knowingly or not) that the market is inefficient. One phenomenon often cited as 'proof' of a market inefficiency that can be exploited for profit is the so-called "January Effect." However, the belief that a particular market inefficiency exists and the ability to actually profit from that inefficiency are usually two very different things.[23]

Since 1926, small company stocks have often outperformed large company stocks in the month of January by amounts far greater than in any other month of the year. Armed with such knowledge, it would seem easy for an investor to profitably capitalize on this seeming inefficiency in the market - just buy small company stocks before January rolls around! So he picks up the telephone and calls his stockbroker because he knows in advance about an opportunity to make some money. However, his desire to profit from a market inefficiency that he has identified is dampened when his broker tells him that there are *other* investors who also know about the January Effect.

So instead of buying stocks in December to take advantage of the January Effect, the investor joins other investors and begins to buy them in July so that he won't miss the boat. *The Wall Street Journal* explains:[24] "As more investors position their portfolios to take advantage of the January Effect, the bounce in small cap stocks has shown up earlier and earlier. Because there really has been a quantifiable January Effect in years past, more investors try to participate in that phenomenon in advance."

This collective behavior by investors who are trying to profit from a perceived market inefficiency creates great demand for the investments (such as small company stocks) that constitute the market inefficiency. The resulting reduction in their available supply and the consequent increase in the market prices of these investments inevitably combine to eliminate for all but those relative few who happened to first identify the market inefficiency any chance to profit from it. Because of this, the all too often brief exploitation of an inefficiency comes to an end when enough investors have been "let in on the secret" about it.

Thus, a well known market inefficiency *always carries the seeds of its own destruction.* Robert D. Arnott, a widely respected investment advisor and author, comments on "disappearing inefficiencies:"[25] "In the early 1980s, the small stock effect was widely publicized; small stocks beat large in three years out of four by an average margin that is quite large. Similar research demonstrated that small company stocks beat large company stocks in almost every January. Subsequent to these well-publicized findings, small company stocks began a seven-year bear market in which a dollar invested in small company stocks was ultimately worth half as much as a dollar invested in large company stocks. Similarly, the January Effect became much less reliable."

Even if small company stocks were to again substantially outperform large company stocks in January, it is unlikely that investors could profit from this phenomenon. The reason why is that they would quickly bid up the prices of the stocks constituting this widely perceived inefficiency, thereby preventing the reoccurrence of any profitable opportunities.

Consequently, it really doesn't matter whether or not the January Effect is still "in existence." What really matters is whether or not investors can profitably take advantage of it. All evidence suggests that they cannot. Thus, the investment strategies recommended by a stockbroker cannot help his clients profit from this inefficiency. This is true even though he may continue to claim that the January Effect is clear evidence of an inefficient market.

Investors Cannot Be Expected To Beat The Market Even By Investing In Less Researched And Inefficiently Priced Stocks

Some 'smart' investors attempt to beat the market by using particularly sophisticated methods of stock picking to carefully analyze less researched and inefficiently priced stocks such as small company stocks and foreign stocks. Although these investors believe that they can search out undervalued and overvalued stocks before others, they generally concede that *large* company stocks such as General Motors are accurately valued and thus correctly priced by the market. Thus, there is widespread agreement among stock pickers that there are just too many analysts following large company stocks for any one stock picker to get a significant edge on others.[26]

However, they insist that less researched and inefficiently priced stocks such as foreign stocks can be a hidden cache of investment gems. Stock pickers maintain that these stocks are just waiting to be uncovered by enterprising individuals in their unceasing search among America's small companies to find the next Wal-Mart. They also believe that such opportunities abound in foreign stocks where the discovery of the next Turkish or Brazilian or Indonesian Microsoft can be just around the corner.

While such reasoning is intuitively appealing, it must be remembered that *all* financial markets (efficient as well as inefficient) are zero sum games. In this kind of game, by definition, before costs, expenses and taxes, half of the active investors investing in any given market will underperform it and half of them will outperform it. (Indexers will earn the market return - or the zero sum.) But once costs, expenses and taxes are taken into account, an unpredictable number of active investors who are the marginal outperformers will achieve less than the market return and become underperformers.

It is important to emphasize that this outcome *does not require that a market be efficient* - it is true of *both* efficient and inefficient financial markets. Because all financial markets are zero sum games, indexers can therefore be confident that they will outperform the (probably heavy) majority of active investors in both efficient and inefficient markets.

Thus, it makes good sense to use index funds to invest in less researched and inefficiently priced stocks such as small company stocks and foreign stocks.[27] Since these stocks often bear high annual expenses and large trading costs,[28] investors who invest in them by employing index funds can realize the greatest potential savings and thus earn a greater net return.

Even those relatively few stocks that outperform the relentless arithmetic of zero sum markets by overcoming heavy costs, expenses and taxes are selected by skillful or lucky stock pickers who cannot be identified until after their superior performances are made known to the investing public. This is a problem that is virtually insurmountable when picking thoroughly researched and efficiently priced stocks *as well as* less researched and inefficiently priced stocks.

> **SIMON SAYS:** *A Sure-Fire Formula To Beat The Market*
>
> Despite the fact that no particular investor who we can identify today can be expected to beat the market, it is actually possible to beat the market. The only requirement is to follow a sure-fire formula that demands essentially impossible proficiency in a whole series of tasks.
>
> The first task involved in trying to beat the market is to accurately predict the future in a consistent way.[29]
>
> The second task is to take public information (it isn't advisable to cheat by using non-public "inside" information because that can mean a stiff jail sentence), equally available to millions (there are more every year) of other resourceful and brilliant people (eager to beat the market and all active investors just as badly as all active investors want to beat the market and them) and interpret it differently and correctly.
>
> The third task requires that an investor not only be correctly different from the great mass of opinion held by his talented competitors, but also that he be right substantially more often than wrong in his correctly different interpretations of this public information.
>
> The fourth task involved in beating the market requires that the consensus of other investors must be wrong and that their mistakes are exploitable, after adjusting for market risk.
>
> An investor who doesn't feel that he can master these tasks that will result in market-beating performance can always hire someone to do it for him. But he must be able to find this person. That shouldn't present too much of a problem because the ability to identify today the next Peter Lynch only requires that an investor eliminate the other 99.98% of active mutual fund managers out there.

Most Investors Who Attempt To Beat The Market Believe That They Will Be Successful

Most investors attempt to beat the market because they believe that they will be successful. If they can make a greater effort than the next person to get more information about individual stocks and their perception is keener in analyzing this mass of data, then they believe that the payoff in market-beating investment performance is likely to follow. A good part of the reason for this widespread attitude among active investors is that American culture (as well as many other cultures) instills in most people the belief that superior intelligence, hard work and perseverance are traits that lead to individual success.

Since "success" in the investment world is usually defined as the ability to beat the market, investors who have these outstanding traits (or can hire someone who has them) believe that they will be successful. The media and the professional money management industry reinforce this belief by telling investors that picking the right stocks and profitably timing markets are not only possible, but necessary to make them successful.

SIMON SAYS: *Even Brilliance Usually Isn't Enough To Beat The Market*

The regular application of intelligence, hard work and perseverance are not much help for the purpose of beating the market. As hard as it may be to believe, these traits are not that scarce in the investment world. Since the market doesn't confer rewards for things that are not scarce, the majority of immensely talented people trying to outsmart each other and the market will fail to beat the market over the long run.

Most active investors scoff at this because it undermines their belief that superior investment performance will go to those who are intelligent, hard working and persevering. Yet if possessing these admirable traits produces superior performance, *why is it that most professional money managers who possess them in abundance regularly underperform the market?*

It is no surprise, then, that most investors are ready to pay good money to find those stocks, mutual funds or money managers that seemingly offer them a chance to beat the market. This behavior can be likened to avoiding "lottery risk" which is the risk of not buying a ticket and thus missing the chance to win the lottery. Peter L. Bernstein, noted economic consultant and founder of *The Journal of Portfolio Management*, explains:[30] "The decision to choose active [money] management is disarmingly simple: Nobody likes to pass up a chance to find the Big One . . . People believe that *somebody* will win, and that somebody might be them."

John C. Bogle notes:[31] "Though expecting investors in the aggregate to outperform the market has been, as Samuel Johnson said about marrying for the second time - 'a triumph of hope over experience' - the idea that 'hope springs eternal' is deeply imbedded in the psyche of the investing public." Thus, most investors pick stocks, bonds and/or mutual funds and/or time markets because they want to be in a position to get market-beating returns rather than "settle" for the market return of index funds.

One of the most common methods employed by investors in their attempts to beat the market is track record investing. Three well known sources of investment information used by track record investors are Morningstar, the Forbes Mutual Fund Honor Roll and mutual fund advertisements. They are all examined in the following chapter. Active investors also turn to sources of investment advice such as stockbrokers, financial roundtables, newsletters and Value Line in their attempts to beat the market. Their success is considered in Chapter Five.

SIMON SAYS: *What An Investment Guide For Trust Attorneys Says About Attempts To Beat The Market*

The Prudent Investor Rule was adopted by the American Law Institute in 1992.[32] It was drafted to bring trust law into conformity with Modern Portfolio Theory and other prudent notions concerning the investment of trust assets. The Rule provides a legal road map for attorneys, trustees and investment advisors to guide them when investing and managing the assets of a trust. Courts throughout the country may cite it as a source of legal authority in the fields of trust law, trust administration and investment management. In addition, the Rule serves as a model for state legislatures in drafting prudent investor laws such as California did in 1995.[33]

The Reporter's Notes to the Rule clearly state the implications of attempting to beat the market:[34] "Economic evidence shows that, from a typical investment perspective, the major capital markets of this country are *highly efficient*, in the sense that available information is rapidly digested and reflected in the market prices of securities. As a result, fiduciaries and other investors are confronted with potent evidence that the application of expertise, investigation, and diligence in efforts to 'beat the market' in these publicly traded securities ordinarily promises little or no payoff, or even a *negative* payoff after taking account of research and transaction costs. Empirical research supporting the theory of efficient markets reveals that in such markets skilled professionals have *rarely* been able to identify under-priced securities (that is, to outguess the market with respect to future return) with any regularity. In fact, evidence shows that there is *little correlation* between fund managers' earlier successes and their ability to produce above-market returns in subsequent periods."

This chapter has detailed why no particular investor who can be identified today can be expected to beat the market. The following chapter examines the validity of the belief held by adherents of track record investing that past market-beating investment performance will continue and produce the same performance in the future.

Chapter Notes

[1] "The Performance of Mutual Funds in the Period 1945-1964" by Michael C. Jensen, *The Journal of Finance*, Volume 23, No. 2, May 1968, pages 389-416. *See* earlier studies: "Mutual Fund Performance" by William F. Sharpe, *Journal of Business*, Volume 39, January 1966, pages 119-138 and *Mutual Funds and Other Institutional Investors* by Irwin Friend, Marshall Blume and Jean Crockett (New York: McGraw-Hill, 1970).

[2] "Returns from Investing in Equity Mutual Funds 1971-1991" by Burton G. Malkiel, *The Journal of Finance*, Volume 50, No. 2, June 1995, pages 549-572.

[3] This is one of the two great principles of investment theory set forth since World War II. (The other principle is that a properly diversified portfolio can reduce investment risk and/or increase return. Its significance is covered in Chapter Eleven.)

[4] Many investors appear to define investment success as something other than the ability to beat the market. So they seek answers about investing for a variety of reasons. For example, some investors look for information about stocks that make the best long term investments. Others invested in fixed-income investments such as bonds want to find out whether interest rates will be going up or down. But what most investors are *really* looking for when they ask these questions is a way to beat the market. Naturally, stock picking and market timing money managers will always be ready with lots of "investment advice" to answer such all-important questions. This advice often goes into mind-numbing detail about how each of them has a "better way" of beating the market than any others in the crowd of professional money managers.

[5] Game theory was developed in the 1920s by physicist John von Neumann and economist Oskar Morgenstern. The "games" that game theory studies range from child rearing to nuclear war. *See Theory of Games and Economic Behavior* by John von Neumann and Oskar Morgenstern (Princeton, New Jersey: Princeton University Press, 1941). The first person to advance the idea that the stock market is a zero sum game was Louis Bachelier, a French mathematician. He introduced it in his Ph.D. thesis at the Sorbonne in 1900. *See Théorie de la spéculation* by Louis Bachelier (Paris: Gauthier-Villars, 1900). The original English translation of this 70-page work appeared in *The Random Character of Stock Prices* edited by Paul H. Cootner (Cambridge, Massachusetts: The MIT Press, 1964). Nobel Laureate Paul A. Samuelson was an early adherent to Bachelier's observation.

[6] Of course, after netting out his wins and losses, any active investor can also wind up earning the market return at the end of any time period. But this is not his investment goal - he wants to beat the market and thus earn more than the market return.

[7] This SIMON SAYS relies heavily on "The Arithmetic of Active Management" by William F. Sharpe, *Financial Analysts Journal*, January/February 1991, pages 7-9.

[8] A related example involves mutual fund ratings (and studies) that exclude from

the group of active money managers those who went out of business during the period under review. Because these managers were likely to have had inferior track records, any track records that "survive" tend to be superior. These better track records become the inputs which create the erroneous averages that misleadingly outperform the average actively-managed dollar. *See* page 128 for a discussion of "survivorship bias."

[9] *Bogle on Mutual Funds* by John C. Bogle (Burr Ridge, Illinois: Irwin Professional Publishing, 1994), page 178. *See* "Selecting Equity Mutual Funds" by John C. Bogle, *The Journal of Portfolio Management*, Winter 1992, pages 94-100 and "The Arithmetic of Active Management" by William F. Sharpe, *Financial Analysts Journal*, January/February 1991, pages 7-9.

[10] "The Behavior of Stock Prices" by Eugene F. Fama, *The Journal of Business*, Volume 37, No. 1, January 1965, pages 34-105.

[11] Stock pickers also use technical analysis.

[12] For example, if the market price of Varccek Industries stock is $15, its true underlying investment value is also $15.

[13] This example is presented in a very simplified way to illustrate a concept. As such, it doesn't account for the unknowable (and thus incalculable) pieces of other information that can affect the market price of a stock.

[14] Rex A. Sinquefield in "Active or Passive: The Debate about Investment Management Styles," a speech at the International Association for Financial Planning Success Forum, Boston, Massachusetts, September 12, 1994.

[15] "Fund Managers As Fruit Flies" by Catherine Barron, *Investors Chronicle*, March 22, 1996, pages 16-18. This quotation has been edited for greater clarity.

[16] *Ibid.*

[17] One thing that illustrates this is the number of people seeking to obtain the Chartered Financial Analyst (CFA) designation. This designation, awarded after the successful completion of three annual examinations and the fulfillment of required work experience, is the most prestigious that can be earned in the fields of financial analysis and investment management. Over the last decade, there has been a three-fold increase in the number of people taking these rigorous exams. In addition, the test sites where they are administered are no longer limited to North America. They now reach into almost every other part of the world including numerous locales in Africa. The presence of more CFAs every year even in such relatively remote areas makes it more, not less, likely that fewer and fewer stocks will escape the attention of stock pickers. This should reduce the number of less researched and inefficiently priced stocks. That, in turn, will tend to drive financial markets toward greater efficiency. (A study examined the average mutual fund and found that its investment performance was dominated by the market return regardless of whether the mutual fund managers making up the average were CFAs or non-CFAs. *See* "Are CFA Charterholders Better Equity Fund Managers?" by Ravi Shukla and Sandeep Singh, *Financial Analysts Journal*, November/Decem-

ber 1994, pages 68-74.)

[18] *See* "Pascal's Wager and the Efficient Market Hypothesis" by Peter L. Bernstein, *The Journal of Portfolio Management*, Fall 1996, page 1.

[19] *See* "Theory of Speculation" by Louis Bachelier in *The Random Character of Stock Prices* edited by Paul H. Cootner (Cambridge, Massachusetts: The MIT Press, 1964), page 28.

[20] "Diversification: Old and New" by James H. Lorie, *The Journal of Portfolio Management*, Winter 1975, pages 25-28.

[21] "If General Motors posts disappointing earnings or if Merck announces a major new drug, stock prices do not stand still while investors contemplate the news. No investor can afford to wait for others to act first. So they tend to act in a pack, immediately moving the price of General Motors or Merck to a level that reflects this new information. *But new information arrives in random fashion.* Consequently, stock prices move in unpredictable ways." *Against the Gods: The Remarkable Story of Risk* by Peter L. Bernstein (New York: John Wiley & Sons, Inc., 1996), page 145.

[22] "There is no question that, after prices in a market have fallen drastically, we can with hindsight conclude (or define) that prices had been too high." "Bubbles, Theory, and Market Timing" by Harold Bierman, Jr., *The Journal of Portfolio Management*, Fall 1995, pages 54-56.

[23] Identifying the ways that the market has been inefficient in the past does not necessarily help to profit from them in the future. Robert D. Arnott comments: "Market inefficiencies likely exist and are relatively easy to identify in *historical* perspective. But how many of these historical inefficiencies will prove profitable in the *future?*" *The Portable MBA In Investment* edited by Peter L. Bernstein (New York: John Wiley & Sons, Inc., 1995), pages 212-214. This quotation has been slightly edited and rearranged in sequence for greater clarity and context.

[24] "January Effect May Arrive Late, If It Comes At All" by Molly Baker, *The Wall Street Journal*, January 8, 1996, page C7.

[25] *The Portable MBA In Investment* edited by Peter L. Bernstein (New York: John Wiley & Sons, Inc., 1995), pages 212-214. This quotation has been slightly edited and rearranged in sequence for greater clarity and context.

[26] Although this is true, many active investment advisory firms (and mutual fund managers) continue to pick only 100 or fewer of the 500 large company stocks that make up the S&P 500. So even though there is widespread agreement that active money managers cannot beat the market by picking stocks from the S&P 500, they nevertheless continue to select them for their clients' portfolios and charge excessive fees for doing so.

[27] Investors who seek to invest in small company stocks and foreign stocks usually find that there is comparatively little available information about them. This scarcity of information often results in low trading volume for these stocks which translates into high annual expenses and trading costs.

[28] For example, trading-related costs such as brokerage commissions, market impact costs and bid-ask spread costs are notoriously large in many foreign stock markets. In addition to trading costs, the annual expenses of the average active fund that invests in foreign stocks were 1.58% and those of the average emerging markets fund were 1.92% in 1995. World Equity Benchmark Shares (WEBS) are sometimes offered as alternatives to index mutual funds that invest in specific foreign markets. Introduced in March 1996 by Morgan Stanley, WEBS are single country index portfolios that trade on the American Stock Exchange. There are 17 WEBS that each target a different Morgan Stanley country index (ten countries in Europe, four in Asia plus Australia, Canada and Mexico). However, WEBS have some problems. First, they are about twice as costly as index funds that invest in foreign markets, although still considerably less expensive than such actively-managed funds. Second, they can be riskier than index funds. Although a country-specific WEB is well diversified within the stocks of that country, it is maximally exposed to a drop in value of the country's stock market. In addition, a WEB runs the risk of being exposed to the currency fluctuations of a specific country. In contrast, an index fund mitigates these risks because it is invested in the many different stocks of many different countries.

[29] When an investment guru makes a prediction about the future earnings of any stock, he is really just *guessing* about what he believes will happen in the future since the future, by definition, is unpredictable.

[30] "Measuring the Performance of Performance Measurement" by Peter L. Bernstein in *Performance Evaluation, Benchmarks and Attribution Analysis* edited by Jan R. Squires (Charlottesville, Virginia: Association for Investment Management and Research, 1995), pages 68-71.

[31] John C. Bogle in "Be Not the First, Nor Yet the Last," a speech at the annual conference of the Association for Investment Management and Research, Atlanta, Georgia, May 8, 1996. This quotation has been slightly altered to provide better context.

[32] The American Law Institute (ALI) incorporated the Prudent Investor Rule into the *Restatement (Third) of Trusts*. In existence for over 60 years, the ALI represents some of the most advanced legal thinking in America. Section 227 of the Prudent Investor Rule reads as follows: "The trustee is under a duty to the beneficiaries to invest and manage the funds of the trust as a prudent investor would, in light of the purposes, terms, distribution requirements, and other circumstances of the trust. (a) This standard requires the exercise of reasonable care, skill, and caution, and is to be applied to investments not in isolation but in the context of the trust portfolio and as a part of an overall investment strategy, which should incorporate risk and return objectives reasonably suitable to the trust. (b) In making and implementing investment decisions, the trustee has a duty to diversify the investments of the trust unless, under the circumstances, it is prudent not to do so. (c) In addition, the trustee must: (1) conform to fundamental fiduciary duties of loyalty

. . . and impartiality . . . ; (2) act with prudence in deciding whether and how to delegate authority and in the selection and supervision of agents . . . ; and (3) incur only costs that are reasonable in amount and appropriate to the investment responsibilities of the trusteeship . . ." *Restatement (Third) of Trusts (Prudent Investor Rule),* (Washington D.C.: The American Law Institute, 1992), page 8.

[33] California Probate Code sections 16002(a), 16003 and 16045 through 16054 (collectively known as the Uniform Prudent Investor Act).

[34] *Restatement (Third) of Trusts (Prudent Investor Rule),* (Washington D.C.: The American Law Institute, 1992), page 75. Italics added.

FOUR

TRACK RECORD INVESTING

We know that the past is meaningless, but it is all we have.[1]
- An investment newsletter publisher

Overview

Track record investing is not the solution to the "investor's problem" of trying to find investments today that will beat the market. There are two reasons for this. First, there is no reliable way to predict when (or which) winners from the past will win in the future. Second, winning track records are usually the result of fortuitous asset class exposure, not skillful stock picking. The real solution to the investor's problem is to ignore track records and invest in a properly diversified portfolio of index funds.

Track Record Investing: The Solution To "The Investor's Problem?"

Stock pickers sooner or later encounter "the investor's problem:" how to find investments today that will beat the market. One widely used method for attempting to solve this problem is known as "track record investing." A track record investor is one who identifies some investment (such as a mutual fund) featuring an outstanding track record and invests in it because he thinks that the record will continue.

The fact that nearly 90% of the new money invested in mutual funds in 1995 was placed in funds with 4-star and 5-star Morningstar ratings indicates that track record investing is pervasive among investors. Indeed, track record investing is so common that an entire industry has sprung up to help investors identify future investment winners based on past performance. For example, winning mutual fund managers boast of their track records in newspaper and magazine advertisements. Mutual fund track records regularly appear in such publications as *Barron's, Business Week, Fortune, Money* and *Consumer Reports*. (We will see in the next section that even highly sophisticated pension plan consultants use track records as the most important criterion when recommending active money managers to their clients.)

But track record investing is not the solution to the investor's problem

of finding investments today that will beat the market. There are two principal reasons for this.

Past Investment Performance Does Not Predict Future Performance

The first reason why track record investing is not the solution to the
investor's problem is that past investment performance does not predict
future performance. In fact, no reputable study of mutual fund performance
over the last 30 years has found a dependable way for investors to identify
today, based on a reading of the *past*, *future* winners.[2] As John C. Bogle
warns:[3] "The great idea of the age, to go to [discount brokers such as]
Charles Schwab and trade funds for free, is in the last analysis a dangerous
and bad idea. You can't pick out the best performers of the future based on
past performance."[4]

Thus, there is no reliable way to know when (or which) winners from
the past will win in the future.[5] In addition, because track records are only
reflective of the past they cannot be identified as superior (or inferior) until
after the fact.

SIMON SAYS: *What's Past Is Past*

Active mutual fund managers (as well as any other active money manager)
can only guarantee their *past* success. This is true even though their marketing
plans to attract new investors always infer that past success will guarantee *future*
success. Yet active managers can only promise that their stock picks will pay off in
the future and their clients can only hope that they will keep these promises. In fact,
neither active managers nor their clients can ever be sure in advance of the superiority of their stock picking. These managers can only be sure of their success at the
same time as the rest of us are - in the future - when, after an examination of their
track records, we find that their stock picking turned out to be superior.

Illustration 2 on pages 62 and 63 lists the top five mutual fund
performances for each year of the 10-year period of 1985-1994 and
their subsequent performances. For example, in 1985 Fidelity OTC was
the top-performing general equity mutual fund out of a total of 363
such funds. In each of the following nine years, it ranked as follows:
1986: 302 of 409 funds; 1987: 229 of 466; 1988: 95 of 551; 1989: 151
of 603; 1990: 326 of 647; 1991: 129 of 714; 1992: 155 of 819; 1993:
761 of 1,027; and 1994: 877 of 1,392. This illustration quite clearly
shows that there is no correlation between past superior performance
and future superior performance.[6]

SIMON SAYS: *The Past Is Not Prologue*

One recent study that examined mutual fund performances for the period of 1976-1988 concluded that a mutual fund's track record *is* an important predictor of its future performance.[7] However, the study's findings are limited in scope which make its conclusion of little practical use to investors.

First, its authors admit that "the 'repeat-winner' pattern may not be a guide to beating the market." This finding alone severely undercuts the idea that an investor can find future market-beating mutual funds by identifying superior track records. Second, the repeat winner pattern was good for only *one- and two-year* periods during the thirteen years examined by the study. A short term effect that lasts only 12 or 24 months is a slender reed on which to build an investment strategy. In addition, if investors had to reinvest their portfolios that often, performance could be significantly eroded by commission loads and trading costs. Third, the repeat-winner pattern "does appear to be a guide to beating the pack over the long term." Even if true, this isn't much help to active investors who want to beat the market, not other mutual funds.

Instead of relying on the limited findings of this study, investors would be better served to look to the actual performance of the market and the overwhelming weight of academic evidence which both clearly show that the past does not reliably predict the future.

The Frank Russell Company: The Search For The "Best" Based On Track Records

The following example shows why reliance on track records is not a dependable way to find superior money managers. Although this example is a description of how an institutional pension plan searches for a superior money manager, it can just as easily apply to an individual active investor and the attempt on his own (or with the help of an investment advisor) to find superior managers or mutual funds based on their track records.

Institutional investors such as corporate pension plans control enormous amounts of investment assets. As fiduciaries, pension plan executives are required to maximize the return and/or minimize the risk of these investments for the benefit of current and retired corporate employees. So when a manager retained by a pension plan to actively invest its money underperforms the market enough times and/or by enough of a margin, the pension plan usually begins a search for a new manager to replace it.

One consultant often hired by pension plans to help them in these searches is the Frank Russell Company, a highly respected investment management and consulting firm. A marketing brochure describes its services:

Illustration 2

Top Five Mutual Funds And Their Subsequent Track Records (Ten Years - 1985 Through 1994)

	1986	1987	1988	1989	1990	1991	1992	1993	1994
1985									
1.Fidelity OTC	302	229	95	151	326	129	155	761	877
2.Twentieth Century: Giftrust	8	58	402	7	603	10	89	25	18
3.Evergreen Ltd. Market: Y	205	355	51	423	509	111	320	689	1333
4.Alliance Quasar: A	308	393	25	212	627	324	707	305	1238
5.GIT Equity: Spec. Growth	197	318	66	303	591	555	538	364	1019
Totals - 363 Funds	409	466	551	603	647	714	819	1027	1392
1986									
1.Fidelity Destiny II		82	96	267	232	209	138	47	118
2.Strong Opportunity		29	256	475	525	377	102	138	183
3.Fidelity Growth & Income		101	90	170	417	200	262	183	246
4.Voyager Growth Stock		70	413	167	437	69	595	1016	551
5.Bruce Fund		458	357	531	162	713	294	184	1373
Totals - 411 Funds		466	551	603	647	714	819	1027	1392
1987									
1.Dreyfus Cap Value: A			461	297	81	712	816	503	1011
2.Mathers Fund			337	576	5	707	697	953	1175
3.Hartwell Growth: A			517	72	581	59	723	661	1302
4.John Hancock Cap. Growth: A			150	429	395	257	607	835	1348
5.FPA Paramount			164	376	75	586	335	153	30
Totals - 468 Funds			551	603	647	714	819	1027	1392
1988									
1.Kaufmann Fund				11	382	11	273	233	32
2.SunAmerica: Small Co. Growth: A				364	636	93	66	428	107
3.Columbia Special				117	545	116	194	127	242
4.Parnassus Fund				597	622	106	4	264	21
5.Vista: Growth & Income: A				2	123	71	152	475	958
Totals - 554 Funds				603	647	714	819	1027	1392
1989									
1.Alger: Small Capital					14	92	673	496	1087
2.Vista: Growth & Income: A					123	71	152	475	958

3.GT Global America: A	439	664	8	762	12
4.Twentieth Century: Vista Inv.	587	17	785	863	109
5.Eagle Growth Shares	620	337	395	972	1372
Totals - 607 Funds	647	714	819	1027	1392
1990					
1.Phoenix Capital Appreciation: A		136	435	636	1005
2.Founders: Discovery Fund		58	149	603	1259
3.Progressive: Aggressive Growth		693	818	172	1377
4.Monetta Fund		88	606	982	1190
5.Mathers Fund		707	697	953	1174
Totals - 651 Funds		714	819	1027	1392
1991					
1.CGM Capital Development			100	38	1387
2.Montgomery: Small Cap			356	68	1320
3.American Heritage Fund			76	4	1390
4.Berger One Hundred			408	137	1216
5.United New Concepts			653	608	24
Totals - 719 Funds			819	1027	1392
1992					
1.Oakmark				31	176
2.Heartland: Value				207	274
3.Skyline: Special Equity				95	684
4.Parnassus Fund				264	21
5.Crabbe Huson Special				13	22
Totals - 824 Funds				1027	1392
1993					
1.Govett: Smaller Co.: A					1
2.PBHG Growth Fund					105
3.Oak Hall Equity					1356
4.American Heritage Fund					1390
5.UST Mstr.: Business & Indust.					218
Totals - 1,034 Funds					1392

Source: Lipper Analytical Services, Inc. The mutual funds in this illustration were selected from the Lipper database covering "general equity" mutual funds. This includes capital appreciation, growth, mid-cap, small company growth, growth and income, S&P 500 and equity income mutual funds.

"Many [pension] funds use highly sophisticated consultants to evaluate and recommend money managers and monitor their results. One of the earliest consultants - and now the largest and best known - is Frank Russell Company . . . Russell manages the money managers - evaluating, recommending, and monitoring results on behalf of such clients as AT&T, IBM, Chevron, GM, and J.C. Penney."

For most pension fiduciaries the objective of their search is to hire the best money managers in the business. The "best" are usually defined as those ranked in the top quartile of money management performance over the past three to five years.[8] During a search, "[m]ajor corporations and their pension fund consultants go through a prolonged and elaborate ritual . . . Pretty clearly, however, the single criterion on which at least 80 percent of the selection decision is based is the manager's investment performance during the prior three years."[9] So after a highly paid consultant has screened a large number of money managers in a process that involves a complex set of guidelines, the finalist for the job nearly always seems to be the one sporting a (recent) outstanding track record!

The decision to select a money manager largely on the basis of its track record is understandable from the standpoint of a pension plan fiduciary for a number of reasons.[10] First, it is much easier to justify hiring a money manager with a superior track record than one with a mediocre one. Second, by selecting such a manager it is easier to defend the selection process against criticism from corporate employees/plan beneficiaries if superior performance does not pan out.[11] Third, a track record is the most widely used criterion that pension consultants themselves rely on to select new money managers. Finally, a track record provides an easily understood "box score" for all concerned in the selection process.

But Russell and other pension plan consultants certainly know better than to recommend to their clients that they hire managers on the basis of past performance. A Russell senior research analyst confirms this:[12] "We've long believed that performance alone is not sufficient to predict the future . . . That is not a good or reliable way to pick managers." In fact, there are hundreds of studies showing that past performance is not predictive of future performance including at least one conducted by Russell itself.[13] *The Economist* comments:[14] "Like earlier [studies, this study] shows that apparently gifted investment managers are no more common than lucky cointossers, and that success in one four-year period implies nothing about performance in the next."

SIMON SAYS: *Just Why Doesn't Past Performance Predict Future Performance?*

Investment experts give at least three reasons *why* past performance doesn't predict future performance. The most frequently cited is that any outstanding track record turned in by a money manager is the result of the market favoring his particular investment style.[15] Yet this is as entirely unpredictable as the period of time that such good fortune will last. This means that it is impossible to (1) identify an outstanding track record until after the fact and (2) know when (if ever) a manager's investment style that has produced an outstanding track record will be favored by the market to produce a similar one in the future.

Second, outstanding investment performance is often achieved when a money management firm (or mutual fund) is small. Such performance usually fuels an exponential growth in the amount of money that must be invested. But the "market impact" of trading costs and other costs (examined in Chapter Twelve) generated by the investment of this much larger amount of money can neutralize or even outweigh the margin by which a skillful or lucky money manager may beat the market in the future.

Third, as the management firm grows, the investment "superstar" who was responsible for the outstanding track record often takes on additional administrative duties and leaves more of the stock picking to others. If this individual is truly skillful but can't transfer his skills to other stock pickers, it is highly unlikely that past superior performance will repeat itself in the future.

It is clear, then, that Russell and other pension plan consultants are well aware that past investment performance is not predictive of future performance. Yet even though they admit this in their public utterances and marketing brochures, the very solution - managers with (recent) superior track records - that they usually offer to their clients belies this and confirms the truth of the quotation at the beginning of the chapter: *"We know that the past is meaningless, but it is all we have."*

Since pension consultants know that track records are not helpful in identifying a manager who will be the "best" in the future, the only other criterion that they can use to find the best is to identify *skill*. A Russell analyst states:[16] "If I have to base future expectations, I want to base it on identification of skill as opposed to identification of good performance." The problem with this reasoning is that it is well nigh impossible to determine if a superior track record was due to skill or to luck. It takes a long track record to identify skill; it is not something that can be determined over a three-year or five-year period. In fact, the time period that is required ranges from 15 to 80 years depending on how outstanding the track record.

Even if it was possible to determine that a manager was truly skillful, there is no assurance that his skill would be rewarded *after* this determination. Why? Because the prevailing market environment may not favor the particular investment style at which he is skillful. Furthermore, if it was really possible to identify skillful money managers, then wouldn't all the money be in their hands by now and wouldn't all the money managers lacking skill be out of business? The fact that this obviously is not the case is strong evidence that there is no reliable way to identify a skillful money manager, especially over the short run.

Despite this, pension consultants continue to thrive. In fact, after a manager who has not lived up to his past fails to have his contract renewed, a pension consultant can conduct yet another search for the 'best' money manager and earn yet another healthy fee!

Because there is no reliable way to know when (or even if) a past superior record will produce a future superior record, pension plan fiduciaries are wasting their time and the money of their investors when they hire pension consultants to conduct searches for new managers on the basis of track records. Fortunately, more and more fiduciaries are ignoring track records and indexing greater amounts of the plan assets for which they are responsible.

Investment Winners Are Usually Produced By Fortuitous Asset Class Exposure, Not Skillful Stock Picking

The second reason why track record investing is not the solution to the investor's problem is that a winning performance is usually the result of fortuitous asset class exposure, not skillful stock picking.

"Fortuitous asset class exposure" occurs when an active money manager places money (intentionally or unintentionally) in the right asset class at the right time. (An "asset class" consists of investments in the financial markets such as individual stocks or bonds that have common investment characteristics. Examples of asset classes include the large company stocks of the S&P 500 and foreign stocks. A fuller discussion about asset classes appears in Chapter Nine.) For example, suppose that the manager of an active mutual fund invests primarily in some of the large company stocks that are represented in the S&P 500. In order to boost his fund's performance against the S&P 500, he will purchase en masse those stocks (say, small company stocks) that currently enjoy better returns than large company stocks.

As a result, the fund will generate the superior performance of small company stocks even though it shows up in mutual fund ratings as a large company stock fund. This makes investors think that the large company stock fund manager was a superior stock picker with true investment skill.[17] However, it is much more probable that the manager was only lucky in fortuitously singling out an asset class that was temporarily enjoying superior investment performance. This phenomenon is apparent when we examine the track record compiled by Peter Lynch in the 1980s while he was the manager of Fidelity Magellan.

Nancy L. Jacob, former dean of the School of Business at the University of Washington and long-time trustee of the College Retirement Equities Fund (CREF), reviews Lynch's record:[18] "By all accounts, Lynch gained a reputation as a master stock picker while managing the excellently performing Magellan Fund during the 1980s. The S&P 500 was the performance benchmark used by Fidelity and by virtually everyone who had occasion to assess Lynch's investing prowess. Yet, it was well known at the time that Lynch had invested a significant portion (25 percent or so) of Magellan's assets in foreign stocks, which are not included in the S&P 500. During the last half of the 1980s as the U.S. dollar weakened and Japan's market soared, foreign stocks as a group dramatically outperformed domestic stocks as a group."

This story is not presented to minimize Lynch's accomplishments as a money manager. Rather, it underscores the importance of attempting to distinguish between exceptional stock picking and placing a good portion of invested money in the right asset class at the right time.[19]

The story about Lynch also illustrates the importance of measuring the performance of an active mutual fund against the performance of a *relevant* index.[20] For example, the performance of an active small company stock fund earning outstanding returns should not be compared to the S&P 500 index since it only represents the investment behavior of large American stocks. To do so would be like comparing apples to oranges. Instead, the performance of an active small company stock fund should be measured against a relevant small company stock index.[21]

Once this more accurate comparison is made, the superior performance of the fund usually *disappears* from mutual fund ratings. Why? Because when an active small company stock fund is a superior performer (vis-à-vis the S&P 500, for example), usually *all* small company stocks are superior performers. (This isn't true only of the asset class of small company stocks. It also pertains to other asset classes of stocks such as medium company stocks and technology stocks.) So the fund is only reflecting the currently superior performance of the asset class of small company stocks of which it is a part. This is why it is often fortuitous asset class exposure not skillful (or lucky) stock picking that lands an active fund at the top of the mutual fund ratings pile for any given period of time.

It is doubtful that any discussion of fortuitous asset class exposure will stop an active investor from thinking: "Even if a money manager was entirely lucky in temporarily singling out an outstanding asset class performance, he still made his clients a bundle of money so I'll take good luck any day."

While this kind of reasoning makes sense when playing the lottery, it is not a good idea to base an investment strategy on the hope of such good luck continuing in the future. Why? Because the money that an investor invests in the market (whether in individual stocks or bonds or in asset classes) can be likened to a series of bets, whether placed at monthly, yearly or longer intervals. If an investor believes in luck, he is going to run into some good luck and some bad luck with these bets. But the good luck and the bad luck will tend to cancel out each other over a long period of time. This makes it unlikely that an investor will beat the market, especially when the reality of costs and taxes is recognized.[22]

SIMON SAYS: *Like, Why Are These Guys So Rich?*

Investment magazines such as *Forbes* or *Money* often publish color photos of the current crop of investment gurus in striking poses. The articles frequently relate an assortment of entertaining "war stories" from their distinguished careers. They tell about their advanced degrees from prestigious schools and their high compensation levels. These money managers express great confidence that they can pick investment winners - whether they be stocks and bonds selected for mutual funds or for portfolios of individual investments. Many investors have a real emotional need to believe that someone can actually do this. Alfred Cowles III observed this behavior in active investors more than sixty years ago:[23] "[Active investors] want to believe that somebody knows. *A world in which nobody knows can be truly frightening.*"

So it is easy to see why the people featured in such articles who manage billions of dollars for millions of people are looked on with such awe by the investing public. After all, if they weren't so smart, why would they be entrusted with all that money and why would they be so rich? Well, it certainly isn't because they achieve superior investment returns! In fact, over the last thirty years the collective track record of active money managers, both institutional and non-institutional, has significantly *underperformed* the market. As Rex A. Sinquefield notes:[24] "Poor investment advice is not cheap. You have to pay dearly for it."

So how can the fat fees commanded by these money managers be explained? The only conceivable answer is that they provide active investors (who need to believe in something) with *assurances* that they know all about the mysteries of beating the market. The result? A lot of active investors who are bamboozled into paying a lot of money for investment results (and ultimately, empty assurances) that, on an aggregate net basis, are less than those achieved by indexers. Yet instead of revolting against such poor performance, active investors amazingly continue to shower riches on this bunch of overpaid underachievers.

The uncertainty about whether an investment track record is the result of fortuitous asset class exposure or skillful stock picking can largely be resolved by the use of a simple statistical procedure. The fly in the ointment, though, is that the track record to be measured must cover *many years*. Peter L. Bernstein estimates[25] that it requires a period of about 35 years to have a 95% degree of confidence that a track record outperforming the market by an average annual return of 1.7% is the result of true investment skill.[26]

Other Reasons Why Track Record Investing Is Not The Solution To The Investor's Problem

There are other reasons why track record investing is not the solution to the investor's problem of finding investments today that will beat the market.

First, track records can be *misleading* to investors. Although few investors know it, often the most important factor that separates a winning track record from a losing one is the choice of their starting dates and ending dates.[27] For example, Fabian Financial Services, a well known market timing advisory firm, generated a cumulative gain of 282% for the 10-year period from July 1, 1980 through June 30, 1990. Over the same period, the S&P 500 gained 376%. However, lengthening the period of Fabian's track record by $1^1/_2$ years so that the ending date becomes December 31, 1991 produced a 533% cumulative gain for the $11^1/_2$-year period compared to the S&P 500's cumulative gain of 485%.

In this instance, lengthening a track record from 10 to $11^1/_2$ years *turns a loser into a winner* (just as shortening it $1^1/_2$ years from $11^1/_2$ years to 10 years turns a winner into a loser). So guess which track record was prominently featured by Fabian in advertisements that publicized its market timing expertise? In the world of track record investing, a winner is often crowned as a result of clever marketing.

SIMON SAYS: *Active Investment Advisors Always Have Excellent Track Records - Just Ask Them!*

Needless to say, in their efforts to attract new investment clients or when reporting to existing clients, active investment advisors always put their best foot forward. For example, if an advisor has a poor investment track record over the recent past, he will accentuate his better long term record. If he has an inferior long term record, he can pull out a more recent superior performance. It would be interesting to see if any active investment advisors (or mutual fund managers) have ever admitted that their investment track records were anything *less* than excellent.

Second, investors rarely understand that an outstanding track record always carries an undue amount of *risk*. As Roger C. Gibson, the noted investment authority and financial educator reminds us, investment winners turn out to be those who implemented a nondiversified (i.e., higher risk) investment strategy which concentrated money at the right time in whatever happened to be the top-performing sector of the market.[28] Thus, an outstanding track record is really nothing more than the market's reward for exposure to excessive investment risk.[29]

Third, track record investing can blind investors in assessing the impact of *taxes*. As we will see in Chapter Thirteen, published mutual fund ratings are pre-tax returns which disguise their true net after-tax performance. For example, Fidelity Magellan generated an average annual pre-tax return of 18.3% over the ten-year period from mid-1985 to mid-1995. But once taxes (and commissions) were taken into account, the after-tax return dropped to 12.7%.

The well known retirement expert and investment educator Bruce J. Temkin helps us to understand yet another downside of playing the track record investing game. He observes that after the performances of outstanding mutual funds are posted, the investment information system will always be able to show investors *how they would have been better off* if they had held them.

An example is when an investor looks at the headlines of a financial magazine. He may be thrilled to find out that he holds one or more of "The 25 Best Mutual Funds Ever Created By Mankind That Have Never Lost Money." Yet when this happy investor retrieves the next month's issue of the same magazine, he may see that 25 new "winning" mutual funds have replaced the previous dazzling crop.

Is the investor now supposed to sell off the magazine's previous recommendations that he holds and then buy the new ones or should he add some or all of the new funds to his portfolio? This "Monday Morning Investment Quarterbacking" reduces investing to a process in which finding a particular investment winner or uncovering a 'smarter' investment advisor just depends on the weekly or monthly publication date of the financial magazine which describes the winner or profiles the advisor.

As a result, active investors get caught up in a game where it is hard for them to feel good because they rarely consider themselves winners. But indexers understand that there will *always* be a group of market-beating winners that will prevail in the investment race at the end of any time period. This is why they never worry about the fact that it is always possible to show investors how they would have been better off if they had held the current winning group of mutual funds.

SIMON SAYS: *The Bleak Odds Facing An Investor Who Wants To Beat The Market*

No wonder it is uncommon for an active investor to outperform an indexer over the long run. First, he must face the inescapable fact that any financial market in which he chooses to invest is a *zero sum game*. This destines him to the mathematical certainty that, in the aggregate with other active investors, he will do worse in net investment performance than an indexer.

An active investor can always hope that he will do better than the rest of the herd on an individual basis. But the *Efficient Market Theory* give short shrift to this since it holds that the individual investment performances of most active investors are likely to fall below the market return earned by an indexer.

Moreover, an active investor has little chance of profiting from the occasional *inefficiencies* that appear in the market because they usually disappear before he is skillful or lucky enough to find and profit from them.

Perhaps an active investor can study *track records* to find future investment winners. But track records only reflect the past and do not predict the future so it is unlikely that he will prevail over an indexer using this investment method. Even when an active investor turns to an investment advisor with an excellent track record, what assurance can the advisor offer him about the future other than to say *"trust me?"*

Sources Of Investment Information Used By Track Record Investors

The most well known sources of investment information used by track record investors include Morningstar, the Forbes Mutual Fund Honor Roll and mutual fund advertisements. An examination of each of these sources shows why the hope of superior performance is often dashed by the unpredictability of the future and its failure to live up to the superior performance of the past.

Morningstar

Morningstar Mutual Funds, a mutual fund ratings guide, is probably the source of investment information most widely used by track record investors today. The Morningstar mutual fund rating system tends to give five stars to the most recent outstanding mutual fund performers. For example, in the late 1980s international mutual funds and junk bond funds were the top performers so they were awarded five stars. The same was true in the early 1990s with health care funds.

But when a sector of the market unpredictably goes out of favor, mutual funds invested in that sector are downgraded by Morningstar to fewer stars. A case in point is a particular mutual fund invested in Japanese stocks that received five stars from Morningstar in 1989. In 1990 it got one star. This indicates that when this mutual fund was performing well it enjoyed a 5-star rating and when it was doing badly it got one star. But other than that the stars reveal nothing.

Of course, most investors do not believe this because they regard Morningstar as a kind of investment Bible. After all (as noted earlier in this chapter), nearly 90% of the new money that was invested in mutual funds in 1995 went into funds with 4-star and 5-star Morningstar ratings. But the problem with track record investing of this kind is that the average Morningstar 5-star mutual fund keeps its lofty rating only for about *eight months*.[30] The combination of these two factors - investor appetite for 5-star performance and the relatively short period that a mutual fund actually keeps its five stars - often gets investors into trouble. This trouble takes the form of investment whipsaw.

"Investment whipsaw" occurs when investors select mutual funds near their 5-star peaks because they become enamored with their outstanding track records and then dump them near their 1-star troughs when they become disgusted with their subsequent poor performances. Thus, investment whipsaw is something that investors do to themselves - it is not an outside force of the market.

How do track record investors usually react to a round of investment whipsaw? They go back to Morningstar's ratings guide and redouble their efforts to find a winner! This often means going through another round of investment whipsaw and repeating a losing investment performance. These investors fail to admit the nature of the problem which is that past superior performance has literally nothing to do with predicting future superior performance.

A good example of the unfortunate consequences that can result from investment whipsaw is found in a 1994 study conducted by Lipper Analytical Services, Inc., a widely known mutual fund data firm.[31] Lipper selected those mutual funds that were rated by Morningstar with five stars at the beginning of the year and then measured their performances in the following 12 months against mutual fund averages. This was done for each of four one-year periods in 1990, 1991, 1992 and 1993.

The study found that the majority of Morningstar's 5-star stock mutual funds underperformed against mutual fund averages in each of the four subsequent years. This means that investors can end up in the wrong mutual funds at the wrong time when they select market-beating mutual funds from Morningstar's 5-star list. It not only demonstrates the unreliability of track record investing over a period even as short as one year, but it also shows how *consistently unpredictable* actively-managed mutual funds can be in beating the market (and getting beat by it). The results of the Lipper study are depicted in Illustration 3, below.

Illustration 3

The Percentage Of Morningstar's 5-Star Stock Mutual Funds
Subsequently Underperforming Stock Mutual Fund Averages

Beginning Year	Subsequent Year	Percentage Subsequently Underperforming
1990	1991	52.6
1991	1992	71.1
1992	1993	56.0
1993	1994	63.6

Source: Lipper Analytical Services, Inc.

Specifically, the study found that at the end of 1990 after a long period of superior performance by foreign-oriented mutual funds, 32% (25 of 77) of the total number of 5-star stock funds were listed in Morningstar's "international" and "global" fund categories. Predictably, many investors jumped into these superior-performing 5-star funds fully believing that their track records would be repeated in the future. However, *every one* of these 25 international and global funds subsequently underperformed the average stock fund in the following twelve months.

Conversely, at the end of 1992, after foreign-oriented mutual funds had been poor performers for a year, no international or global funds appeared on Morningstar's 5-star list. Predictably again, few investors were attracted to these international and global funds because they were at the bottom of the Morningstar ratings pile. The result? Investors missed the superior performance of international and global mutual funds that began at the end of 1992.

To its credit, Morningstar advises investors that its mutual fund ratings should not, by themselves, be used to predict future performance. So it seems unfair to hold Morningstar responsible for the way in which investors use its rating system in their investment strategies. Yet it seems equally unfair to blame investors for reasoning that *current* 5-star mutual funds (their high ratings achieved because of *past* success) should deliver *future* 5-star performance.[32] Indeed, Morningstar's 5-star "Seal of Approval" creates the expectation among investors that these funds will be future winners.

SIMON SAYS: *Morningstar Wants The Best Of Both Worlds*

On the one hand, Morningstar advises investors not to use its mutual fund ratings as the sole indicator of future investment performance. On the other hand, though, Morningstar has never been known to forbid the use of these ratings in mutual fund advertisements. These advertisements suggest to investors that because publicized funds have been superior in the past, they will be superior in the future. Logically, Morningstar cannot have it both ways. This is particularly true when it knows full well that millions of active investors take its ratings at face value.

Thus, track record investors will be sorely disappointed when they use Morningstar as a source of information to help them find future mutual fund winners. This is why Rex A. Sinquefield advises: "The answer to smart investing is not found in the stars."

The Forbes Mutual Fund Honor Roll

The Forbes Mutual Fund Honor Roll, another source of investment information used by track record investors, is touted by the media as a dependable way to find mutual funds that will beat the market in the future. Each year since 1973, highly respected *Forbes* magazine has singled out 15-30 stock mutual funds and elevated them to Forbes Honor Roll status. These superior-performing funds are selected on the basis of their total returns over at least a ten-year period, the stability of their investment management over at least seven years and their relative performance both in up markets and in down markets over several market cycles.

A comprehensive 1992 study by John C. Bogle examined the record of the Forbes Honor Roll covering the period of 1974-1990.[33] He sought the answers to these two questions: (1) did Honor Roll mutual funds continue to beat comparable non-Honor Roll funds in subsequent years during the 1974-1990 time period and (2) did Honor Roll funds continue to beat the market in the ensuing years during this time period?

Bogle answered the first question by finding that there was a virtual tie in performance between the Honor Roll funds and the average stock mutual fund in subsequent years during this time period. He answered the second question by finding that, after commission loads were taken into account, the Honor Roll funds subsequently underperformed the market by a significant amount over the 1974-1990 period.[34] Illustration 4 on page 75 and Illustration 5 on page 76 show the results of the study.

Illustration 4

Forbes Honor Roll vs. Indexing
(1974-1990)

	1974	1975	1976	1977	1978	1979	1980	1981	1982	1983	1984	1985	1986	1987	1988	1989	1990	Cumulative Return	Annual Rate of Return
Forbes Honor Roll [a] (Before Commission Loads)	-25.2%	23.6%	24.7%	5.9%	6.9%	40.4%	34.7%	-4.7%	23.5%	23.8%	-4.7%	27.5%	12.1%	2.0%	14.9%	28.4%	-4.5%	604.8%	12.2%
Forbes Honor Roll [a] (After Commission Loads)	-28.9%	23.6%	23.6%	5.3%	4.9%	38.8%	30.4%	-5.8%	21.6%	20.5%	-6.9%	27.4%	10.6%	1.4%	14.9%	26.2%	-6.7%	439.7%	10.4%
Wilshire 5000 Index [b]	-28.4%	38.5%	26.6%	-2.6%	9.3%	25.6%	33.7%	-3.7%	18.7%	23.5%	3.1%	32.6%	16.1%	2.3%	17.9%	29.2%	-6.2%	633.4%	12.4% [c]

a Performance figures exclude international and balanced funds.
b Performance figures are net of .2% annual operating expenses.
c The S&P 500 return for this period was 12.2%.

Source: "Selecting Equity Mutual Funds" by John C. Bogle, *The Journal of Portfolio Management*, Winter 1992. This illustration was slightly modified by the author.

Illustration 5

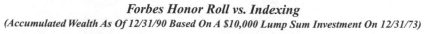

Forbes Honor Roll vs. Indexing

(Accumulated Wealth As Of 12/31/90 Based On A $10,000 Lump Sum Investment On 12/31/73)

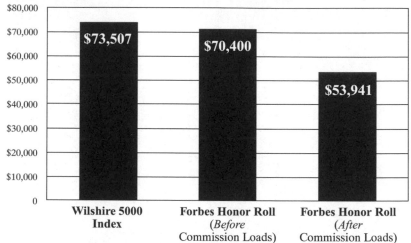

	Wilshire 5000 Index	Forbes Honor Roll (Before Commission Loads)	Forbes Honor Roll (After Commission Loads)
	$73,507	$70,400	$53,941

Source: "Selecting Equity Mutual Funds" by John C. Bogle, *The Journal of Portfolio Management,* Winter 1992.

Winning mutual funds from the past significantly underperformed the market in the future for several reasons. One reason is that the superior performance generated by an active mutual fund manager's particular investment style is dependent on a time period in which the market favors that style. Since the stock market unpredictably favors (and disfavors) different investment styles for unpredictable periods of time, a manager's past superior *performance* is therefore closely tied to a past *time period* in which the market happened to favor his kind of investment style.

A good example of the link between a past performance and a past time period can be found in the 1983 Honor Roll. In that year it contained a large number of small company stock mutual funds because small company stocks had generally outperformed large company stocks over the previous six or seven years. But in the following years beginning in 1984, small company stocks began a dismal run in performance relative to large company stocks. As a result, small company stock funds began to drop out of the Honor Roll after 1983. So while the small company stock funds in the 1983 Honor Roll had great track records, their returns in 1984 and in the following years were, on average, inferior to the market and to the average stock mutual fund.

Another reason why Honor Roll funds subsequently underperformed the market is that they came back to earth after their high-flying years and turned in below average performances. (This is the story of the inevitable "regression to the mean" which will be covered in Chapter Six when we examine Peter Lynch's investment record.)

A final reason why Honor Roll funds underperformed the market in ensuing periods is that they are actively-managed funds which often bear heavy commission loads that cut into gross investment performance.

Bogle's study of the Forbes Honor Roll reached two conclusions: (1) investors cannot pick out a future winning mutual fund based on its superior track record and (2) over the long run, the market outperforms even highly rated active mutual funds.

Mutual Fund Advertisements

Mutual fund advertisements, although not as seriously relied on by investors, are another source of investment information used in track record investing. Mutual fund advertisements convey this implicit message: "Since These Funds Have Done Well In The Past They Will Do Well In The Future So Buy Them Today."

Active mutual funds boasting of their "No. 1" status run in countless advertisements. This makes it appear that there aren't any *losing* mutual funds. Indeed, since there are now nearly 7,000 mutual funds[35] featuring so many investment objectives spread out over so many time periods in so many categories, something must be wrong if each and every mutual fund weren't No. 1 at some point in time! As William F. Sharpe, a co-recipient of the 1990 Nobel Prize in Economic Science, jokes:[36] "It is like the Academy Awards: Best actress under the age of 30 in a low-budget film made by a producer in India."

Mutual fund advertisements are required to carry an SEC-mandated disclaimer which states that "past performance is no guarantee of future performance." While some investors may acknowledge this, most of them *act as if* these disclaimers were not true at all. They fall for the implied message of mutual fund advertising that past superior performance will be duplicated in the future by continuing to purchase and sell mutual funds based on track records.

Index Mutual Funds: The Solution To "The Investor's Problem"

The solution to the investor's problem of trying to find investments today that will beat the market is to invest in a properly diversified portfolio of index funds. This allows an investor to *ignore* investment track records and give up trying to beat the market. The implementation of an indexing strategy is simply an acknowledgment of what even many professional active money managers privately admit: there is no reliable way to predict future market-beating investment performance based on track records.[37]

This chapter has demonstrated the shortcomings of a traditional method of investing - the idea held by track record investors that the excellence of the past will be repeated in the future. The next chapter analyzes some sources of investment advice widely used by investors in their attempts to beat the market.

Chapter Notes

[1] *The Wall Street Journal*, April 5, 1995, page R4, quoting Michael Stolper, publisher of a San Diego-based investment newsletter.

[2] Two of the most recent of these studies are "On Persistence in Mutual Fund Performance" by Mark M. Carhart, *The Journal of Finance*, Volume 52, No. 1, March 1997, pages 57-82 and "Does Historical Performance Predict Future Performance?" by Ronald N. Kahn and Andrew Rudd, *Financial Analysts Journal*, November/December 1995, pages 43-52. The first study concluded: "Persistence in mutual fund performance does not reflect superior stock-picking skill. Rather, common factors in stock returns and persistent differences in mutual fund expenses and transaction costs explain almost all of the predictability in mutual fund returns . . . While the popular press will no doubt continue to glamorize the best-performing mutual fund managers, the mundane explanations of strategy and investment costs account for almost all of the important predictability in mutual fund returns."

[3] "Firebrand John Bogle Envisions Pain Ahead From 'Greed' at Funds" by Robert McGough, *The Wall Street Journal*, April 4, 1996, page R1.

[4] Burton G. Malkiel adds: "I guarantee you that there is no way today, using investment track records or any other method that can be found, that you will be able to predict which mutual funds will be in the top one-quarter. I also guarantee you that 20 years from now, an index fund tracking a broad-based market index will be in the top one-quarter of all mutual funds still left around during that period." "Some Like It Hot, Some Like It Cheap" by Thomas Easton, *Forbes*, February 12, 1996, page 114. This quotation has been slightly edited to provide more context and greater clarity.

[5] *See* "Persistence in Performance" by Ernest M. Ankrim, *Russell Research Commentary*, January 1992 and "Volatility and Predictability of Manager Alpha" by John A. Christopherson and Andrew L. Turner, *The Journal of Portfolio Management*, Fall 1991, pages 5-12. However, there is one correlation between the past and the future which seems to hold true in some cases. Past *poor* performance of some mutual funds tends to persist in the future primarily because of the high costs charged by these funds. *See* "A Matter of Cost and Style" by William F. Sharpe, *Investment Advisor*, October 1994, pages 83-89. An example of this is the Steadman Group. This is a mutual fund group that is legendary on Wall Street for turning in consistently poor performance. Three of the four funds in this group have lost money in the last five years of the current bull market. In addition, they were ranked as the three worst performing mutual funds in the entire country during that period. The formula for such persistently bad performance is enormously high fund expenses and risky, bad investments. *See* "At Dead-Last Steadman, Past is Prologue" by Robert McGough, *The Wall Street Journal*, April 15, 1997, page C1.

[6] Even if there was a correlation, active investors can never be sure that it will hold up in the future. The inability to discern a predictive pattern between past superior

performance and future superior performance is not confined to mutual funds. It is also present in the year by year performance rankings of large institutional pension plans. "In looking at . . . [1987 investment performance] - in particular at the list of 1987's 'losers' of pension fund business - it is very disturbing, but not at all surprising, to see among those losers many firms that were among the big winners only a few years ago." "Hiring High, Firing Low" by Robert Kirby, *Institutional Investor*, May 1988, page 29. This statement could apply to *any* year's list of losers.

[7] "History Does Repeat Itself" by Roger G. Ibbotson and William N. Goetzmann, *Financial Planning*, February 1995, pages 95-96.

[8] "The Steinbrenner Syndrome and the Challenge of Manager Selection" by Michael L. Troutman, *Financial Analysts Journal*, March/April 1991, pages 37-44.

[9] "Hiring High, Firing Low" by Robert Kirby, *Institutional Investor*, May 1988, page 29.

[10] "The Steinbrenner Syndrome and the Challenge of Manager Selection" by Michael L. Troutman, *Financial Analysts Journal*, March/April 1991, pages 37-44.

[11] At the personal level, it would be very difficult for a spouse charged with the responsibility of finding an investment advisor to justify to the other spouse the hiring of one that was a recent loser, especially if that loser continued to lose in the future!

[12] "Russell Focuses on Criteria Other Than Returns" by Hillary Durgin, *Pensions & Investments*, March 30, 1992, page 24.

[13] "Persistence in Performance" by Ernest M. Ankrim, *Russell Research Commentary*, January 1992 (at the time this study was published, the author was a Frank Russell Company employee). The following studies (representative of hundreds of others) have also found no discernible patterns that allow investors to predict when (or even which) superior track records will be repeated in the future. *See* "Volatility and Predictive Ability of Manager Alpha" by Jon A. Christopherson and Andrew L. Turner, *The Journal of Portfolio Management*, Fall 1991, pages 5-12 (at the time this study was published, both authors were Frank Russell Company employees), "How Consistently do Active Managers Win?" by Patricia C. Dunn and Rolf D. Theisen, *The Journal of Portfolio Management*, Summer 1983, pages 47-51 (the authors of this study used data supplied by the Frank Russell Company) and "Investment Policy Review," Collins Associates, April 1989, Newport Beach, California.

[14] *The Economist*, March 7, 1992, page 81.

[15] This usually has a much larger bearing on a manager's track record ranking than any skill. Thus, even a skillful money manager will produce an inferior track record if the market doesn't happen to favor his particular investment style.

[16] *See* "Russell Focuses on Criteria Other Than Returns" by Hillary Durgin, *Pensions & Investments*, March 30, 1992, page 24.

[17] Nevertheless, the fact that a stock picker at the top of the heap in one time period has a very real tendency to be average or even occupy the bottom in the next time

period is strong evidence that stock pickers possess little, if any, market-beating investment skill. This is not to flatly suggest that stock pickers who beat the market have no skill whatsoever. But the insurmountable problem is that even assuming that an element of skill exists, we still cannot know who, out of many existing stock pickers, actually possesses it.

[18] *The Portable MBA In Investment* edited by Peter L. Bernstein (New York: John Wiley & Sons, Inc., 1995), pages 337 and 418, footnote 17.

[19] Active investors would no doubt argue that it really doesn't matter whether or not Lynch was a good picker of individual stocks in this example. But they must admit that there is a big difference between picking the right 10 individual stocks out of an asset class of, say, 135 stocks and being fortuitously invested in 125 of these stocks.

[20] In the example previously cited in this section, the relevant index against which Lynch's record should have been measured would have been a blend of U.S. and international stocks, not the S&P 500. The use of this more accurate benchmark would have reduced (or perhaps eliminated) Lynch's outperformance of the market during this period.

[21] Even when the performance of an active small company stock fund is measured against a small company stock index such as the Russell 2000, it may not be a true apples-to-apples comparison. For example, in early 1997 the average active small company stock fund invested 18.5% of its assets in technology stocks compared to 12.8% for the Vanguard small company stock index fund which tracks the Russell 2000 index. The average active small company stock fund was therefore more oriented toward fast growing, high priced growth stocks than the index. This difference is one of the reasons why some active funds turned in better performances at that time than index funds tracking the Russell index. Another difference is that over the past few years, most active small company stock funds were invested in some stocks that were significantly larger than those in the Russell 2000 index - in other words, they weren't small company stocks. During this period, having just a minor portion of the assets of an active small company stock fund invested in these larger stocks substantially boosted its performance. An index fund manager does not make these kinds of bets. *See* "Funds Haven't Done Well By Indexing Small Stocks" by Karen Damato, *The Wall Street Journal*, January 28, 1997, page C1.

[22] This is why it is not good enough just to be a *lucky* investor.

[23] *Capital Ideas* by Peter L. Bernstein (New York: The Free Press, 1992) page 38. Italics added.

[24] Rex A. Sinquefield in "Active or Passive: The Debate about Investment Management Styles," a speech at the International Association for Financial Planning Success Forum, Boston, Massachusetts, September 12, 1994.

[25] *The Portable MBA In Investment* edited by Peter L. Bernstein (New York: John Wiley & Sons, Inc., 1995), page 327.

[26] Two investment gurus whose track records generally fit these requirements are

John Neff and John Templeton. Neff managed the Vanguard Windsor Fund for over 31 years from June 1964 through December 1995. During this period, he comfortably outperformed the 10.5% average annual compound return of the S&P 500 by generating a return of 13.8%. Another skillful investment guru who beat the market over the long run was John Templeton. During his more than 32-year tenure at the Templeton Growth Fund from December 1954 through March 1987, he compiled an average annual compound return of 15.4% in comparison to the 11.4% return of the S&P 500. For this entire period, the mutual fund carried an 8.5% commission load and a very high 2.5% average annual expense ratio. Despite these huge drags on performance, Templeton managed to easily beat the market. Yet even the fact that we can be sure that these two investment gurus were both truly skillful in the past doesn't help us find *other* skillful money managers *today* so that we can end up being enriched by them from here on into the *future*.

[27] For an excellent real-life example of the ramifications of time dependency in track record investing, *see* "Does the Emperor Wear Clothes or Not? The Final Word (or Almost) on the Parable of Investment Management" by Philip Halpern, Nancy Calkins and Tom Ruggels, *Financial Analysts Journal*, July/August 1996, pages 9-15.

[28] ". . . investors often have a hard time seeing risk when they look back at historical results. The stock or mutual fund that has had great performance will not necessarily have frightening statistical risk measures, even though it actually may have been quite risky. The reason is that the risks that could have devastated the position simply did not mature. There is only one way to handle those risks: broad diversification. But as soon as you follow the broadly diversified path, you will never get the best result if 'best' is defined as winning the performance race. That race will always be won by a nondiversified strategy that concentrated money in whatever happened to be the top-performing sector at the time. The problem is that this is not something that is predictable at the start of the race - the risks that did not mature are not seen as risks looking back in time." "Roger C. Gibson on Portfolio Management" by Jeffrey H. Rattiner, *Journal of Financial Planning*, February 1996, pages 44-50. In other words, *any nondiversified investment strategy is inherently risky but if it turns out to be a winner it isn't seen as being risky in retrospect!*

[29] The same excessive risk that made possible an outstanding track record today can turn against investors and produce a miserable track record in the future once the market begins to favor other sectors.

[30] *Forbes*, December 6, 1993, page 275.

[31] "Selling the Future: Concerns About the Misuse of Mutual Fund Ratings" by Lipper Analytical Services, Inc., Summit, New Jersey, May 16, 1994.

[32] "Are Five-Star Funds Black Holes?" by Eric J. Savitz, *Barron's*, June 6, 1994, page 35.

[33] "Selecting Equity Mutual Funds" by John C. Bogle, *The Journal of Portfolio Management*, Winter 1992, pages 94-100.

[34] The same results were found for the 1976-1991 period in a 1995 study. *See* "Returns from Investing in Equity Mutual Funds 1971 to 1991" by Burton G. Malkiel, *The Journal of Finance*, Volume 50, No. 2, June 1995, pages 549-572.

[35] The Investment Company Institute, the trade association for mutual funds, had 6,170 open-end and 443 closed-end mutual funds on its membership roster as of the end of December 1996. However, according to Lipper Analytical Services, Inc., there were 7,607 mutual fund "choices" as of March 31, 1995. For example, Lipper counts one mutual fund as having three choices when it offers investors three different share classes (A, B and C). Note that these choices are really only different ways for investors to pay commission loads.

[36] "A Matter of Cost and Style" by William F. Sharpe, *Investment Advisor*, October 1994, pages 83-89.

[37] Although track record investing is not a good way to invest money, there will always be some investors who will succeed at it. However, such success is guaranteed only if (1) they can skillfully or luckily identify early enough in their investment lives those that will turn out to be winners and (2) continue to invest with them through thick and thin.

FIVE

SOURCES OF INVESTMENT ADVICE USED IN ATTEMPTS TO BEAT THE MARKET

. . . most [stock pickers and market timers] should go out of business - take up plumbing, teach Greek . . .[1]
- Paul A. Samuelson (1915 -   )
  Economist, author and the first American to receive the
  Nobel Prize in Economic Science

Overview

Some sources of investment advice widely relied on by investors in their attempts to beat the market include stockbrokers, financial roundtables, newsletters and Value Line. However, those involved in offering this advice to investors can only guess about what might happen in an unpredictable future. Since the ability to predict the future in a consistent way is the essential prerequisite for beating the market, these sources of investment advice are unlikely to help investors achieve this goal.

Stockbrokers

Many investors rely on their stockbrokers for investment advice. Based on the recommendations made by their stockbrokers, investors make purchases that they hope will produce future market-beating performance (and sell investments that they are advised will be future losers). Usually, though, a stockbroker can only recommend that his clients buy or sell those stocks which appear on a list preapproved by the brokerage firm that employs him.

As a practical matter, then, a stockbroker is often largely a mere conduit between the securities analysts who analyze these stocks and his clients. Since we have seen that such analysts can only make crude estimates about what might happen in the future, a stockbroker who relies on them for stock picking recommendations is no more likely to have the ability to help investors beat the market than anyone else.

SIMON SAYS: *Gangsta Wrap*

The stockbrokerage industry has admitted that it hasn't done a very good job of training stockbrokers (now renamed "financial consultants") to manage investment portfolios and give impartial advice to investors. The industry's diabolical solution to this problem is called a "wrap account." There are two kinds of wrap accounts: (1) those that invest in individual stocks and bonds and (2) others that invest in mutual funds.

In wrap accounts that invest in individual stocks and bonds, financial consultants match their clients with independent money managers who are hired to pick individual stocks and bonds and engage in market timing. The cost for the services of the financial consultant and the money manager plus all custodial costs and trading commissions are "wrapped" into one fee. The annual management wrap fee for stocks is usually 3% of the money under management, with a slightly smaller fee for larger accounts.

Wrap accounts are popular among investors because their cost structure is easy to understand - one simple fee. Financial consultants are also wild about wrap accounts. First, they can remain "pure" and never charge commissions (although they do levy a 3% management fee). Second, they can shift the responsibility for periods of poor investment performance to outside money managers who can always be fired for such transgressions. Third, financial consultants only have to make a one-time sale which is a lot easier than repeatedly coming back to their clients to sell different stocks, bonds and mutual funds.

Wrap accounts that invest in mutual funds require smaller minimum investments than those that invest in individual stocks and bonds. This broadens their appeal, particularly for investors who are confused by the proliferation of mutual funds.

About the only appreciable difference between wrap accounts that invest in individual stocks and bonds and those that invest in mutual funds is the way that their costs are presented to the investing public. Generally, a mutual fund wrap account seems to be the better bargain because it 'only' levies a 1% or 1.5% annual management fee while the other kind of wrap account levies a 3% fee. This is a difference without distinction.

A stockbroker (or an outside active investment advisor) who places a client in a mutual fund wrap account typically receives the following compensation: (1) The client pays an annual fee of 1% to 1.5% which is based on the amount of money under management. Sometimes he must also pay a 1% "surrender charge" if he cashes out of the wrap account in the first year. (2) The amount that a mutual fund pays differs according to the fund family. Some funds pay the stockbroker or outside investment advisor a front load commission which typically ranges from 3% to 5.75%. Others pay a front load commission of 1% as well as an annual 1% trail commission. Naturally, the client gets stuck with paying higher annual mutual fund expenses to offset these costs.

So when all is said and done, either kind of wrap account is really *just another very expensive product* that fattens the wallets of stockbrokers (and outside active investment advisors) at the expense of active investors.[2]

No doubt many stockbrokers are professional, honest and hard-working people who are genuinely concerned about their clients. However, it should be remembered that the system in which they operate forces them to sell in order to survive. So *first and foremost, stockbrokers are salespeople*. Salespeople sell something for a reason and that reason is to make money which will be extracted from a "prospect" in some way. The incentive to trade stocks in order to generate commissions can directly interfere with a stockbroker's delivery of impartial investment advice to his clients. This creates a conflict of interest or, at the very least, the appearance of a conflict of interest.

Because of the nature of this system, stockbrokers all too often must pose as possessors of "superior" information about certain stocks or bonds that they predict will make their clients "a bundle" and/or beat the market.[3] This is never openly stated (except by the greenest of stockbrokers) but it is clearly implied by the authoritative and knowledgeable manner that stockbrokers are trained to assume when they pitch investment products to their clients.

Sometimes stocks and bonds with obviously poor investment prospects are sold to unsuspecting investors so that stockbrokerage firms can clear them out of their inventories. Yet even though stockbrokers know that such investments are poor ones, they are motivated to unload them by the promise of high commissions.

Financial Roundtables

Many investors want to know the latest thinking from the current crop of stock picking and market timing gurus. One way that this desire is fulfilled is by "financial roundtables" which are periodically featured in the investment media. Probably the most well known financial roundtable is that which appears in *Barron's* twice a year.

The participants in the *Barron's* Roundtable are generally acknowledged to be the cream of the crop in the investment advisory world. These pundits make predictions about individual stocks and bonds and the future course of financial markets for the upcoming quarter or the new year. If it is possible for investors to beat the market by following published predictions about the future behavior of stocks, the *Barron's* Roundtable should be the place to find them.

A 1995 academic study, conducted by two scholars from Tulane University, examined the investment performances of 1,599 common stocks recommended by 65 different participants in the *Barron's* Roundtable from its inception in 1968 through 1991 - a period of 24 years.[4] The participants in this period included mutual fund superstars Mario Gabelli (12 years), John Neff (17 years) and Peter Lynch (6 years), stock analysts, proprietors of private money management firms and successful private investors.

Typically, 8-12 money managers participated in the *Barron's* Roundtable which meets in late December or early January (there is also a mid-year review). This is defined as the "meeting day." Usually about 14 days elapsed between the meeting day and the "publication day," which was the day (always a Monday) that the Roundtable's recommendations were officially published in *Barron's*. (However, *Barron's* was available to investors at newsstands the weekend previous to the publication day.)

The Tulane study made numerous findings. First, a *Barron's* reader who followed all the buy recommendations, purchased the stocks one trading day after the publication day and held them for a year would have earned, in the words of the study's authors, "essentially zero" or just 21/100ths of a percentage point (.21%) more than a sample control group of stocks. Furthermore, over following two- and three-year periods the Roundtable buy recommendations did slightly *worse* than the control group.

Second, the Roundtable recommendations did 2.12% better than the control group when their performances were measured *from the meeting day* until one year after the publication day.

Third, .87% of this excess 2.12% gain came during the period from the meeting day through the Friday before Monday's publication day. The study's authors believe that the gain occurred because word of the recommendations leaked out. But *Barron's* readers would not have been able to participate in this gain since the earliest that they could have entered the market to act on the recommendations was on Monday - publication day.

Fourth, 1.04% of the 2.12% excess gain came on Monday, the publication day. Since *Barron's* is available to investors over the weekend, it was very likely that the prices of the recommended stocks would have *already* incorporated this gain when the market first opened or within the first few trades.

Fifth, *Barron's* readers therefore had no practical way to participate in 1.91% (.87% before publication day and 1.04% on publication day) of the 2.12% excess return which occurred between the meeting day and one year after the publication day. This means that they were effectively barred from the possibility of profiting from about 90% of the excess return.

Last, since the excess return achieved by the Roundtable stock pickers was about two percentage points (1.91%) from meeting day through the end of publication day, the study's authors wondered whether this meant that some of the participants had real stock picking skills. They found that even if they did possess skill, the relatively small size of the excess returns may not have been large enough to cover the research and trading costs spent to find the stocks that earned those returns.

The Tulane study came to this principal conclusion: "An investor, who reads the recommendations in *Barron's* and invests accordingly, would not profit by investing in the buy recommendations at the Roundtable. Thus, the so-called 'superstars,' on average, do not seem to possess superior skills in recommending stocks." The study's authors are careful to point out that their findings do not imply that there are no money managers with superior skills. But they caution that even if they do exist, it would take many years of investment performance to be sure that such managers were skillful rather than lucky.

This study (the conclusion of which is representative of many others) demonstrates that what passes for solid investment advice from the "best and the brightest" usually amounts to little more than idle predictions about the future which, by definition, is unpredictable. Evidence of such statements abounds in the problematic forecasts made by the *Barron's* Roundtable participants: "I predict," "I guess," "I feel," "I hope," "I think" and "I believe." Thus, it is difficult to see how these pundits can help investors beat the market. Unfortunately, all too many investors seriously believe that the advice provided by financial roundtable participants is gospel truth and actively incorporate it into their investment strategies.

SIMON SAYS: *"Wall $treet Week" Stock Picks - Dart Throwing At Its Best*

A study conducted in 1993 by *Market Logic* examined about 2,000 stock buy recommendations made from December 1980 to September 1992 by guests on the television show, *Wall $treet Week.*[5] Its principal findings are remarkably similar to those of the Tulane study. First, the stocks recommended by the guests on *Wall $treet Week* tended to rise in price during the two weeks *before* the shows. Second, the prices of the recommended stocks jumped up on Mondays, the first trading day after the shows were broadcast, stayed there for a week and then dropped back to the market average. Third, while some of the recommended stocks did well, there was no way to know in advance which ones would do well. The study concluded: "Viewers could do better selecting stocks by flipping coins or throwing darts at *The Wall Street Journal* stock pages than buying after the recommendations air on *Wall $treet Week.*"

Investment Newsletters

It is hard to see how editors of investment newsletters can help investors beat the market. Peter Lynch notes that in the twentieth century there have been 53 declines of 10% or more in the stock market (on average, about one every two years). Of those 53 declines, 15 have been 25% or more (on average, about one every six years).[6] Of course, there is no way to accurately predict the occurrences of any future declines. But on a purely statistical basis, the editor of an investment newsletter who makes a prediction twice a year over the next six years that the market will decline 25% or more beginning within the next six months, should, on average, get it right once over the six-year time period.

Assuming that this 'prediction' comes true and is spectacular enough, it will be characterized by the investment media as an omniscient forecast of a major down market. (The eleven other predictions will be ignored.) Yet such a fabulously correct market call was invariably just a vague prediction buried among many other such uncertain utterances about the future. The newly crowned guru was simply very wrong many times over a period of time before he quickly became very right (for the wrong reason) only once. This is why it is wrong to suggest that a newsletter editor's prediction that has come true has anything to do with an ability to beat the market. All that it really proves is that if someone "cries wolf" enough times, eventually the wolf will show up as a market downturn.

This point is examined from a different angle by a professor of mathematics at Temple University:[7] "Let's suppose that some would-be investment advisor puts a logo on some fancy stationery and sends out 32,000 letters to potential investors. The letters tell of his company's elaborate computer model, his investment expertise and inside contacts. In 16,000 of these letters he predicts that a certain market index such as the S&P 500 will rise, and in the other 16,000 he predicts a decline. No matter whether the index rises or falls, a follow-up letter is sent, but only to the 16,000 people who initially received a correct 'prediction.' To 8,000 of them, a rise is predicted for the next week; to the other 8,000, a decline.

"Whatever happens now, 8,000 people will have received two correct predictions. Again, to these 8,000 people only, letters are sent concerning the index's performance the following week: 4,000 predicting a rise; 4,000, a decline. Whatever the outcome, 4,000 people have now received three straight correct predictions. This is repeated a few more times, until 500 people have received six straight correct predictions. These 500 people are now reminded of this and told that in order to continue to receive this valuable information for the seventh week they must each contribute $500.

"If from some stock market advisor you received in the mail for six weeks in a row correct 'predictions' on this certain stock index and were asked to pay for the seventh such prediction, would you? If they all pay, that's $250,000 for our advisor. If this is done knowingly and with intent to defraud, it is an illegal con game. Yet it is considered acceptable if it is done unknowingly by earnest but ignorant publishers of stock newsletters. *There's always enough random success to justify almost anything to someone who wants to believe.*"

A ground-breaking study released in late 1994 by two scholars from the University of Utah and Duke University confirms that even highly touted market timing investment newsletters have compiled miserable records in their attempts to help investors beat the market.[8] The study is significant because it is the first (and only so far) to analyze the specific market timing recommendations made by investment newsletters. (It did not examine stock picking recommendations.)

The Utah/Duke study evaluated the performance of 237 newsletter investment strategies over the $12^1/_2$-year period from June 1980 through December 1992. It found that when the performances of the newsletters were risk-adjusted, 77.2% (183 of 237) of them were beaten by the S&P 500.

Specifically, the study established that an investor who was invested in an S&P 500 index fund over this $12^1/_2$-year period would have generated a 15.9% (15.8% after transaction costs) average annual compound return. However, if he had held an equally weighted portfolio consisting of all the newsletter portfolios examined by the study, he would have achieved an 11.3% (10.9% after transaction costs) return. When the equally weighted newsletter portfolio was adjusted so that its volatility matched the volatility of the S&P 500, it still only generated an 11.7% return. This was 26% less than the 15.8% return of an S&P 500 index fund.

SIMON SAYS: *The Short Shelf Life Of Investment Newsletters*

Only 5.5% (13 of 237) of the newsletters existed for the entire $12^1/_2$-year period examined by the Utah/Duke study. Among other things, this illustrates the instability of the investment newsletter business in which many newsletters are started up and many others go out of business. It also reveals quite another dimension to the problem of accurately predicting the future in a consistent way: which *newsletters* will manage to survive?

The Utah/Duke study came to four conclusions about the market timing recommendations made by investment newsletters. First, few newsletters can beat the market. Second, there is no evidence that they can correctly forecast the future direction of the market as a whole (time the market). Third, their records demonstrate that there is no correlation between
past superior performance and future superior performance. Fourth, there
is formidable evidence of persistent bad performance. These last two conclusions are consistent with studies of mutual fund investment track records:
*there is no reliable way to predict when (or which) "winners" will win
again, even though "losers" often lose again.*

It is important to note that the Utah/Duke study didn't examine the
effect that taxes would have had on the performances of the recommendations made by the newsletters.[9] If taxes had been taken into account, a *far
higher* percentage of investment newsletters would have been beaten by the
market than the nearly 80% of them that actually underperformed it.

A different study analyzed the 15-year track records of investment newsletters. The study's author marvels:[10] "If we were to get together 15 years
from today and rank all of our performances over the last 15 years, 80% of
you will be behind where you would have been had you simply been invested in an S&P 500 index fund. Isn't that an overwhelming thought?
*What other pursuit in life is there where you can do better than 80% of your
peers without even trying?*"

Despite the subpar records turned in by the great majority of investment
newsletters, many investors continue to turn to them for help in simplifying
their investment lives. In our "sound-bite" culture, it is not difficult to see why
they can be readily influenced by newsletter promises of quick and easy profits. By claiming special powers of insight and knowledge, even newsletter pundits with exceedingly bad records are often able to convince many investors
that they are superior forecasters who can help them beat the market.[11]

There are more than one thousand newsletters read by perhaps two
million subscribers annually paying $500 million[12] to read what generally
amounts to, at best, superficial investment advice. (This is not to say that
many newsletters are not entertaining. In fact, they are often well written
and highly amusing. But if investors are relying on them for help in beating
the market, they are likely to be disappointed.)

Value Line

Probably the best-known investment advisory service in the world is the *Value Line Investment Survey*. It ranks about 3,500 stocks based on the price gains that they are predicted to achieve over the next year. Although the Value Line ranking system was created solely to foster the selection of stocks that will outperform the market, it is hard to see how it can help investors reach that goal.

Under the Value Line system, stocks ranked in Group 1 are predicted to be the best performers. For example, if an investor had invested $10,000 in all 100 of the Group 1 stocks on April 15, 1965 and updated his list every week,[13] he would have amassed $3.54 million by June 30, 1995 (a gain of 35,341%).[14] During this same period, the S&P 500 was up about 1,900%.[15]

Obviously there is a huge difference between the Group 1 paper portfolio's 30-year cumulative return of over 35,000% and the market's cumulative return of just less than 2,000%. Does this mean that the stock pickers at Value Line are that outstanding? In a word, no. While the historical performance of the stocks in the Group 1 paper portfolio is truly awesome, no real live investor could have duplicated it since it is based on *hypothetical* stock picking.

In an attempt to match the enormous hypothetical returns of the Group 1 paper portfolio, Value Line set up a mutual fund in late 1983 called Value Line Centurion Fund. Unfortunately, the Centurion Fund has not only failed to duplicate the record of the Group 1 stocks,[16] it has also been soundly beaten by the market. From its inception on November 15, 1983 through June 30, 1995, the Centurion Fund generated an average annual compound return of 11.4% while the Group 1 stocks returned 15.2%. In comparison, the return of the S&P 500 was 14.7%.[17]

There are three reasons to explain the shortfall in performance of the Centurion Fund in comparison to the Group 1 paper portfolio.

First, the Centurion Fund actually incurs trading costs such as brokerage commissions, market impact costs and bid-ask spread costs which all savagely eat into performance. But the Group 1 paper portfolio *ignores trading costs*. These real-life costs do not show up when designing portfolios on paper by the mere stroke of a pen. This is primarily why the astonishing returns on paper do not hold up in the real world.

Second, the popularity of Value Line has forced the Centurion Fund's managers to compete for market trades with its subscribers. This increased competition to buy and sell the stocks that move in and out of Group 1 has made it more difficult for the Centurion Fund managers to obtain favorable trading prices. For example, the scramble to buy stocks recently blessed by Value Line to enter Group 1 heaven pushes up their prices which is unfavorable to the Centurion Fund because it must then pay more to purchase them.

The fund's managers also find it difficult to sell its Group 1 stocks when Value Line casts them into non-Group 1 purgatory because all the Value Line subscribers are dumping them at the same time. This pushes down their prices which is unfavorable to the Centurion Fund because it must then sell these stocks at lower prices.

Third, because the Value Line Centurion Fund is an actively-managed mutual fund it maintains healthy cash reserves to facilitate transactions such as paying off departing shareholders. These cash holdings create a drag on return when the market is rising, thereby contributing to the Fund's shortfall in performance in comparison to the Group 1 paper portfolio which holds no cash.

So while it is true that Value Line's Group 1 paper portfolio outperformed the market by a huge margin, investors could not have actually profited from this performance. Even the mutual fund Value Line set up to duplicate the performance of the Group 1 paper portfolio substantially underperformed it as well as the market. Thus, investors may want to stop relying on Value Line's unrealistic stock picking system to help them in their attempts to beat the market.[18]

This chapter has shown that some of the most well known sources of investment advice used by investors in attempting to beat the market do not help them reach this goal. The next chapter examines a subject that investors do not perceive as a drawback - investing with a guru. Yet the problems experienced by investors can be many when they follow an investment guru.

Chapter Notes

[1] "Challenge to Judgment" by Paul A. Samuelson, *The Journal of Portfolio Management*, Fall 1974, pages 17-19.

[2] The investment performances of wrap accounts are not audited by the SEC, unlike those of mutual funds. Thus, a common marketing ploy used by brokerage firms is to show the records of only the best-performing wrap accounts.

[3] In fact, far from being able to predict the future, stockbrokers must focus on the *present* given the nature of the sales system which requires them to peddle commissioned products.

[4] "An Analysis of the Recommendations of the 'Superstar' Money Managers at Barron's Annual Roundtable" by Hemang Desai and Prem C. Jain, *The Journal of Finance*, Volume 50, No. 4, September 1995, pages 1257-1273. This study is discussed in "Think Twice Before Taking Stars' Advice" by Roger Lowenstein, *The Wall Street Journal*, January 11, 1996, page C1. There were actually 79 different participants in all. However, 14 of them did not make any common stock recommendations so they were not included in the study. In addition, some of the common stock buy recommendations made by the Roundtable participants were excluded from the study due to unavailability of data.

[5] "How to Make Money From Wall Street Week," *Market Logic*, Reprint #2, September 1993, Ft. Lauderdale, Florida. *See* "The Big Tease" by Jane Bryant Quinn, *Newsweek*, August 7, 1995, pages 64-65.

[6] "The 5 Percent Solution" by Peter Lynch, *Worth*, April 1996, pages 33-36.

[7] *Innumeracy: Mathematical Illiteracy and Its Consequences* by John Allen Paulos (New York: Hill & Wang, 1988) pages 32-33. This quotation has been slightly edited and italics have been added.

[8] "Market Timing Ability and Volatility Implied in Investment Newsletters' Asset Allocation Recommendations" by John R. Graham and Campbell R. Harvey, National Bureau of Economic Research Working Paper No. 4890, October 1994. The authors of the study relied on a database of newsletter performance supplied by Mark J. Hulbert, *Forbes* columnist and editor of the *Hulbert Financial Digest*, an investor service that tracks the performance of investment newsletters.

[9] Mark J. Hulbert in "Lessons Drawn From Tracking Investment Advisors' Performance," a speech at the National Endowment for Financial Education national conference, July 27-29, 1995, Denver, Colorado.

[10] *Ibid*. The 80% figure used by Hulbert comes from data on active mutual funds that does not include how taxes and commission loads adversely impact their performances. This percentage would rise (probably a lot) if these additional factors were taken into account. *See* pages 9-11 for a detailed discussion of this issue.

[11] Performance "puffery" is prevalent in the investment newsletter industry. *The Wall Street Journal* didn't even start accepting advertisements for newsletters until the late 1980s partly because their claims were - and continue to be - difficult to

substantiate. "Fear of Crashing" by Peter Lynch, *Worth*, September 1995, pages 124-130.

[12] *Forbes*, January 30, 1995, page 128.

[13] In a typical week, four of the 100 Group 1 stocks drop out of the group and have to be replaced by four new Group 1 stocks. "Paying the Piper" by William Baldwin, *Forbes*, October 19, 1987, page 208.

[14] Dividends excluded and before commissions, expenses and taxes.

[15] Dividends included and reinvested and before commissions, expenses and taxes.

[16] The Value Line Centurion Fund invests in the top 100 of the 300 stocks in Group 2, as well as all 100 stocks in Group 1.

[17] From its inception through the end of July 1997, the average annual return of the Centurion Fund was about 13.6% while the performance of the S&P 500 was about 17.3% over the same period. Thus, the fund increased its underperformance of the market.

[18] Value Line's "Timeliness" rankings, updated each week, are essentially determined by a stock's earnings growth and stock price momentum. Yet stocks with high ranks for Timeliness (Groups 1 and 2) frequently have subpar 3-5-year appreciation potential. Why? Because stocks in Groups 1 and 2 often have below average long term capital growth potential since recent stock price gains have pushed their prices well toward the projected 3-5-year range. This is Catch-22 investing at its best. On the one hand, Value Line advises investors that they should hold stocks that are ranked in Groups 1 and 2, but on the other hand it advises them not to hold long term those stocks with low 3-5-year appreciation potential. In other words, the stocks in Groups 1 and 2 are the best of the bunch, but because they are so *good* their longer term prospects are often *bad*. This leaves investors with only two options. The first option is to immediately sell the stocks in Groups 1 and 2 and completely avoid the Catch-22 situation created by Value Line's method of stock picking. The second option is to remain invested in these stocks. What can happen if investors follow the second option? Well, when investors hold, say, small company stocks from Groups 1 and 2, they hold stocks that generally do not pay dividends. Any earnings generated by these stocks are plowed back into their companies to help build them. Hence, investors usually do not make any money from dividends by holding small company stocks. Also, because small company stocks often have poor 3-5-year prospects (according to Value Line), it is unlikely that investors will make any money from their longer term appreciation in value. So if they cannot make any money from dividends or capital appreciation, why would investors ever hold small company stocks from Groups 1 and 2? The only possible answer is that as long as they remain invested in these stocks, "hope springs eternal" that they will outperform the market in the future. The story becomes a bit better if investors hold large company stocks from Groups 1 and 2 because at least most of them usually pay dividends. But they don't need Value Line to show them that - they can just look at stock quotations in a newspaper. Value Line's method of

ranking stocks represents one of the worst aspects of today's investment information system: a short term investing mentality that generates a lot of trading costs and capital gains taxes.

SIX

INVESTING WITH A GURU

All the time and effort people devote to picking the right fund, the hot hand, the great manager have, in most cases, led to no advantage.[1]
- Peter Lynch, (1943-   )
  Beating the Street, 1993

Overview

Track record investing with an investment guru creates unexpected problems for investors. First, since there is no correlation between past and future performance, investors can never know when (if ever) the future will repeat the excellence of the past. Second, investors cannot tell whether an outstanding track record was achieved because of skill. Third, relatively few investors are enriched by an outstanding track record. Fourth, outstanding track records regress to the mean. Investors can avoid all these problems by investing in index funds.

Peter Lynch: The Most Famous Investment Guru Of Our Time

Peter Lynch is the most famous investment guru of our time. He managed the Fidelity Magellan mutual fund from 1977 to 1990. Many investors think that they will achieve market-beating performance if they read Lynch's books and apply his investment methods. However, the stock picking system that glorifies the track record of Lynch or any other investment guru creates many unexpected problems for investors. This chapter is an examination of these problems and how they are illustrated by Lynch's track record.

First, *an outstanding track record is only a reflection of past performance*. This is a problem because there is no correlation between a past outstanding performance and a future outstanding performance. Thus, investors can never know when (if ever) the future will repeat the excellence of the past. The great uncertainty as to whether an excellent track record will continue into the future is illustrated by the following example.

A person investing in the stock market for the *first* time in the 1980s would naturally be attracted to the track record of a superstar such as Lynch. But if a new investor first invested in 1985 or even in 1988 (in 1984 and 1987 the S&P 500 outperformed Lynch) he saw, *at each of those points in time*, that Lynch had turned in a subpar performance. This might have given him second thoughts about investing with Lynch since there was no way that he could be sure that he would climb back to the top of the rankings.

The uncertainty about the excellence of a track record continuing into the future can also extend to experienced investors already investing with a superstar. For example, there is little doubt that investors withdrew almost $4 billion from Magellan's $11 billion asset base at the time of the Crash of '87 in part because they thought that Lynch had lost his Midas touch.

SIMON SAYS: *The Initial Lengthy Obscurity Of A Legend*

Peter Lynch's fame as a stock picker didn't start to spread until after his most spectacular years which were in 1979 and 1980. In fact, he was only beginning to be widely known in 1982 and 1983. Prior to August 1982, investment magazines mentioned Lynch only once. As late as the beginning of 1982, there was just $107 million invested in Fidelity Magellan. But Lynch began to receive prominent national attention when he first appeared on *Wall $treet Week* in October 1982.[2] Until then, he was just another mutual fund manager who had labored in relative obscurity for the first 5-6 years of his 13-year term as head of Magellan. So two or three years after his very best years (or almost half-way through his investment career), Lynch was still relatively unknown to the investing public!

Second, *investors have no way to tell whether an outstanding track record was achieved because of skill.* This becomes a problem when an investor who relied on what he thought was a skillful investment guru finds out that he had only hit a lucky streak.

About midway through his 13-year investment career, Lynch began to cool off and was beaten by the market in three of the last seven years (1984-1990) that he ran Fidelity Magellan. Does this mean that Lynch lost his skill or that he never had any skill in the first place and just ran into some bad luck after a string of good luck? Peter L. Bernstein answers that we can be 99% certain that Magellan's managers (Lynch was succeeded in 1990 by Morris Smith who was succeeded by Jeffrey Vinik in 1992) beat the market over the 11-year period of 1983-1993 as a result of their skillful stock picking.[3]

Alternatively, it could be argued that after the sizzling first half of his tenure at Magellan, Lynch's 4-3 record against the market during the second half is about the same result that we would expect from a random game of coin flipping. Even Lynch's hot start, when he beat the market for seven years in a row (1977-1983), might be attributed to random chance. Mathematician John Allen Paulos observes that if two people each flip a coin once every day for about nine weeks, then it is more likely than not that both coin flippers will have each had a streak of five winning flips in a row. If they stretch this contest out to five or six years, it is likely that *each* will have won ten coin flips in a row.[4] Most investors would probably concede after watching this purely random contest that these coin flippers were exceptionally skillful just as they would conclude that Lynch was skillful.[5]

However, what looks like enormous skill is often just luck in disguise. In fact, admission to membership in the "Winning Stock Pickers Club" rarely has anything to do with investment skill. Instead, it is usually a short term *random and rotating* phenomenon as lucky new winners unpredictably join the club and replace unlucky losers (who formerly were lucky winners).

SIMON SAYS: *Lucky Money Managers And Michael Jordan*

Most investors assume that active money managers who beat the market are skillful and those who do not lack skill. Yet there is no evidence that those who beat the market demonstrate the same level of relatively consistent skillful performance as, say, Michael Jordan or Garry Kasparov, the reigning human world chess champion ("Big Blue," the IBM supercomputer, beat him 31/2 to 21/2 games in May 1997). In fact, active money managers do not play in a game that measures genuine skill such as basketball or chess, but in a game that not only has a large element of chance but may be almost entirely random in conferring long term investment success on its players.

For example, if particular market conditions favor growth stocks for a year or a decade, the manager who excels at picking good growth stocks will rank high in any comparisons with other managers who do not invest in these stocks. But if market conditions don't favor such stocks, the growth manager will turn in a bad performance compared to another manager whose non-growth investment style is then favored by the market. This is true even though the growth manager may actually be a skillful picker of stocks!

Thus, some markets will make a money manager look good and some will make him look bad *independent* of his skillful (or lucky) stock picking abilities. This is why an investor who selects an active money manager will usually turn out to be a winner or a loser as a result of the behavior of the market itself rather than the manager's skill (or luck) at picking stocks.

Still, even if Lynch or any other investment guru has real skill, Peter L. Bernstein reminds us that *investors themselves* cannot skillfully select mutual funds for their portfolios:[6] "The problem is that investors had no way of knowing back in 1983 what Magellan's track record would be from 1983 forward. So, even if an investor decided to buy Magellan shares in 1983, how can that investor seriously claim to know now that the decision was a matter of skill rather than luck?"

There is really no way to dispute Bernstein's compelling logic. After all, nobody had ever heard of Peter Lynch *at the time* he began to manage Fidelity Magellan in 1977. So how could any investor have possibly known that he (or any other mutual fund manager) would turn out to be an investment legend?

Third, *relatively few investors are enriched by an outstanding track record*. This is an obvious problem. Since investors cannot identify, at its inception, what will turn out to be an outstanding investment performance, they cannot be there *from the beginning* to maximally benefit from it. Lynch understood this harsh fact of investing all too well. He referred to it in 1990 at the end of his career with Magellan: "Magellan is up 26-fold in 13 years. *But no one was in it 13 years ago*. In 10 years, it is up nine or 10-fold. *But no one was in it 10 years ago*."[7]

13 years before 1990, at year-end 1977, Magellan had only 9,227 shareholder accounts while 10 years before at year-end 1980 (immediately following Lynch's best two years), the number had decreased to 6,791.[8] Thus, there were very few investors in Magellan that could have actually taken advantage of Lynch's most spectacular years. (Yet, like those millions who claim to have been in Atlanta Stadium when Hank Aaron hit his 715th home run to break Babe Ruth's record, many millions of investors would say that they were with Lynch right from the beginning.)

Even when investors are able to identify a fabulous record and attempt to get a piece of it, the winning mutual fund has usually already peaked in performance. New investors impressed by Lynch's outstanding track record poured increasingly larger amounts of money into Magellan *after* his best years.[9] This unceasing flow of money directed at Magellan in the hope that Lynch would duplicate the excellence of his past (which turned out to be largely fruitless), coincided with the period when Lynch was only 4-3 against the market.

Fourth, *the performances of outstanding mutual funds regress to the mean ("march toward the average") performance of the stock market*. This is a problem for investors because when they see the performances of their mutual funds march toward the average, they dump them and replace them with Morningstar-rated 5-star funds. By doing this, they climb on the merry-go-round of track record investing yet again. Even mutual funds that have outstanding track records and are managed by superstars such as Peter Lynch cool off as they are inexorably pushed by the enormous forces of the market to march toward the average.

Actively-managed mutual funds march toward the average for various reasons. The main reason is due to the higher costs and taxes that typically impact the performance of active funds.

A second reason is that the investment styles of winning active mutual fund managers are unpredictably disfavored by the market for unpredictable periods of time. Consequently, their superior track records gradually turn average as the losses of the bad years begin to level out the gains of the good years.

A third reason is that, over the long run, a stock's rate of return is largely determined by the rate of growth in its earnings. This growth must eventually slow down and when it does, the stock's performance tends to regress to the market's average rate of return. In the same way, the performance of an active mutual fund that holds stocks will march toward the average.

A fourth reason for an active mutual fund's march toward the average involves "copycat" investors. Once investors begin to see a hot investment record, they jump on the bandwagon and attempt to imitate it. Some of thcsc copycats will be successful in duplicating and thus "stealing" the performance of a Peter Lynch and divide it up among themselves. When this happens, a Peter Lynch is not exceptional anymore - he marches toward the average.

SIMON SAYS: *Copycat Investors*

It may very well be that there has been an acceleration of regression to the mean by active mutual funds over the last twenty years. Why? Because today, copycat investors have a greater ability to instantly spot potentially lucrative investment performances than when Peter Lynch started his fabulous run in 1977. This is primarily due to technological advances in computers and an enormous increase in the quantity of on-line databases as well as the addition of faxes and e-mail.

As they march toward the average, it is likely that actively-managed mutual funds will settle for the average market return on a gross basis and less than the market return on a net basis. So in Lynch's case, we could expect that his long term gross investment performance would have been about the same as that achieved by an indexer: the average performance of the stock market. Also, we could expect that, over the long run, Lynch's net performance would have been less than that of an indexer, once deductions were made for Magellan's commission loads and annual expenses as well as for the taxes paid by Magellan shareholders.

We will never know if these theoretical assumptions would have proved correct over the long run since Lynch's track record was relatively short. However, by looking at the second half of his record that followed the peak of his performance, we can see that Lynch was *well on his way* to validating these assumptions. Not only was he beaten by the market in three years of that seven-year stretch (1984-1990), but even in the four years that he beat the market, Lynch beat it by a smaller margin in each successive year (except for one year when he virtually tied the previous winning year). Thus, we can see that even a superstar such as Peter Lynch marches toward the average with the passage of time. Illustration 6, below, clearly reveals this phenomenon.

SIMON SAYS: *What Goes Down Doesn't Always Come Back Up*

Our discussion about regression to the mean would seem to imply that less than average mutual funds should be marching up toward the average. But studies show that what actually happens is that a good number of poorly performing mutual fund managers tend to *remain inferior* due to high costs.[10] Thus, the performance gap between hot mutual fund managers such as a Peter Lynch and many poorly performing managers will persist over time even as a hot gross investment record gradually moves to the average. So in the world of mutual fund performance, what goes up must eventually come down, but what goes down doesn't always come back up.

Illustration 6

Peter Lynch And Fidelity Magellan: "The March Down Toward The Average"

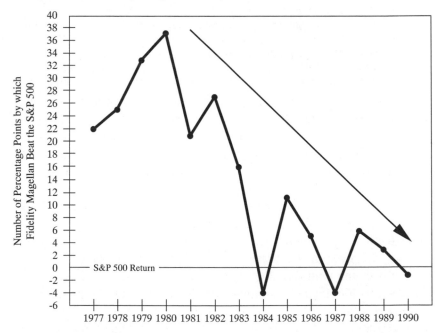

Source: Based on Fidelity Investments data

SIMON SAYS: *"Regression To The Mean" And The "Random Walk" Are Not Contradictory Descriptions Of The Stock Market's Behavior*

The inevitable regression to the mean of actively-managed mutual funds makes it seem that the aggregate performance of the stock market follows some kind of *order*. But as we saw in Chapter Three, the Random Walk Theory maintains that changes in individual stock prices are entirely *random*, thereby making the performances of individual stocks unpredictable.

While it may appear to the contrary, this doesn't create an inherent contradiction in describing the behavior of the stock market. The reason why is that although the long term behavior of the stock market is characterized by regressing to a relatively more stable average performance, its short term behavior is a random walk of unknowable investment performance. In this light, the chaos of significant short term declines in the market becomes meaningless since it is the stability of long term average returns that really counts in investment performance.

The Inability Of Pontificating Prognosticators To Help Investors

Of course, a true believer in Peter Lynch and in the ability of stock pickers to outperform the market will say: "You have presented a good argument in favor of the idea that I cannot expect to beat the market. But the bottom line is that Lynch was up a total of 2,475% in his 13 years at Fidelity Magellan while the S&P 500 was up only 518% over the same period.[11] Since Lynch beat the market and index funds invested in the market portfolio by a wide margin, why should I invest in index funds which will only guarantee me the mediocrity of the market return?"

This important question deserves an answer. The response that follows is a sobering recognition of the significant limitations that investors face today both in drawing conclusions from the past and in predicting the future.

In terms of the *past*, it is self-evident that Lynch came to our attention because he produced an outstanding track record. This offers pontificating prognosticators a golden opportunity to declare that he beat the market. Yet showcasing a money manager with a market-beating track record (whether long term or short term) is welcome news only to those (too often lucky few) who were actually invested with him. Otherwise, such claims are of little practical use to the great majority of investors. The most that can be said about the fact that Lynch (or at least someone) beat the market is that other active investors can always hope that they too will be similarly successful.

In terms of the *future*, indexers fully acknowledge that there will always be someone who will be skillful (or lucky) enough to beat the market for any given investment period. After all, in any group of competitive human beings such as stock picking mutual fund managers, some will achieve above-market returns just as others will achieve below-market returns. (An above-market return can be likened to a football that is "passed around" and gets "caught" by an unpredictable winner. While this winner will "run" with this return for an unpredictable amount of time, it will eventually be passed to another unpredictable winner who will hold it for an equally unpredictable amount of time. The same phenomenon applies to those who earn below-market returns.)

But there is no evidence to indicate that investors can actually identify *today* those few who will be future Peter Lynches. It is simply impossible to pick out of the many thousands of money managers (including those who run nearly 7,000 mutual funds) the small number who will reign supreme over the next 5, 10, 20 or 30 years. This is why investors are left in the dark not only as to how to find a future Peter Lynch but also how to know whether a money manager who is *already* a proven winner will *continue* his past market-beating performance.

SIMON SAYS: *Yes, But What Have You Done For Me Lately?*

Active money managers not only attempt to beat the market, but they must also actually do it. As a Fidelity mutual fund manager puts it:[12] "I'm flipping burgers if I don't beat the Vanguard index fund . . . There's not a lot of tolerance here for underperformance." Apparently not.

Jeffrey Vinik, who succeeded Peter Lynch's successor as fund manager at Fidelity Magellan, began his tenure there in July 1992. In early 1996, instead of betting on stocks, he made the mistake of betting on cash and bonds.[13] For the first four months of 1996 Magellan posted a gain of 2.4% compared to the 6.9% return of the S&P 500. As a result, Vinik was forced out by Fidelity in May 1996.

The moral of the story? Fidelity rid itself of Vinik because he got beat by the market for a period of four months by four and a half percentage points, even though he had outperformed it on a cumulative basis for almost four years. When an investor invests in index funds, he doesn't have to concern himself with this nonsense. He is only interested in the long term reliability of the market itself, *not soap operas at widely followed mutual funds involving changes in personnel that ultimately mean nothing to his long term investment performance.*

Thus, admiring Peter Lynch's outstanding track record and claiming that it is proof that the market can be beaten is of little help to an investor who is looking today for a reliable, workable and understandable investment strategy that will continue to be viable in the future. An indexing investment strategy that is appropriately tailored to an investor's unique circumstances is the solution to this search. By switching to indexing, an investor is relieved of two burdens at once. First, he can give up track record investing which, try as it may, cannot derive meaning from the *past*. Second, an indexer can avoid the guesswork of trying to predict the *future* in order to identify the next Peter Lynch or market-beating mutual fund or individual stock.

SIMON SAYS: *Ask The Right Question*

In the continuing debate about whether it is possible to beat the market, active investors often point to Peter Lynch and ask indexers: "How do you explain Peter Lynch?" The answer to this is that Lynch was a statistical anomaly who widely beat the market either with great skill or with great luck. But this begs the right question: "Why aren't there more Peter Lynches?"

Although many investment gurus (such as Peter Lynch) do not believe in market timing, there are plenty of professional market timing advisors that sing its praises. The next chapter shows investors why they may not wish to play the market timing game.

Chapter Notes

[1] *Beating the Street* by Peter Lynch with John Rothchild (New York: Fireside/ Simon & Schuster, 1993), page 60.

[2] *Ibid.*, page 113.

[3] "Measuring the Performance of Performance Measurement" by Peter L. Bernstein in *Performance Evaluation, Benchmarks and Attribution Analysis* edited by Jan R. Squires (Charlottesville, Virginia: Association for Investment Management and Research, 1995), pages 68-71.

[4] *A Mathematician Reads the Newspaper* by John Allen Paulos (New York: Basic Books, 1995), page 75.

[5] The coin-flipping example involves a streak of *days* within a multi-year period while Lynch established a streak of *years* within such a period. This really isn't a meaningful distinction. Rather, the real significance of these two examples is that in *both* of them people automatically attribute skill to those who may very well be only the luckiest of the lucky in a random process.

[6] "Measuring the Performance of Performance Measurement" by Peter L. Bernstein in *Performance Evaluation, Benchmarks and Attribution Analysis* edited by Jan R. Squires (Charlottesville, Virginia: Association for Investment Management and Research, 1995), pages 68-71. A portion of this quotation has been omitted for greater clarity.

[7] "Is There Life After Babe Ruth?", *Barron's*, April 2, 1990, page 15. Italics added.

[8] In contrast, by year-end 1995, Magellan had 4.044 million shareholder accounts. Fidelity apparently does not publicly release figures indicating the number of individual shareholders, but only the number of shareholder accounts. For example, one shareholder may hold two accounts - his taxable account and his IRA account. (In mid-1997, Fidelity had 28.2 million accounts.) Keeping this in mind, it is safe to say that Magellan has at least several million investors.

[9] The fact that Magellan was closed to new investors during Lynch's tenure until June 1981 obviously played a part in distorting the rate and amount of money invested in the fund. Still, the great bulk of the money flowing into Magellan over the ten-year period of 1982-1991 occurred at the end of that decade - *long after* Lynch's best years and *long after* his record became well known. During 1982- 1991, $18.3 billion in new money flowed into Fidelity Magellan. More than half of it wasn't even invested until 1989-1991 and more than a third of it wasn't invested until 1991 (after Lynch's departure in 1990).

[10] "A Matter of Cost and Style" by William F. Sharpe, *Investment Advisor*, October 1994, pages 83-89.

[11] This 13-year period ran from April 1, 1977 through March 31, 1990.

[12] "Magellan Falls Below S&P's 3-Year Return" by Robert McGough, *The Wall Street Journal*, May 2, 1996, page C1.

[13] As of February 1996, only 70% of Magellan's assets were invested in stocks. The remainder was invested in long term bonds (20%) and cash (10%).

SEVEN

MARKET TIMING: A FOOL'S GAME?

Market timers make astrologers look respectable.
- Anonymous

Overview

All studies indicate that market timing is an investment strategy that is doomed to fail over the long run. However, an indexer can exceed the market timing records of even the 'best' market timers. He does this by following the most important market timing 'call' of them all - remaining fully invested in the market at all times in a portfolio of index funds. An investor who does not heed this call and engages in market timing is playing a fool's game.

The Definition Of Market Timing

A market timer shifts allocations of money in and out of investments in the hope of profiting from short term cyclical events in financial markets. These investments range from specific asset classes of stocks or bonds (such as small company stocks or long term bonds) to all stocks or bonds as a group. For example, a market timer who wants to successfully market time all stocks as a group would be fully invested in the stock market when it is rising in value and fully invested in the safe haven of 90-day Treasury bills or money market funds when it is falling in value.

While the definition of market timing is straightforward, the investment industry has not yet come up with a common definition of a "rising" market and a "falling" market. This definitional mushiness, which prevents the precise measurement of market highs and lows, means that a rising market such as the great bull market of the 1980s or a falling market such as the Crash of 1987 can be measured in different ways. For example, one market timing advisor may say that the falling market preceding the Crash of 1987 began in August while another may insist that it began in September. If it is defined as beginning in August, the first advisor who had his clients entirely out of stocks in August will have a better market timing record than the second advisor who had his clients fully invested in stocks. Yet the complete opposite may be true if the falling market is defined as beginning in September.

SIMON SAYS: *Beware Of Report Cards Turned In By Market Timing Advisors*

One of the results of being unable to agree on a common definition of a rising market and a falling market is that market timing advisors have more leeway in compiling their report cards for presentation to existing and potential clients. Naturally, these self-graded marks will always be favorable ones. Another result is that market timing advisors have more "wiggle room" in explaining away their earlier vague and incorrect market timing forecasts.[1]

The Seduction Of Market Timing

Market timing carries great seductive appeal for many investors. They look at the historical returns of the market and see the wide swings in gains and losses. These investors know that if they can get out of a falling market early and get back into a rising market early they can make a lot more money than if they merely stay fully invested in the market at all times. It is this potentially large difference in investment performance that motivates the market timer.

Market timing also appears to be a relatively easy investment strategy. Its technical jargon of "trend lines," "momentum indicators" and the like creates a certain quantitative elegance and simplicity. This makes it seem that an investor only needs to follow the mechanical buy and sell signals of a market timing advisor to get rich. The combination of potentially vast profits and the apparent simplicity of market timing (not to mention its sometimes raw emotional excitement) are enticements that make it hard for many investors to resist playing the game.

The Ability To Predict The Future Is Necessary For Successful Market Timing

We saw in Chapter Two that the basic prerequisite for successful stock picking requires that an investor be able to accurately predict the future in a consistent way. This is also true of market timing where money can be made only by successfully predicting when to be invested in a rising market.[2] It is particularly important that a market timer be accurate in predicting the *start* of a rising market. The reason why is that much of a rising market's gains tends to be concentrated in short and intense upsurges at its beginning.[3]

Yet it is a real problem for a market timer to capture any of these upsurges. While the start of a rising market is right after the end of a falling market, *the end of a falling market is the point of maximum pessimism among investors*. In such an atmosphere it is virtually impossible for a

market timer to invest in a rising market soon enough to capture the upsurges that will help him *build real wealth*. The media helps create this
atmosphere by headlining an endless succession of investment gloom and
doom stories.

Because of this, market timing advisors rarely maintain that they can
help investors predict the start of a rising market. Instead, all they usually
lay claim to is the ability to predict the start of a falling market in order to
limit losses. But even when a market timer is fully convinced that he has
identified a falling market, he must wait for some period of time for a
downward market trend to establish itself so that he can confirm his initial
conviction. Of course, the longer he waits to get out of a falling market, the
more his losses mount.

The steep cost paid by an investor who is wrong in predicting the best
times to be fully invested in the market and when to be out of it is demonstrated by a 1993 SEI Corporation study.[4] It examined the 2,528 stock market trading days over the exceptionally good investment decade of the 1980s.
During this period, the market (the S&P 500) produced an average annual
return of 17.5%.

If an investor had been out of this market for the 10 trading days with
the largest gains, his average annual return would have dropped from 17.5%
to 12.6%. Being out of the market for the best 20 trading days would have
reduced his return to 9.3% and eliminating the 30 best trading days would
have left him with a 6.5% return. An investor would have averaged only
3.9% annually if he had been out of the market for the best 40 trading days
(or only 1.6% of the total number of trading days). So whether it is a case of
a rising market or a falling market, there is no reason to believe that a
market timer has any more chance to accurately predict the future than a
stock picker.

Indexers Have Superior 'Market Timing' Records

Indexers have better 'market timing' records than those achieved by
professional market timing advisors. Yet indexers do not believe that any
market timing system works for investors. This seeming paradox is resolved
once it is understood that an indexer who remains fully invested in the
market at all times is like an *optimistic market timer* who thinks that the
market will be up every year.[5] This means that an indexer will likely be a
successful market timer about two-thirds of the time since, on average, the
market is up about two of every three years over long periods of time. There

is no credible evidence that this average can be matched by market timers over the long run.

It is also true that an indexer fully invested in the market at all times will be an *unsuccessful* market timer on average about one out of every three years over the long run. However, the losses of these less numerous and *temporary* (yet unpredictable) down years are far outweighed by the gains of the more numerous (and equally unpredictable) up years. There are other advantages enjoyed by an indexer who remains fully invested in down markets that are not available to a market timer. Unlike a market timer who exits a down market and locks in losses on his mutual fund shares, an indexer can buy more shares at cheaper prices. In addition, there is no need for an indexer to pay taxes to the IRS on any realized capital gains nor incur hefty trading commissions. Finally, an indexer can avoid high market timing advisory fees.

Indexers understand that they can build real wealth only by maintaining a constant fully invested presence in the market during the good times *and* the bad times. This makes them better 'market timers' than market timers who dart in and out of markets in attempts to anticipate where they are heading in the future.

SIMON SAYS: *Good Investment Performance Does Not Require Market Timing*

Whenever the investment media shows the long term performance of market indexes, it is useful to remember that no market timing was involved in generating these impressive numbers. Instead, this data shows the effect of being fully invested at all times in the investments that are represented by these indexes.

The Long Term Climb Of The Stock Market Makes Market Timing Unnecessary

The stock market has had many unpredictable ups and downs in the past and it will continue to have them in the future. Despite these fluctuations, the market has experienced an upward climb in value over the long run. *The fact that the stock market has provided reliable long term performance is precisely what makes market timing so unnecessary.* The best way for an investor to maximally take advantage of this performance is to remain fully invested in the market at all times by holding a portfolio of stock index funds. This becomes clear when we examine the "big picture" of the stock market over the last half century.

There has been a vast increase in the Gross Domestic Product (GDP) of the United States since World War II. Yet this period included the Korean War, the Vietnam War, four major wars in the Middle East, the Cold War, Desert Storm, high inflation, double digit interest rates, two world oil price shocks, domestic wage and price controls, ten recessions, stock market plunges, race riots, the Kennedy assassinations, the King assassination, the Nixon resignation, the Reagan attempted assassination, record budget deficits and huge tax increases.

During this period of turmoil, American business continued to increase its production of goods and services, which in turn produced real growth in the GDP. The stock market reflected all this economic activity by continuing its long term climb, despite the fact that there were many good reasons during those years not to invest in it.

Unless our whole capitalist system collapses, it is a good bet that America's GDP will continue to expand in the future and that the stock market will reflect this expansion. Index funds are the best way to capture this growth. Although market timers attempt to exceed this growth, we will now see that such efforts amount to little more than a fool's game.

Market Timing Studies Of Actual Market Behavior

A review of the most important academic studies detailing actual stock market behavior shows that market timing is not a viable investment strategy. Even under the more optimistic market timing scenarios described in these studies, the chances of profitably timing market movements long term are overwhelmingly against investors.

The goal of a 1986 New York University study was to determine which kind of market was more critical for an investor to correctly time - a rising market or a falling market.[6] Specifically, would an investor's gains derived from entering a rising market at the right time outweigh the losses he avoided by exiting a falling market at the right time?

The study concluded that it is more important to correctly time the beginning of a rising market. Three findings account for this conclusion. First, much of the gain achieved in a rising market is often concentrated at its beginning. Second, there are about twice as many up years than down years in the market over long periods of time. Third, gains in rising markets exceed losses in falling markets. These findings suggest that market timing advisors aren't concentrating on the most important aspect of market timing - fully reinvesting at the start of a rising market in order to build real wealth. Instead, they focus on an opposite strategy - disinvesting in a falling market to limit losses.

This study also calculated minimum "batting averages" necessary for a market timer to outperform a continuously and fully invested indexer. In order to achieve this, a market timer would need to have a minimum forecasting accuracy of at least 80% for rising markets and 50% for falling markets or 70% for rising markets and 90% for falling markets. In effect, a market timer would be required to bat about .700 to beat an indexer fully invested in the market at all times.

Nobel Laureate William F. Sharpe conducted a study in 1975 to determine whether investors can successfully time the market.[7] He concluded: "A manager who attempts to time the market must be right roughly three times out of four, merely to match the overall performance of those competitors who do not. If he is right less often, his relative performance will be inferior. There are two reasons for this. First, such a manager will often have his funds in cash equivalents in good market years, sacrificing the higher returns stocks provide in such years. Second, he will incur transaction costs in making switches, many of which will prove to be unpredictable." Sharpe warned that the odds against successfully timing the market are so great that it is advisable not to even try it.

A 1992 study by SEI Corporation updated the data used by Sharpe and came to the same conclusion.[8] The study found that in order to merely equal the average annual stock market return of 9.4% over the 90-year period from 1901 through 1990, a market timer needed to correctly time 69% of the rising markets and the falling markets. An investor who was 100% right about falling markets and 50% right about rising markets couldn't even match the market return.

A critical assumption made by the SEI study was that market timing moves were made *instantaneously* on January 1 of every up year and down year. However, if each of these moves was delayed for just *one quarter* of a year (as is usually the case in actual timing decisions where market timers wait for market trends to develop), then the market timing accuracy necessary to merely equal the market return rose to 91%. These already poor odds would have been worse had trading costs related to getting in and out of the market and capital gains taxes generated by the market timing been taken into account.

A 1994 study by Trinity Investment Management Corporation measured ten post-World War II peak-to-peak market cycles.[9] The first of these began in 1946 and the last ended in 1990. The study is important because it shows why a market timer has such difficulty in knowing *at the time* whether or not he is in a falling market or a rising market.

This difficulty originates when "false signals" identified by the study such as the 3 to 4 up months in the average 12-month down market and the 13 down months in the average 40-month up market appear in market cycles. For example, a few months of explosive gains can constitute a series of false signals within an otherwise depressed falling market. These gains can rapidly recover many of the losses previously suffered in the falling market. This is why a falling market may not appear to be falling anymore and can even look like a rising market! The reverse is true when down months falsely signal the end of a rising market. In either case, a market timer can't be sure whether the market that he is currently experiencing is *beginning, continuing or ending.*

This study also demonstrates how the false signals that appear in any market can breed uncertainty between a market timing advisor and his clients. For example, how can an advisor know that there is light at the end of the tunnel when he is surrounded by false signals such as 13 down months in an average 40-month rising market? If the advisor keeps his clients out of a rising market based on these signals, how likely is it that they would follow any of his recommendations after that?

Even if an advisor were able to actually know when a falling market was ending, how could he ever convince his clients to reenter the market at that time? As we know, the bottom of a falling market is the best time to be fully invested to maximally profit from the ensuing rising market, but it is also where the prospects for a market upturn are the bleakest. It is not likely that an advisor's clients would heed his advice in this situation.

A review of these academic studies detailing actual market behavior shows that successful market timing requires far more of a person than the mere ability to avoid losses in falling markets. Even more importantly, it demands that a market timer be able to build real wealth by catching the unpredictable short and intense bursts of gains at the beginning of rising markets. The odds against being successful at this are overwhelming. They become even worse with the passage of time and the frequency of market timing moves.[10]

The Unfair Taxes Generated By Market Timing Mutual Funds

Many investors who time markets do not have their own market timing advisors (who usually charge their clients 2-3% of the value of their investment portfolios every year[11]). Instead, they invest in market timing mutual funds. These funds often produce high trading costs. They can also generate capital gains when liquidations are made by the fund to pay off departing market timers. Obviously such gains will be taxable to these investors.

However, a little known fact is that these same gains are also distributed at year-end to fund shareholders who chose to remain invested in the fund and engaged in no market timing at all.[12] This means that non-market timing shareholders in mutual funds *also* have to pay taxes on the realized gains triggered by departing market timing shareholders. Investors can avoid the cost-generating and tax-creating market timing moves made by managers and shareholders of active mutual funds by remaining fully invested in the market at all times in index funds.[13]

Market Timing Gurus Are Made By Falling Markets

Market timing gurus who have made a successfully fabulous market call usually get awarded 15 minutes of fame not because they got in a rising market at its beginning and built real wealth, but because they avoided (or reduced) losses in a falling market. Therefore, what passes for 'successful' market timing is often one headline-grabbing lucky guess to pull out of a falling market. An analysis of the market timing 'records' of the following three individuals clearly shows that this is true.

Joseph Granville

In profiling the exploits of a market timing guru, the media focuses only on the part of the story that contains the good news. But it might be even more interesting if we could scrutinize a guru's *past* record as well as his *subsequent* record. We are fortunate in that we can do both by examining the career of one such guru. He is Joseph Granville who is the editor of the *Granville Market Letter*, an investment newsletter that he started in 1963.[14]

In April 1980, many of those on Wall Street attributed a 31-point market rally to Granville's dramatic prediction that the market had finally reached bottom. Granville also declared at this time:[15] "I don't think that I will ever make a serious mistake on the stock market for the rest of my life." Then in January 1981, Granville advised his newsletter subscribers to sell everything just as the Dow Jones Industrial Average was pushing through the 1,000-point barrier for the first time in years.[16] Many followed his advice and the resulting tide of sell orders was thought to be largely responsible for causing the Dow to fall 24 points.

What is not well known is that *prior* to his 'correct' predictions in 1980 and 1981, Granville doesn't seem to have made any accurate market timing calls at all. He even completely missed calling the prolonged 1973-1974 down market which, in the twentieth century, was second in severity only to the one experienced during the Great Depression.

Subsequent to his 1980 and 1981 claims to fame, Granville's record is just awful. For the 12½-year period ending on December 31, 1992, one of his portfolios, the *Granville Market Letter - Traders Portfolio*, lost an annual average of 5.4%.[17] Furthermore, in the decade ending April 30, 1995, all the market timing and stock picking portfolios recommended by the *Granville Market Letter* produced a total loss of 96.7%.[18] Both of these periods included the roaring bull market of the 1980s - one of the greatest of the century![19]

Elaine Garzarelli

Elaine Garzarelli was the manager of a mutual fund that was set up just before the sharp downturn in the stock market in October 1987. Garzarelli's fund was able to avoid a plunge in value presumably because her indicators told her to stay out of the market. Her employer, Smith Barney Shearson, immediately took steps to capitalize on this and made sure that its stockbrokers waxed enthusiastic about Garzarelli's fund to their clients. This, and the fact that she gave a large number of media interviews subsequent to the October collapse, helped to rapidly swell the mutual fund's assets to $700 million.

But subsequent to her 1987 'call,' Garzarelli's fund was the *worst* performing growth stock mutual fund of all in 1988. In addition, from 1988 to 1990, her fund underperformed the S&P 500 by 43 percentage points. Thus, the few investors who were in Garzarelli's fund prior to the 1987 Crash (when it beat the S&P 500 by 26 percentage points) and remained in it until the end of 1990 (or after) still wound up in a negative position.[20]

More recently, in late July 1996, Garzarelli made another call to get out of the market by saying that it was due for a 15-20% correction. In October 1996, Garzarelli appeared on CNBC and was asked to be more specific about when to expect a market correction. Her reply was that when the market reached its peak, it would decline by 15-25%. (Garzarelli's followers presumably found this exchange to be less than helpful in that it was like asking what time it will get dark and then being told when the sun goes down.)[21]

Unfortunately for the newsletter subscribers and money management clients of this market maven, the market then rose about 30% by the end of January 1997. At that time, Garzarelli rescinded her call and turned bullish. The fact that her subscribers lost out on such a profitable run-up in stock prices didn't faze Garzarelli. Although she admitted that her call was wrong, she explained that the reason why she was wrong was that certain companies did not report their cash flow earnings on a timely basis. In other words, no one (including the millions of investors that make up the market) cooperated with Garzarelli to ensure that her crystal ball predictions would come true.

Investors with access to the Internet can visit various "chat rooms" that have been set up by Garzarelli's devotees. However, a perusal of the chat room archives that display messages sent between investors in the second half of 1996 reveals an increasingly bitter attitude towards Garzarelli and her bearish stance during the market's advance. Their collective sentiment by the end of 1996 that "Garzarelli is worthless because she is always wrong" also spread to other financial soothsayers such as Michael Metz of Oppenheimer and CNN favorite Jim Rogers.

Yet, all too many investors seemed to have learned the *wrong* lesson from the Garzarelli saga: "These soothsayers are wrong, but let's continue the search for others who will be right." Instead, the *right* lesson can only be this: "No one can meaningfully predict the future behavior of individual investments, much less entire asset classes, in complex financial markets so it makes no sense to listen to any soothsayers at all."

Roger Babson

Yet another example (although more distant in time) of a market timer who became well known because of a 'correct' market timing call was Roger Babson, an investment advisor who 'predicted' the stock market crash of 1929. However, Babson started prophesying crashes starting in 1925 - four years before the real Crash. So Babson's clients who followed his advice in 1925 and bailed out of the market (missing the huge bull market in the second half of the 1920s) were probably hurt as much as those who ignored his many earlier incorrect calls, remained invested in the bull market and then went through the '29 Crash. Although Babson may have become rich and famous because of his one-time claim to fame in 1929, he never made another 'correct' market timing call.

The Possibility Of The Existence Of Successful Market Timers

Naturally, we must allow for the possibility that there are successful market timers who can beat the market (after fees, commissions and taxes) over the long run. But even conceding this possibility, investors who identify past successful market timing systems, advisors, or mutual funds based on their track records have no reliable way of knowing today who the market timing winners of the future will be. Another problem faced by market timers is that even when a 'successful' market timing system, advisor or mutual fund is seemingly identified, the time period needed to tell whether such success is based on skill or is just the result of luck is longer than human life expectancy.[22]

SIMON SAYS: *The Perfect Market Timing System*

A market timer who can *really* tell when the stock market will hit its highs and lows would keep the secret of his perfect market timing system out of the hands of others. He would never sell it for the simple reason that he could become immeasurably richer by keeping the system to himself. This is why it doesn't make sense that a market timing system that really worked would be sold by its inventor to other investors. Consequently, investors should look with a jaundiced eye at any market timing system being peddled by its guru-creator.

This chapter has cited numerous academic studies of actual stock market behavior to demonstrate one of the general disadvantages of active investing - the fool's game of market timing. The next chapter analyzes why the investment information system, from which most individual investors get their knowledge about investing, is not enthusiastic about index funds.

Chapter Notes

[1] "Learning to Live With Bear Markets," Trinity Investment Management Corporation, Boston, Massachusetts, October 1994.

[2] There is really no practical difference between market timing and stock picking. After all, saying that a rising market has peaked or that a falling market has bottomed out are just different ways of saying that stocks are overvalued or undervalued by the market.

[3] "Timing Strategies And The Risk Of Missing Bull Markets" by P.R. Chandy and William Reichenstein, *AAII Journal*, August 1991, pages 17-19.

[4] "The Asset Allocation Decision," SEI Corporation position paper, April 1993.

[5] "Likely Gains From Market Timing" by William F. Sharpe, *Financial Analysts Journal*, March/April 1975, pages 60-69.

[6] "Gains From Stock Market Timing" by Jess H. Chua and Richard S. Woodward, Monograph 1986-2 of Monograph Series in Finance and Economics, edited by Anthony Saunders (Salomon Brothers Center for the Study of Financial Institutions at the Graduate School of Business Administration of New York University: New York, 1986), pages 12-13.

[7] "Likely Gains From Market Timing" by William F. Sharpe, *Financial Analysts Journal*, March/April 1975, pages 60-69.

[8] "Technical Note: Calculation of Forecasting Accuracy," SEI Corporation position paper, April 1992.

[9] "Learning to Live With Bear Markets," Trinity Investment Management Corporation, Boston, Massachusetts, October 1994.

[10] "The Folly Of Stock Market Timing" by Robert H. Jeffrey, *Harvard Business Review*, July/August 1984, pages 102-110.

[11] There is an *additional* layer of expenses that market timers incur when they use mutual funds.

[12] When mutual fund shareholders in an "open-end" mutual fund decide to "cash out" their shares, they turn them over to the mutual fund. The fund then sells the shares and gives the cash that it receives to the departing shareholders. Naturally, if these shareholders have generated any capital gains they must pay taxes on them. But what is not well understood is that the mutual fund itself must also pay taxes on the gains. According to the federal tax code, the only way for a fund to avoid this is to pass through these gains to its *non-liquidating* shareholders who remain in the fund. "These realized gains, although incurred on behalf of the departing shareholders, who will pay their own capital gains taxes, are distributed at year-end to the remaining [i.e., non-liquidating] fund shareholders and are taxable to them. The little known result [among the investing public] is that *the Treasury temporarily collects two taxes on essentially the same gain*. (The second tax is temporary - assuming a stepped-up cost basis at death does not arise in the interim - because the [non-liquidating] continuing shareholders' cost bases are increased

by the amount of the capital gains and dividends)." *The Portable MBA In Investment* edited by Peter L. Bernstein (New York: John Wiley & Sons, Inc., 1995), page 419, chapter note 12. *See* "Is Your Alpha Big Enough to Cover Its Taxes?" by Robert H. Jeffrey and Robert D. Arnott, *The Journal of Portfolio Management*, Spring 1993, page 24, footnote 7. The tax that must be paid by non-liquidating shareholders who remain invested in the fund is obviously unfair to them. They are penalized by having to pay taxes on capital gains that they never generated simply because they chose to hold on to their mutual fund shares. Such investors typically have no intention of selling their shares in the short run, if ever. The unfairness of this can be mitigated by another provision in the tax code. This provides that whenever a non-liquidating shareholder later decides to cash out his mutual fund shares, the adverse effect of any capital gains distributions is canceled out by adding them to his cost basis. For example, suppose that a non-liquidating shareholder holds a mutual fund share worth $12 with a $5 cost basis. If he receives a $1 long term capital gains distribution from a mutual fund due to the actions of liquidating shareholders who depart from the fund, then he must involuntarily pay a capital gains tax of $.20 on the $1 gain (20% of $1). The $1 distribution is added to the $5 cost basis of his investment for a new cost basis of $6. This reduces the amount of the gain from $7 to $6 which thereby decreases the potential tax that may have to be paid from $1.40 to $1.20. But even though a non-liquidating shareholder who later cashes out "gets back" the $.20 tax that he was forced to unfairly pay, he still must pay a tax of $1.20 on the subsequent cash out. If this shareholder holds his shares until death, though, he escapes the $1.20 tax entirely. In addition, if he is an indexer he is invested in mutual funds that have low portfolio turnover (defined in Chapter Nine) which not only minimizes capital gains taxes *but also trading costs. This is why it makes so much sense to invest in low turnover index funds and hold them for life.*

[13] Full investment in the market at all times not only gives an indexer an immediate advantage each time the market "comes back" after it has bottomed out, but also allows him to participate in the market's long term climb in value.

[14] "Joe Granville: Messiah or Menace?" by Michael Spivvy, *Financial World*, June 15, 1980, pages 18-22.

[15] *Ibid.*

[16] "Fear of Crashing" by Peter Lynch, *Worth*, September 1995, page 127.

[17] "Market Timing Ability and Volatility Implied in Investment Newsletters' Asset Allocation Recommendations" by John R. Graham and Campbell R. Harvey, National Bureau of Economic Research Working Paper No. 4890, October 1994.

[18] "Fear of Crashing" by Peter Lynch, *Worth*, September 1995, page 127.

[19] Granville missed another call - he predicted that Los Angeles would be destroyed by an earthquake in May 1981. *See* "Joe Granville: Messiah or Menace?" by Michael Spivvy, *Financial World*, June 15, 1980, pages 18-22.

[20] The author of this book spoke with an attorney who was attracted to the hype

surrounding Garzarelli's mutual fund. She invested in the fund only *after* the 1987 Crash and thus failed to benefit from its outperformance of the market. Unfortunately, she remained in the fund and endured its nightmarish performance during 1988-1990. This experience fully cured the attorney of any belief in market timing.
[21] In November 1996, Garzarelli sent out a direct mail piece to get investors to subscribe to her investment newsletter. *The Wall Street Journal* called it "one of the most alarming pieces of junk mail in [Wall] Street history . . . " It describes the mailing: "'SELL NOW!' the envelope warned in red. 'Get OUT of all U.S. stocks and mutual funds now.' The mailing noted that the warnings came from a guru who had 'predicted *every* bear market crash of the last 20 years.' There has been only one crash in that time, but let's not get picky. If the market crashes any time in the next 20 years, the guru, or at least her public-relations people, can say she was right again." "Crystal Ball I: Garzarelli on A Roll," *The Wall Street Journal*, January 2, 1997, page R8.
[22] "Measuring Market Timing Strategies" by G.L. Beebower and A.P. Varikooty, *Financial Analysts Journal*, November/December 1991, pages 78-84 and 92.

EIGHT

WHY THE INVESTMENT INFORMATION SYSTEM IS NOT ENTHUSIASTIC ABOUT INDEX FUNDS

Insidious Indexing: How Robot Investors Are Undermining the Market[1]
- A headline in *Barron's*, 1990

Overview

The investment information system, from which most individual investors get their knowledge about investing, is generally not enthusiastic about index funds. The reason for this is that no part of the system can make any money from them. As a result, relatively few individual investors know about the indexing revolution and the many advantages offered by index funds.

The Investment Information System Cannot Make Money From Index Mutual Funds

The investment information system, from which most individual investors get their knowledge about investing, includes the media, the professional active money management industry, mutual fund ratings guides such as Morningstar and other sources of information. This system tends to ignore or even discredit the idea of index fund investing.

The reason why the investment information system is generally not enthusiastic about index funds is that no part of it can make any money from them. If the investment media was truly enthusiastic about index funds it would deliver the indexing message in a consistent and meaningful way. There would be no need for it to feature stories describing the investing adventures of colorful stock picking and market timing personalities. However, this would reduce the investment media's revenues and might even decrease its power. If investment salespeople such as stockbrokers were to favor indexing, most of them would go out of business since index funds do not carry commission loads. If Morningstar was to embrace indexing, track record investing would lose some of its popularity. As a result, investors would have less need for Morningstar's mutual fund ratings guide.

The Message Conveyed By The Investment Information System

The message generally conveyed by the investment information system is that smart and aggressive stock pickers and market timers can beat the market. Although some parts of this system occasionally describe the benefits of indexing,[2] fundamentally it does not take seriously the idea that investors cannot be expected to beat the market. Much more typically, the system derisively labels this idea as the acceptance of "guaranteed mediocrity." Richard Fentin, former manager of the Fidelity Puritan Fund, sums up this attitude perfectly:[3] "Why would anyone not want to be aggressive with your money? If you didn't want to be aggressive, why go into mutual funds? Don't you want to beat the market? Do people want to achieve only average returns?"[4]

Because of the investment information system's built-in bias against indexing, relatively few investors have been exposed to the message of the indexing revolution and the many advantages offered by index funds. One indication of this is that only *seven percent* of all investments in stocks and bonds made by individual investors are placed in index funds.

The investment information system consists of many parts. As we will now see, each part of this system in its own way generally conveys the message that (1) investors (or those that they hire) can beat the market and therefore (2) indexing investment strategies make little sense.

The Investment Media: One Part Of The Investment Information System

The investment media, which is comprised of magazines, newspapers, television and radio, is a very powerful part of the investment information system. Since the media wishes to maximize its revenues just like any other business, it must be responsive to the consumers of its products.

What these consumers want is access to information about investing. But in responding to this demand, the investment media is forced to compete for the attention (i.e., the money) of consumers. The surest way for it to successfully grab some of this attention is to be more entertaining in selling its products. As a result, the media generally presents investment *entertainment* as investment *information*.

This entertainment often consists of a heavy dose of spellbinding stories that detail the market-beating schemes of colorful, rich and well respected stock picking and market timing gurus. These gurus seem to live such fascinating lives that it is easy to see why most investors would "find it exciting and fun to pick stocks and time markets, to be paid high fees and to do it all with someone else's money."[5] Newspaper columnists, newsletter editors, magazine writers, television correspondents and radio commentators all cooperate in the effort to chronicle the exploits of these winners. (Occasionally, losers are profiled. But this only occurs when describing the spectacular fall of those who used to be winners.) This sells more newspapers, newsletters, magazines and books and boosts TV and radio ratings.

The formula used in the stories that record such feats remains the same - a, b or c beat the market over the last x, y or z time period. The cumulative impact of these stories can cause investors to be misled because it convinces many of them that the market is beaten day in and day out by the *same* money managers: "Whadda ya mean you can't beat the market, I see stories about these guys who do it all the time!" All too many investors don't understand that the winners who triumph each year at the expense of the losers in the zero sum game of a financial market are almost always *different* - they are only transitory members that make up a continuously changing group.

Of course, this is very much in the interests of the media since it will always have somebody new to profile and thus always something *new to sell*.[6] Fundamentally, this is why the investment media has a tremendous financial interest in reinforcing the belief that investors can beat the market.

In contrast, indexing does not seem very exciting to investors who equate investment information with profiles of colorful investment personalities.[7] There are no stories describing how an index fund manager 'called' a major down market and saved his clients a bundle or how his fund went up 200% in six months. Because the indexing story does not fit into the media world in which there is a constant need for new and exciting entertainment (and advertising revenues), the media is not enthusiastic about index funds.

The many advantages of indexing become even more apparent when an investor has a long investment time horizon. However, the significance of this is usually lost in the media's mad rush to report short term investment performance.[8] (Even when it reports long term performance, the media gets it wrong since it usually defines "long term" investing as a period of five or ten years. But at a minimum, it should be twenty years and more probably thirty years or longer.)

The problem with focusing on the short term is that it creates a conflict between the media's interest in enhancing its revenues and the interest of the investing public in obtaining meaningful investment information. For example, many investors read *Barron's* and watch *Moneyline* which report tremendous quarterly or annual performances by a few (temporarily winning) individual stocks or mutual funds. These investors then compare their own investment performances to the winners and some become convinced that they should change investment strategies. This can become very costly if they begin to fall for the pitches of, say, mutual fund salespeople pushing the latest No. 1 funds. As the next wave of outstanding short term track records rolls in, the futile cycle of chasing yesterday's winners repeats itself.

In sum, the investment media's primary purpose is not to supply useful investment information or deliver sound long term investment advice to investors. Instead, its main function is to provide entertainment in the guise of investment information (which is largely meaningless) and gear it to short attention spans. Consequently, long term indexing strategies stand little chance of getting meaningful and sustained attention from the investment media.

The Professional Active Money Management Industry: A Second Part Of The Investment Information System

A second part of the investment information system is the vast professional active money management industry. Those employed in this industry include mutual fund managers and commissioned salespeople such as stockbrokers. Most professionals in this industry could not financially survive if they were to recommend index funds to their clients. For example, investment salespeople are compensated only if they can sell commissioned investment products such as stocks, bonds, mutual funds and annuities. Since index funds carry no commission loads, these salespeople are not seriously interested in offering them to their clients. In fact, about the only time that they mention index funds is when they put down the idea of indexing as a "no-brainer."[9]

According to *Fortune* magazine,[10] some individuals in the professional active money management industry "are among the most overpaid people in the country" employed by money management firms that have "the most awesome profit margins in U.S. industry." It is no wonder, then, that no one in this industry is too keen on letting investors know about the many advantages of indexing. Why should they threaten their high profit margins by placing clients in index funds?

Morningstar: A Third Part Of The Investment Information System

A third part of the investment information system is made up of mutual fund ratings guides such as *Morningstar Mutual Funds*. Morningstar cannot be enthusiastic about indexing because its continued existence largely depends on providing a service to those who pursue investment strategies designed to beat the market. For example, Don Phillips, Morningstar's president, is obviously no fan of indexing:[11] "The blind belief that indexes can be taken from the past and projected into the future [is dubious] . . . If you believe blindly in indexing, you stop looking for better answers. If we don't bother to look at the ways people like Warren Buffett beat the market, I can guarantee you we won't find it."

Yet *there is no good reason to look for these answers*. Regardless of whether a given financial market is efficient or inefficient, it is still a zero sum game and that dictates only one outcome - the average actively-managed dollar will *always* underperform the average indexed dollar after costs and taxes. The only thing left, then, is to search within these averages for those that we think will turn out to be winners and invest with them today (much of the 'advice' churned out by the investment information system purports to help investors find success in these searches).

But the problem is that no one has yet discovered a way to find such winners. It can't be done by identifying winning track records because there is no way to know when (or even if) these winners (or others) from the past will win in the future. Nor can it be done by attempting to identify skillful money managers since a track record sometimes longer than human life expectancy is needed to be sure that any success that was uncovered was based on skill and not just luck.[12]

The dubious attitude towards indexing taken by Morningstar's president seems to extend to the kinds of investment options offered to Morningstar employees in their 401(k) plan.[13] All the options are actively-managed mutual funds. (One seeming exception is the Pimco StocksPlus Fund, an "enhanced" index fund. But as we will see in Chapter Nine, an enhanced index fund is really not an index fund but an active fund.) For example, over 30% of the plan's assets are invested in two particularly aggressive mutual funds. Morningstar employees, who are mostly in their 20s and 30s, thus appear to be risk-taking investors intent on outperforming the market.

Thus, it is clear why Morningstar isn't enthusiastic about index funds. If indexing became too popular it would likely see a drop in its revenues and maybe even become a less powerful part of the investment information system.

Survivorship Bias In Mutual Fund Ratings: The Stacked Deck Against Index Funds

Another highlight way in which the investment information system fails to show the superior performance of index funds is found in published mutual fund ratings. These ratings create a "survivorship bias" in favor of actively-managed mutual funds and thus the average active fund.

Mutual fund ratings usually show how the performances of individual mutual funds compare to an "average" mutual fund. This average is made up of active funds that have *survived* from the beginning to the end of a particular measurement period. But other active funds also started up during this period. Over time, these funds turned in poor performances and either went out of business, were merged into other mutual funds or in some way dropped out of the surviving group. For example, 242 (or 5%) of the 4,555 mutual funds tracked by Lipper Analytical Services were merged or liquidated in 1996.

Because these funds failed to survive to the end of the period, their inferior track records were not included in the calculation for figuring the investment return of the average mutual fund. The effect of this is to award the average mutual fund a published return *superior* to the one that it actually achieved. This creates a bias in favor of the average active fund by misleadingly enhancing its relative attractiveness in comparison to index funds.

A recent study reveals how non-surviving funds can distort the computation of the average active mutual fund return.[14] Its findings, based on an analysis of the 34-year period from 1962 through 1995, are as follows: (1) Of the 2,071 stock funds that were open to investors at some time during this period, 35% (or 725) went out of business. This is an annual mortality rate of 3.6%. (2) The average fund (which included only surviving funds) had an average annual compound return of 10.7% compared to the 10.6% return of the S&P 500. But when non-surviving funds were included in the computation, the average dropped to 9.5% - a return that averaged a full percentage point below the market return over the span of a third of a century. This changed the average fund from a winner into a loser. (3) 29% of the funds outperformed the S&P 500 when only surviving funds were counted, but when non-surviving funds were also included just 23% of all funds beat the index.[15]

Another effect of survivorship bias is that mutual fund averages markedly improve with age which *further* boosts their return against index funds. For example, Lipper reported in 1986 that 568 diversified U.S. stock funds earned an average return of 13.39%. But in 1996, Lipper listed the 1986 return as 14.65%. The reason why the return improved from 1986 to 1996 is that the new number is only based on the performance of the 434 funds from the 1986 group that remained in business through 1996. The presumably inferior returns of the 134 funds that went out of business since 1986 disappeared from the 1996 average.

SIMON SAYS: *Survivorship Bias And Track Record Investing*

Survivorship bias underscores the ultimate problem with track record investing: there is no way to know today which mutual funds will even *survive* in the future, much less which ones will be winners.

A fairer approach to evaluating the performance of the average mutual fund would be to include in the calculation of the average *all* mutual funds that were in business at the beginning of the time period in question. This comparison would thus include, not exclude, the poor records of the non-surviving mutual funds. That in turn would lower the investment performance of the average mutual fund and help underscore the superiority of index funds.

A little known effect of survivorship bias relative to stock mutual funds is that, in addition to overstating the *return* of the average active fund, it also understates its *risk*. According to Morningstar, the level of risk contained in the stocks that are represented in the S&P 500 and the Wilshire 5000 indexes is about 25% less than the risk in the average active stock fund.[16] The reason for this is that active stock mutual fund managers have become more aggressive in their search for higher ratings. As a result, these funds have taken on risk profiles that are increasingly dissimilar to those of the S&P 500 and Wilshire 5000. This means that the average active stock fund is riskier than the index funds that track the performances of these two major stock indexes.

"Creation bias" may play an even bigger role in misleadingly enhancing the performance of the average mutual fund at the expense of index funds.[17] Mutual fund regulators allow some newly formed mutual funds to include as part of their track records the performances that they achieved when they existed as limited partnerships or other such non-fund entities. Since mutual fund companies only make the track records of such funds available for inclusion in the computation of an average if they are outstanding, the performance of the average mutual fund is falsely inflated even more.

Survivorship bias and creation bias both demonstrate that the past performance numbers of the average mutual fund are really only approximations. Indeed, while mutual fund ads may warn that "past performance is no guarantee of future performance," it appears that the past performances of mutual funds aren't even good indicators of what has happened in the past.

This chapter has analyzed the reasons why each part of the investment information system is not enthusiastic about index funds. The following section of the book provides a detailed understanding of why index funds are the best investment choice for most investors. The first chapter of this section examines the "nuts and bolts" of index funds as well as concepts related to indexing.

Chapter Notes

[1] *Barron's*, January 15, 1990, page 8.

[2] By mid-1997, indexing was receiving more attention than ever before. This was primarily due to the abnormally high returns produced over the previous two years by the large company stocks of the S&P 500. But on the whole, indexing receives little notice from the investment information system. Even when it does, the effort is little more than a cursory examination of indexing's advantages.

[3] *John Bogle and the Vanguard Experiment* by Robert Slater (Chicago, Illinois: Irwin Professional Publishing, 1997), page 166.

[4] Over the decade ending in 1995, Fentin underperformed the S&P 500 by an average of about two percentage points. Thus, he failed to achieve "only average" returns. He did, however, achieve "less than average" returns. For this privilege, Fidelity Puritan investors only had to pay annual expenses more than three times the amount charged by a low cost index fund. They also had to pay taxes generated by portfolio turnover that exceeded 100%. *Ibid.*, page 161.

[5] Rex A. Sinquefield in "Active or Passive: The Debate about Investment Management Styles," a speech at the International Association for Financial Planning Success Forum, Boston, Massachusetts, September 12, 1994.

[6] Mark J. Hulbert in "Lessons Drawn From Tracking Investment Advisors' Performance," a speech at the National Endowment for Financial Education national conference, July 27-29, 1995, Denver, Colorado. *See* "The No-Nonsense Meeting" by Robert N. Veres, *Investment Advisor*, September 1995, pages 122-131.

[7] The one exception is John C. Bogle of Vanguard. But even though Bogle champions indexing in media interviews, his larger message centers on the deficiencies (such as overweening greed) of the mutual fund industry.

[8] Even the most well respected investment publications are guilty of focusing investors on the short term. For example, *The Wall Street Journal* publishes the top performers over the last 20 trading days and the next day it shows the top performers over the last 90 calendar days. Another day it features six-month performance while yet another, one-year returns.

[9] Merrill Lynch began to offer index funds to its 401(k) customers in early 1997 and to other customers later that year. One way that Merrill Lynch offers index funds is through a wrap account. (*See* page 86 for a description of the horrors of a wrap account.) But this completely negates one of the principal advantages of index funds - low costs. Merrill Lynch also offers four no load index funds to its retail clients as a "loss leader." This is designed to lure new investors who want to climb on the indexing bandwagon into Merrill Lynch offices to invest in their index funds. Since there is no commission on the sale of these funds, though, it isn't long before the sales force - once it gets into "relationship" with the new clients - pushes commissioned products at them. Furthermore, Merrill Lynch's index funds are not particularly low cost. Their annual operating expenses range

from .85% to 1.15% (all include an annual .25% 12b-1 fee) with the annual expenses of the S&P 500 fund pegged at .90% - or more than four times the cost of a low cost S&P 500 index fund.

[10] "The Coming Investor Revolt" by Jaclyn Fierman, *Fortune*, October 31, 1994, page 66.

[11] "Debate: Active vs. Passive Investing," *Financial Planning*, December 1996, page 22.

[12] Even assuming that *all* stock picking winners really are skillful (an assumption that the most rabid active money managers would not make) still doesn't mean that they will always win. As we saw in Chapter Six, the market can make the most skillful stock picker look bad if it doesn't favor his particular investment style for the time period under consideration.

[13] "An Inside Peek At The Experts' Mutual Funds" by Karen Damato, *The Wall Street Journal*, May 10, 1996, page C1.

[14] "Mutual Fund Survivorship" by Mark M. Carhart, Marshall School of Business Working Paper, University of Southern California, May 1997.

[15] This figure would be sharply lower had the study taken into account the effect of commission loads and taxes on mutual fund performance. *See* pages 9-11 for more discussion of this issue.

[16] John C. Bogle in "Be Not the First, Nor Yet the Last," a speech at the annual conference of the Association for Investment Management and Research, Atlanta, Georgia, May 8, 1996.

[17] "Ghosts of Dead Funds May Haunt Results" by Karen Damato, *The Wall Street Journal*, April 4, 1997, page R1.

SECTION II

INDEX MUTUAL FUNDS: A REVOLUTIONARY CALL TO ARMS

THEME OF THE SECTION:

INDEX MUTUAL FUNDS ARE THE BEST INVESTMENT CHOICE FOR MOST INVESTORS

UNDERSTANDING THE BASICS

NINE

THE NUTS AND BOLTS OF INDEX FUNDS

A woman went to her doctor because she wasn't feeling well. The doctor examined her and said: "You only have two months to live."
The woman asked: "What do you think I should do?"
He said: "Get a second opinion."
The woman went to another doctor and asked: "What do you think?"
She said: "I've got good news and bad news for you."
The woman asked: "What's the bad news?"
She said: "You've only got 30 days to live."
The woman asked: "Oh my gosh, what's the good news?"
She said: "You could marry an index fund manager and it would seem like 50 years."
 - Rex A. Sinquefield
   Co-Chairman of Dimensional Fund Advisors Inc.

Overview

It is essential to acquire some basic knowledge about the nuts and bolts of index funds as well as to understand certain indexing-related concepts. This helps investors to fully appreciate the many advantages of index funds.

The Definition Of An "Index"

An "index" is a statistical measurement of the collective investment performance of an asset class. (An "asset class," a group of stocks or bonds with common investment characteristics, is more fully defined in the following section.) An index "keeps score" of the collective performance of the investments that comprise an asset class. A well known index is the Standard & Poor's 500 Composite Stock Index ("the S&P 500") which represents 500 important stocks listed and traded in the stock markets of the United States.[1] The stocks *represented in* this particular index *comprise* an asset class - large company, "blue chip" stocks. An index is not invested in (nor does it physically hold) any of the stocks or bonds that comprise an asset class; it is simply a statistical representation of the performance of these investments.

Currently, about 25 commonly recognized indexes are tracked by index funds in this country and others all over the world. Some of these indexes are listed in Illustration 7, below, and a description of them as well as others is contained in the Appendix. (A "passive" mutual fund is a "first cousin" to an index fund. The principle distinction between them is subtle. All index funds are passive funds - i.e., neither try to predict the future for the purpose of attempting to beat the market. But not all passive funds track a recognized index, so not all are index funds in the strict sense.)

Illustration 7

Published And Commonly Recognized Indexes

U.S. Total Market Indexes
Wilshire 5000 Index
Russell 3000 Index

U.S. Large Company Stock Indexes
Standard & Poor's 500 Composite Stock Index
Schwab 1000 Index
Russell 1000 Index

U. S. Small Company Stock Indexes
Russell 2000 Index
Standard & Poor's SmallCap 600 Index
CRSP 9-10 Index

"Style" U.S. Stock Indexes
Standard & Poor's/BARRA Growth Index
Standard & Poor's/BARRA Value Index
Russell 1000 Value Index
Russell 1000 Growth Index

U.S. Bond Indexes
Lehman Brothers Aggregate Bond Index
Lehman Brothers Long Treasury Bond Index
Salomon Brothers Broad Investment Grade Bond Index

Foreign Large Company Stock Indexes
Morgan Stanley Capital International EAFE Index
Financial Times All-Share Index

Foreign Bond Indexes
J. P. Morgan Government Bond Index
Salomon Brothers World Government Bond Index

Unlike the S&P 500, the Dow Jones Industrial Average ("the Dow") is not an index. It is a "price-weighted" *average* of 30 blue chip stocks issued by companies such as Caterpillar and General Electric. The Dow measures the movements in the market prices of these stocks by adding their prices and dividing that sum by a continuously adjusted denominator.

One of the differences between the Dow and the S&P 500 is the way that the Dow is calculated and the effect that this may have on its performance. Because it is price-weighted, the Dow's performance can be more heavily impacted by a higher priced stock such as Caterpillar than by a lower priced stock such as General Electric, even though the total market value of GE stock is greater. A big change in the market price of just one of the 30 stocks in the Dow can therefore cause a disproportionate shift in the performance of the average. This is unlikely to occur with the S&P 500.

Another difference between the Dow and the S&P 500 is that many of the Dow stocks have individual or cyclical characteristics that may not accurately reflect the broader stock market as well as the more numerous and representative stocks of the S&P 500. All 30 stocks in the Dow are represented in the S&P 500 and all are listed on the New York Stock Exchange.

The Definition Of An "Asset Class"

An "asset class" consists of investments such as individual stocks or bonds that have common investment characteristics. The investment characteristics common to the most well known asset class in America - the large company stocks represented in the S&P 500 stock index - are: (1) large market capitalization which is a result of being widely held and highly valued by investors, (2) a demonstrated history of stable dividend payments[2] and (3) a well established record of continued business operations.

Other examples of asset classes include foreign stocks, small company stocks, emerging markets stocks, real estate securities and various fixed-income investments such as long term Treasury bonds.[3]

Reviewing The Definition Of An "Index Mutual Fund"

We learned in Chapter One that the manager of an index mutual fund attempts to provide the investment performance of the fund's underlying index by holding all (or a sample) of the individual stocks or bonds that are represented in the index. These investments comprise an asset class. Thus, an index fund captures the return and reflects the risk of the asset class whose collective performance is measured by the fund's underlying index.[4]

How well an index fund meets the goal of providing the performance of its underlying index is determined by how closely its manager matches the composition of the stocks or bonds held by the fund to the composition of the stocks or bonds represented in the index. Furthermore, an index fund is just like an actively-managed mutual fund in that it invests in individual stocks or bonds, although it radically differs from an active fund in the sense that its investment goal is not to beat the market.

"Asset Class Investing" With Index Mutual Funds

"Asset class investing" is the process of investing in asset classes with the use of index funds. An index fund is a very efficient and low cost way for an investor to virtually duplicate the investment performance of an asset class. Investors can use index funds as "building blocks" to construct uniquely different portfolios of asset classes ranging from very conservative to very aggressive.

It would seem that asset class investing with index funds entails a modest investment goal: providing the respective investment performances of those asset classes invested in by an indexer. Nothing could be further from the truth. As we will see in the next chapter, investment experts widely agree that the way in which an investor allocates the assets in his portfolio drives virtually all long term investment performance, not stock picking and market timing. The most efficient and effective way for an investor to implement these asset allocation decisions is by asset class investing with index funds.

The Construction And Maintenance Of An Index Mutual Fund

Mathematical formulas and computers assist an index fund manager in the construction and maintenance of his fund. A manager's job largely consists of ensuring that the fund holds the same investments in the same proportionate amounts as those represented in the index tracked by the fund. One of the difficulties in achieving this is that the composition of the investments represented in an index fund's underlying index changes for a variety of reasons.[5] For example, a stock index can undergo alteration because of stock offerings or stock repurchase programs. Stocks can even be removed from an index because of corporate mergers, spin-offs, acquisitions or the occasional bankruptcy.

An index fund manager also ensures that the fund's capital gains taxes and trading costs remain low by minimizing the fund's "portfolio turnover" (the rate at which a fund manager buys or sells stocks or bonds for the fund during the course of a year). In sum, an index fund manager must be prepared to counter anything that may cause the index fund to stray from its goal: to provide the investment performance of its underlying index. The two methods used to construct index funds are full replication and sampling.

Full Replication

"Full replication" is the most common way to construct an index fund. Using this method, an index fund manager invests in all the same investments as those represented in the fund's underlying index in the same proportionate amounts. These proportionate amounts are based on the market value of the investments.

The "market value" of an investment is the total number of shares of the investment owned by all investors multiplied by the market price of one share of the investment. For example, one of the 500 stocks represented in the S&P 500 is General Electric (GE). Suppose that 100 million shares of GE stock are held by investors and each share is worth $100. The market value of GE stock would therefore be $10 billion. If the total market value of GE stock constitutes 3% of the total market value of all 500 stocks in the S&P 500 index, then its "weighting" (or proportionate representation) in the index would be 3%. Likewise, GE stock would constitute 3% of the total value of the investments held by an S&P 500 index fund.

Thus, each of the stocks represented in the S&P 500 is weighted (or proportionately represented) in the index based on its market value. These weightings make each stock's influence on the performance of the S&P 500 directly proportional to its market value. So the smaller (or larger) the market value of a stock in comparison to the other 499 stocks in this index, the smaller (or larger) its weighting in the index fund that tracks the performance of the index.

Sampling

A second method used to construct an index fund is to invest in a "sample" (a representative portion) of the investments in the fund's underlying index. This method, used to save costs, is employed by index funds that either hold a large number of investments or that have small market value. There are two types of sampling methods used by index fund managers: (1) stratified sampling and (2) mean-variance optimization.

An index fund manager who uses "stratified sampling" selects certain stocks from an index that, in the aggregate, will have the same proportionate industry sector and market value characteristics as the entire index. This allows the index fund manager to avoid the cost-prohibitive problem of holding all the investments that are represented in the fund's underlying index.

Stratified sampling may be used to construct index funds such as those that invest in small company stocks. For example, an index fund designed to track the performance of a small company stock index such as the Russell 2000 may hold 75% of the stocks that are represented in that index. Other small company stock index funds may sample a lower percentage of the stocks represented in their underlying indexes.

A second method of sampling is called "mean-variance optimization." This method employs a mathematical model known as a mean variance optimizer. Mean-variance optimization attempts to predict (1) how the various risk factors of a stock such as its market value, volatility and quality of its earnings will impact each other and (2) the exposure of each stock in the index to these various risk factors. If an index fund manager is successful in using this method of sampling, he can create an index fund that should, under all circumstances, perform similarly to the index.

The downside of constructing an index fund using mean-variance optimization is that the predictive inputs often contain mistakes. This can lead to bizarre outputs which increase tracking error. Because the inputs used in a mean-variance optimizer are derived from the past, the future must duplicate the past to ensure that tracking error is small when using this sampling method.

The S&P 500: The Index Most Commonly Tracked By Index Funds

As we know, the S&P 500 is a well known index of 500 stocks listed and traded in the stock markets of the United States.[6] It is the oldest and most widely followed barometer that is used to measure the performance of "the market." This is why it has become the preeminent standard against which the investment performance of mutual funds is compared. (The Dow is also a well known gauge of the market but it is not used as a standard for comparing the investment performance of mutual funds. Instead, it is widely followed as a daily indicator of the market's performance.) Most index funds today track the performance of the S&P 500.

Many of the stocks in the S&P 500 are representative of companies that tend to be leaders in their respective industries and are important to the entire American economy.[7] The S&P 500 encompasses about 90 specific industry groups that are part of four major industry sectors divided into Industrials, Utilities, Financials and Transportation.[8]

However, there are three reasons why the S&P 500 is an incomplete barometer of the stock market in the United States.[9]

First, it only represents stocks that make up about 70-75% of the total market value of all U.S. stocks. Consequently, the S&P 500 fails to mirror the investment performance of a significant number of stocks available to investors.

Second, the S&P 500 is biased in favor of large company stocks. In a year in which small company stocks outperform large company stocks, the large company stocks that comprise the S&P 500 may not be the best gauge of market behavior.[10]

Third, there is corporate cross-ownership of some stocks in the S&P 500 which can cause distortions in the market value of the index. "Cross-ownership" occurs when stock in a company represented in an index is held by another company which is also represented in the index. For example, if Hale-Bopp Corporation and Gouda Corporation are both included in the S&P 500 index and Hale-Bopp owns 100% of Gouda's shares, then the value of these shares is included in the market values of both Hale-Bopp and Gouda. The value of Gouda's shares is thus "double counted" which overweights the market value of Hale-Bopp. This may cause a distortion in the value of the index.

The "Tracking Error" Of An Index Mutual Fund

"Tracking error" refers to the amount by which an index fund's performance falls short of the goal of providing the performance of its underlying index. (More rarely, tracking error measures the amount of performance by which an index fund exceeds the performance of its underlying index.) An index fund's tracking error is primarily attributable to its annual operating expenses plus the trading costs associated with investing new cash flow from investors and reinvesting their dividends or interest. The closer an index fund "tracks" its underlying index, the more directly its investment performance will rise and fall in correlation to the index.

The Vanguard Index 500 is a good example of how well an index fund can minimize tracking error. This index fund tracks the investment performance of its underlying index - the S&P 500. In 1995, the large company stocks represented in the S&P 500 index generated a total return of 37.58%. In comparison, the total investment return of the Vanguard Index 500 was 37.45%. This means that the index fund had a tracking error of only thirteen basis points, or 13/100ths of one percentage point. (One "basis point" is equal to 1/100th of one percentage point (.01%).) Consequently, the Vanguard Index 500 index fund provided 99.7% of the performance of its underlying index.[11]

At times, an index fund manager may be tempted to save trading costs by not purchasing the investments represented in an index that have smaller market value. Giving in to this temptation, though, may lead to tracking error. This is why an index fund manager must always carefully balance the potential for higher trading costs against the potential for higher tracking error in assessing the effect of each on his fund's performance.

Customized Index Mutual Funds

Most index funds seek to provide the performance of investments that comprise published and commonly recognized indexes such as the S&P 500. However, stocks that are not large company stocks (such as small company stocks or foreign stocks) are not represented in this index. Consequently, some investment management firms have developed customized indexes for investors who wish to obtain the advantages of indexing other kinds of stocks or bonds. (These firms also sometimes operate customized index funds that track such indexes.)

This may seem an arbitrary approach to building an index, but it is no more so than the techniques used to construct the most well known indexes. For example, Standard & Poor's did not include Microsoft in the S&P 500 until mid-1994, long after it had become one of the nation's largest companies.[12] In addition, the historical performance of the Dow Jones Industrial Average would probably have been far different had IBM been kept in the average during its high growth years. (It was replaced in 1939 by American Telephone & Telegraph and did not return to the index for 40 years.)

One kind of customized index fund is a "tilt" index fund. Instead of fully replicating or sampling a broad market index such as the S&P 500 or the Wilshire 5000, some very specialized index funds tilt toward a given investment style such as "growth" or "value." For example, there are style-tilted index funds linked to the S&P 500/BARRA Growth index and the S&P 500/BARRA Value index. These kinds of index funds allow indexers to gain exposure to a given investment style while minimizing the high costs of actively-managed growth or value mutual funds.

An "enhanced" index fund is really not an index fund but an actively-managed fund. The manager of an enhanced index fund uses either stock picking or futures and options in attempts to boost its return so that it can outperform its underlying index. At the same time, he tries to hold constant the risk characteristics of the index. Although the costs to operate an enhanced index fund are less than actively-managed funds, they are substantially more than plain vanilla index funds. An example of an enhanced index fund is the Pimco StocksPlus Fund. The manager of this fund seeks to beat the performance of the S&P 500 by an average annual one percentage point over a 5-year period by making selective bets on undervalued bonds.

How An Index Mutual Fund Manager Trades Stocks And Bonds

As will be discussed in greater detail in Chapter Twelve, the biggest advantage of index funds is their low cost. This is largely the result of two factors: low portfolio turnover and the use of inexpensive techniques when trading stocks and bonds.

Since index funds do not buy or sell stocks or bonds based on insights about future investment performance, their portfolio turnover remains low in comparison to actively-managed mutual funds. This saves costs (and taxes). The turnover generated by an index fund is caused by (1) shareholders who invest new money, reinvest their dividend or interest income and redeem their shares, (2) index fund managers who purchase futures contracts to equitize cash holdings and (3) the fund's underlying index when changes are made in its composition.[13]

The techniques used by index fund managers to trade stocks and bonds are much less expensive than those employed by active mutual fund managers intent on beating the market. One of these techniques is to "cross trade" with other index funds. For example, if one index fund needs to add a stock to its holdings and another is required to unload the same stock, buy and sell orders are matched up to make a crossing trade. Index fund managers can do this within their own families of mutual funds at no cost and with outside index fund managers through computerized trading networks at very low cost.

The use of "basket trades" is another technique employed by index fund managers to inexpensively trade stocks and bonds. Because the goal of an index fund is to provide the investment performance of the fund's underlying index, the best way to achieve this is to quickly and cheaply invest in the investments that are represented in the index. But purchasing all (or just some) of these investments may involve hundreds, sometimes thousands, of market trades which can be expensive and time-consuming. A basket trade solves this problem by inexpensively bundling these many disparate orders for nearly instantaneous execution in the market.

Yet another technique for keeping trading costs low is to purchase futures contracts in the "derivatives" market. "Futures contracts" such as S&P 500 stock index futures are short term substitutes for investing in the stocks that are represented in an index. By purchasing futures instead of stocks, index funds can get immediate investment exposure to the market while vastly reducing the number and cost of purchases necessary to gain that exposure.[14]

"Equitizing" The Cash Held By An Index Mutual Fund

We know that an index fund is fully invested in the market at all times. Yet at the same time, it can temporarily hold large amounts of cash.[15] This seeming paradox can be explained by understanding how an index fund equitizes its cash holdings. "Equitizing" cash involves the purchase of stock index futures equal in value to the cash to be invested by the fund. For example, if an index fund holds $450,000 in cash its manager would place a $10,000 margin deposit[16] to purchase a futures contract valued at $450,000. This would leave $440,000 available for investment in low risk, short term investments such as Treasury bills. As the index fund builds up more cash, its manager would begin to sell off the futures positions and buy the stocks represented in the fund's underlying index. This process would keep repeating itself as long as the index fund generated net cash flow.

Equitization of cash allows an index fund to have the best of both worlds. First, by "synthetically" investing in the stock market it can remain fully invested and thus earn stock market returns rather than less favorable money market rates that would be earned in a cash account. This eliminates the problem of "cash drag." (Since cash has a lower expected return than stocks, any cash held by a stock mutual fund *drags down* the fund's long term investment performance.) Second, equitization of cash allows an index fund to maintain the necessary amount of liquidity so that it can reimburse with cash any shareholders who depart from the fund.

Most managers of actively-managed mutual funds do not equitize cash. They give two reasons for this. First, they need cash to quickly implement their stock picking schemes that are designed in the hope of beating the market. Second, they must keep cash on hand to pay off their shareholders (who are more likely to switch to other funds in their efforts to beat the market).

Neither of these are good reasons for active funds not to equitize cash. The fact is that active fund managers do not equitize cash simply because their collective mindset does not allow for it: "We have never equitized cash before so why begin now?" Because of this inflexible thinking, the typical actively-managed fund with 10-12% of its net asset value invested in cash has greater long term cash drag than index funds.

This chapter has presented a basic understanding of what makes an index fund tick as well as indexing-related concepts. The rest of this book is an examination of the many advantages offered by index funds. Collectively, these advantages are the reason why index funds are likely to perform better and more reliably than most actively-managed mutual funds. The next chapter explores one of the principal advantages of index funds - why they are the best way to implement an asset allocation policy.

Chapter Notes

[1] These are traded on the New York Stock Exchange, the American Stock Exchange and the NASDAQ Over-The-Counter Market.

[2] Some stocks represented in the S&P 500 do not pay dividends.

[3] Precious metals, jewelry, art and other such investments also constitute asset classes. However, this book only focuses on asset classes comprised of stocks or bonds that are traded in financial markets.

[4] A Standard & Poor's Depositary Receipt ("SPDR") is a share in a unit investment trust that holds a portfolio designed to provide the performance of the stocks represented in the S&P 500 index. Although individual investors can invest in SPDRs, most of them are purchased by institutional investors for such purposes as "equitizing" cash (explained in Chapter Nine). Individual investors who want to obtain the investment performance of the large company stocks of the S&P 500 would do better to invest in an S&P 500 index fund. The main reason why is that the trading costs of an S&P 500 index fund are lower than a SPDR. Also, SPDR's are designed for investors who engage in short term trading. Thus, they are not appropriate for indexers who are oriented to longer investment time horizons.

[5] However, these changes are not affected by changes in prices when full replication is used to construct an index fund. For example, if General Motors stock doubles in price, its proportionate representation in the S&P 500 index also doubles. This is reflected in the holdings of an index fund tracking the index. So even though a stock represented in the index changes in price, there is no need for an index fund manager to react to this change. Instead, the fund automatically rebalances itself so that its proportionate holdings will reflect the change in the price of General Motors stock.

[6] As of December 31, 1996, there were thirteen companies not headquartered in the U.S. that were represented in the S&P 500. About two-thirds of these were Canadian companies and two were major Dutch multinationals.

[7] The S&P 500 is one of the Commerce Department's 11 leading economic indicators.

[8] At year-end 1996, there were 381 Industrials, 67 Financials, 40 Utilities and 12 Transportation stocks represented in the S&P 500.

[9] *See* page 21, Chapter Note 23 to see why the Wilshire 5000 is a better barometer of the market.

[10] The great majority of stocks represented in the Wilshire 5000 index are small company stocks. When small company stocks outperform the S&P 500, about 50% of the time the Wilshire 5000 will also outperform it.

[11] Subtracting the index fund's annual operating expenses of .20% (20 basis points) from its total return shows that it still provided 99.1% of the performance of its underlying index.

[12] "Indexing: Still a Good Investment Approach?" by Weston J. Wellington, *Per-*

sonal Financial Planning, November/December 1995, pages 21-25.

[13] All these sources of turnover are reflected in the NAV of a mutual fund share.

[14] Some investors may wonder why index fund managers don't just purchase futures contracts so that they can avoid having to buy and sell stocks. There are two simple reasons why they don't. Futures contracts are costlier than stocks and they do not track indexes as well.

[15] This cash comes from new money invested by fund shareholders as well as from dividends or interest that are generated by the investments held by the fund. An index fund also holds cash to pay off departing shareholders when they sell their shares back to the fund.

[16] The margin amount is also invested in Treasury bills.

THE SPECIFIC ADVANTAGES OF
INDEX MUTUAL FUNDS

TEN

INDEX FUNDS ARE THE BEST WAY TO IMPLEMENT AN ASSET ALLOCATION POLICY

Do not fight forces; use them.
- R. Buckminster Fuller (1895-1983)
  American inventor, futurist and author

Overview

Asset allocation is the most important determinant of variance in investment re-
turns. The best way to implement an asset allocation policy is by using index mu-
tual funds rather than actively-managed funds. This is because an index fund re-
mains constantly invested in the investments that comprise a specific asset class
while the typical active fund unpredictably invests in different asset classes. Only
by investing in reliable index funds can investors obtain the full benefits of asset
allocation.

Asset Allocation

"Asset allocation" is the way in which an investor allocates investable
money among asset classes in his portfolio. These asset classes can include
stock asset classes such as foreign stocks, bond asset classes such as long
term Treasury bonds and/or cash. There is general agreement among investment experts that asset allocation is the overwhelmingly most important determinant of variance in investment performance.[1]

Any investor can establish a written "asset allocation policy" for his
portfolio. This document maps out a five-step process for implementing
and then managing and monitoring a portfolio's asset allocation. The first
step required of an investor is the overall determination of how he will
"split" his portfolio into stock and/or bond asset classes and/or cash. Second, he must choose what specific stock and/or bond asset classes are to be
included in the portfolio. Third, he must decide what percentages of the
portfolio are to be allocated to each asset class. Fourth, he must select those
mutual funds (an indexer naturally selects index funds) that best reflect the
investment characteristics (such as patterns of return and volatility) of these

asset classes. Fifth, an investor must manage and monitor his portfolio's asset allocation over time through changing market conditions.

It should be noted at the beginning of this chapter that investment in *individual* stocks and bonds means little for purposes of asset allocation. As we will see in the next section, the way in which an investor allocates his investable money among stock or bond asset classes is far more important in determining variance in investment performance than picking particular stocks or bonds. Thus, the fact that an investor holds individual stocks (such as Microsoft) or bonds (such as Westinghouse corporate bonds) has virtually no significance in determining variance in investment returns. But the fact that an investor is more heavily invested in stock asset classes than in bond asset classes (or vice versa) is of great importance.

If an investor fails to manage his portfolio's asset allocations himself, the financial markets will do it for him.[2] That is, normal market fluctuations will cause the percentage weightings of his portfolio's asset allocations to markedly differ from the percentages established by his asset allocation policy. The result is an "unbalanced" portfolio. This is undesirable because the markets will automatically ensure that the portfolio is overexposed to asset classes at their market highs and underexposed to them at their market lows.

The Brinson Study: The Real-World Confirmation Of Asset Allocation

The Brinson study, reported in 1986, provides real-world confirmation of the critical role played by asset allocation in the investment process.[3] Gary P. Brinson and his research colleagues examined the investment performance of 91 large pension plans for the ten-year period of 1974-1983. They sought to answer this question: "Why did some of these pension plans perform better and some worse?" The study found that three factors accounted for the variation in investment returns among the pension plans. These factors are: stock picking, market timing and asset allocation.

The Brinson study concluded that asset allocation is the overwhelmingly most important determinant of variance in investment returns. On average, it found that asset allocation accounted for 93.6% of this variance among the 91 pension plans.[4] In comparison, stock picking accounted for 4.2%, market timing 1.7% and other factors (including luck) .5%. This means that the way in which an investor allocates his investable money among asset classes will determine over 90% of the variance in his portfolio's return.[5] Illustration 8 on page 151 presents the findings of the Brinson study.

Illustration 8

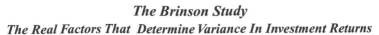

The Brinson Study
The Real Factors That Determine Variance In Investment Returns

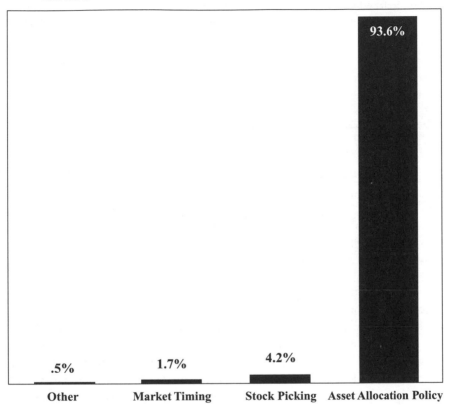

Source: "Determinants of Portfolio Performance" by Gary P. Brinson, et al., *Financial Analysts Journal*, July/August 1986.

The major implication of these findings is that *stock picking and market timing are essentially irrelevant to a portfolio's investment performance.* Thus, the Brinson study invalidates the idea that an investor can be expected to beat the market by picking stocks and/or timing markets. This is startling because investment strategies based on stock picking and market timing dominate the active money management profession and the investment media. It is widely believed that such strategies are far and away the most important in achieving superior investment performance. See Illustration 9 on page 152.

Illustration 9

Truth And The Perception Of Truth In Investing

Factors Determining Portfolio Variance	What Investors Are Told	What The Brinson Study Found
Stock Picking	65.1%	4.2%
Market Timing	7.6%	1.7%
Asset Allocation	7.6%	93.6%
Other	19.7%	.5%

Source: Indexes to feature articles in the *American Association of Individual Investors Journal*, 1989-1991 and "Determinants of Portfolio Performance" by Gary P. Brinson, et al., *Financial Analysts Journal*, July/August 1986.

SIMON SAYS: *Irrelevant Investment Advice Is Not Cheap*

The findings of the Brinson study raise a question. If a stock picking investment strategy is responsible for less than 5% of a portfolio's variance in investment return, why would any investor hand over large fees to an actively-managed mutual fund or to an active investment advisor?

Another important implication of the Brinson study is that once an investor has implemented his asset allocation policy, he has largely determined the long term risk and return characteristics of his portfolio. This is true because a portfolio's asset allocation is the engine that drives its degree of diversification which influences its risk which inevitably determines its performance. For example, if an investor decides that his portfolio's asset allocation policy is to hold 70% stocks and 30% bonds, then over the long run the portfolio will be riskier and thus have a higher return than if the policy had been to hold 30% stocks and 70% bonds.

The Reliability Of Implementing Asset Allocation Policies With Index Funds

Index funds are the best way to implement asset allocation policies because they are more *reliable* in carrying out such policies. The reliability of an index fund arises from the fact that it invests solely in the investments that comprise a particular asset class. It can therefore efficiently capture the investment performance of the entire asset class. This is desirable because it allows each index fund in a portfolio to closely execute its assigned goal. For example, suppose that one of the investment goals of an investor's asset allocation policy is to obtain the performance of the large company stocks of the S&P 500. When the investor holds an index fund that tracks the performance of the S&P 500, he is assured that he will efficiently capture the long term performance of the asset class of large company stocks.

Rex A. Sinquefield explains the reliability of index funds:[6] "For most asset classes there is an extensive historical record that allows you to estimate the risk and return components of each particular asset class and how the resulting performance of each asset class correlates with the performance of other asset classes. You can take this data and then form different combinations of asset classes to find the portfolio of index funds that will best suit your unique circumstances. This allows you to structure a long term strategic plan that will reliably carry out your investment goals."

In contrast, actively-managed mutual funds are an *unreliable* way to implement asset allocation policies. This unreliability comes from the fact that the typical active fund experiences "asset class drift." That is, it doesn't remain constantly invested in a specific stock or bond asset class like an index fund. Instead, it frequently invests in a number of different asset classes at different times in the quest for market-beating performance. For example, over the last ten years Fidelity Magellan showed dramatic changes in its composition as it drifted in and out of different asset classes. Some asset classes entirely disappeared from its holdings while others showed significant percentage fluctuations. During the same period, the Vanguard Index 500 index fund stayed reliably invested in the large company stocks represented in the S&P 500.

Sinquefield explains the unreliability of actively-managed mutual funds:[7] "The problem with actively-managed portfolios, whether they contain individual stocks or mutual funds, is that they do not capture (or often even bear any relation to) the risk and return components of an asset class. It is therefore extraordinarily difficult to estimate the risk and return levels of an actively-managed portfolio or to really know how such a portfolio will relate to various asset classes. The reason for this is that actively-managed portfolios often experience significant unpredictable shifts in their investment style or composition."

An example of such an unpredictable shift is when an active mutual fund stops employing a manager who followed a "growth" stock picking style and hires one who uses a "value" style. Since these are two entirely different investment styles, investors who are invested in such a fund are always playing "catch up" in trying to figure out its risk and return characteristics or how its performance will compare to that of any given asset class. This is why portfolios that are comprised of active funds often produce returns far different than those of established asset classes. Thus, it is essentially impossible to set up a long term strategic investment plan if the building blocks for that plan are active mutual funds or individual stocks.

A recent event that demonstrates the unreliability of active funds in carrying out an asset allocation policy was Jeffrey Vinik's departure as the manager of Fidelity Magellan. Part of the reason why he left in mid-1996 was that he had made some unlucky bets on bonds. This was news to many investors who thought that Magellan only invested in *stocks*.[8] An investor who wanted to obtain the performance of stocks saw some of this particular goal of his asset allocation policy remain unfulfilled because a significant portion of the fund was invested in bonds. It is these kinds of bets made by active mutual fund managers that make it impossible for their funds to capture the investment performance of entire asset classes. This underscores their unreliability in carrying out asset allocation policies.

The Factors That Make Index Funds The Best Choice To Implement Asset Allocation Policies

Certain factors that characterize index funds make them the best choice for implementing asset allocation policies. These factors include: (1) low portfolio turnover resulting from a commitment to long term investment in asset classes, (2) the relative certainty of achieving the expected return of an asset class invested in by an index fund, (3) minimal costs and taxes that maximize market-driven investment performance, (4) broad diversification that reduces investment risk and (5) full investment in the market at all times due to the absence of cash reserves and any market timing activity.

By contrast, factors that characterize active mutual funds make them undesirable choices for implementing asset allocation policies. These factors include: (1) costly portfolio turnover resulting from short term attempts to beat the market with stock picking and market timing, (2) the unpredictability of what asset classes an active fund will be invested in, (3) high costs and taxes that reduce transaction-driven investment performance, (4) inadequate diversification that increases investment risk and (5) less than full investment in the market because of cash reserves and market timing activity.

> **SIMON SAYS:** *What Good Are Stock Picking And Market Timing Money Managers?*
>
> If index funds can more reliably implement an asset allocation policy, have lower costs and taxes and are better diversified, what good are active money managers? Well, they provide a lot of entertainment with their stock picking and market timing hype. But that seems to be about all they are good for since, according to the implicit findings of the Brinson study, stock picking and market timing are essentially irrelevant in determining variance in investment returns.

The Active Money Management Industry And The Investment Media Misrepresent The Brinson Study

The active money management industry and the investment media misrepresent the Brinson study's implicit finding that stock picking and market timing are of almost no consequence in determining variance in investment returns.[9] This is not surprising since the Brinson study essentially invalidates the dominant message that these two powerful parts of the investment information system convey to investors. This message is that investors can beat the market by picking stocks and/or timing markets.

When the Brinson study first appeared, it caused some concern in the active money management industry. After all, this industry's continued robust health depends on its ability to convince vast numbers of investors that the best way to deliver superior investment performance is to pick stocks and time markets. Because it was bad news for the industry that the Brinson study implicitly found that this claim was not true, it had to find a way to counter such an alarming finding.

The industry chose not to attack the Brinson study's implicit finding that stock picking and market timing are essentially irrelevant in determining variance in investment returns. Instead, it emphasized the study's general finding about the critical importance of asset allocation. Those in the active money management industry as well as the investment media usually state that finding like this: "Over 90% of your portfolio performance results from the way that you set up your basic asset allocation policy."

Yet invariably, the sentence following this statement offers advice about which individual stock or mutual fund or what new market timing system is sure to beat the market.[10] By adding that sentence, the active money management industry and the media instantly transform the two factors implicitly found by the Brinson study to be *essentially irrelevant* in determining variance in investment returns - stock picking and market timing - into the *best methods of implementing* asset allocation.

SIMON SAYS: *Irrelevant Investment Advice Is Not Cheap, Part Deux*

The Brinson study identified two factors - stock picking and market timing - that generate fat commissions and management fees. Yet the study implicitly found that both of these factors are essentially irrelevant in determining variance in investment returns. Active money managers cannot make a living from the one factor that is by far the most important in this determination - asset allocation.

This allows the active money management industry and the media to have their cake and eat it too. First, they agree that asset allocation is all-important. Second, they ignore the essentially irrelevant role played by stock picking and market timing in determining variance in investment returns. Third, they assure investors that the surest path to asset allocation salvation is via stock picking and market timing. Thus, the industry and the media can proclaim the virtue of asset allocation and at the same time validate the two factors that the Brinson study implicitly found to be essentially irrelevant - stock picking and market timing.

The following example summarizes the difference between the false *perception* created by the industry and the media about the importance of stock picking and market timing and the *reality* of what actually drives investment performance - asset allocation. Suppose that an active money manager invests 100% of a client's money in stock asset classes for a 30-year period. The odds are overwhelming that the client will have more (probably a lot more) money at the end of that period than if he had been invested 100% in bond asset classes.

The active money manager will argue that these tremendous gains came about because of his skillful stock picking and/or mutual fund selections. He says that this is the way to make asset allocation work for investors. However, it makes *no real difference what particular stocks or mutual funds* that an active money manager chooses for a portfolio. In fact, it is the portfolio's asset allocation policy of being invested 100% in stock asset classes that was the factor almost entirely responsible for the outcome. This being the case, investors would be well advised to select those investments that secure the performance of stock and bond asset classes in the most reliable and cost efficient way. Such investments can *only* be index funds.

Asset Allocation Funds: The Active Money Management Industry's Response To Brinson

In addition to its misrepresentation of the Brinson study, the active money management industry responded to it in a concrete way by introducing asset allocation mutual funds. "Asset allocation funds" are really only jazzed-up versions of "balanced" mutual funds (i.e., funds that invest in both stocks and bonds) with two major drawbacks. Their expenses are greater to cover the glamour of being an asset allocation fund and, to add insult to injury, their performances are no better than balanced funds.

But the biggest problem with asset allocation funds is that they are really nothing more than *market timing* funds. Managers of asset allocation funds usually condition their stock picking decisions on the thinking and market forecasting models of the funds' resident economists. These forecasters try to predict the unpredictable - the future - and tell fund managers where they think "the market is heading." Based on this advice, fund managers shift allocations of money in and out of investments in attempts to profit from short term cyclical events in financial markets. This is precisely the definition of market timing.

Philip S. Wilson of Wilson Associates International, an established leader in developing asset allocation systems for financial professionals (and no friend of indexing), observes:[11] "There is not a single asset allocation mutual fund manager in America today who implements an asset allocation policy in the appropriate way. Instead, all that these [active] fund managers have are collections of stocks, bonds and cash that they just arbitrarily and very subjectively decide to allocate."

The fact that index funds so efficiently and effectively reflect the risk and return of the asset classes in which they are invested clearly makes them the superior way to implement an asset allocation policy. Establishing an asset allocation policy is also the starting point in formulating a plan to diversify the risk of an investment portfolio. The next chapter shows why the use of index funds is the best way to reduce investment risk.

Chapter Notes

[1] For example, William F. Sharpe states: "[It] is generally agreed by theoreticians and practitioners alike that the asset allocation decision is by far the most important made by the investor." *Managing Investment Portfolios: A Dynamic Process*, second edition, edited by John L. Maginn and Donald L. Tuttle (Boston: Warren, Gorham & Lamont, 1990), page 7-3. In addition, Charles D. Ellis notes: "The single most important dimension of investment policy is asset mix, particularly the ratio of fixed-income investments to equity investments." *How to Win The Loser's Game*, second edition, by Charles D. Ellis (Homewood, Illinois: Business One Irwin, 1993), page 3.

[2] *The Portable MBA In Investment* edited by Peter L. Bernstein (New York: John Wiley & Sons, Inc., 1995), page 216.

[3] "Determinants of Portfolio Performance" by Gary P. Brinson, L. Randolph Hood and Gilbert L. Beebower, *Financial Analysts Journal*, July/August 1986, pages 39-44. This study was updated and its conclusions were reaffirmed in 1991. The 1991 study examined 82 large pension plans over the ten-year period of 1978-1987 and found that the asset allocation decision accounted for 91.5% of the variation in plan performance, market timing for 1.8%, stock picking for 4.6% while the balance of the variation, 2.1%, was due to luck and other factors. *See* "Determinants of Portfolio Performance II: An Update" by Gary P. Brinson, Brian D. Singer and Gilbert L. Beebower, *Financial Analysts Journal*, May/June 1991, pages 40-48.

[4] Bruce J. Temkin reminds us that this is just another way of saying that *if an investor is invested in stock asset classes, he will get the returns of stocks and if he is invested in bond asset classes, he will get the returns of bonds*. An investor's belief that financial markets work differently than this usually means that he invests in bonds to reduce risk while hoping that they will generate the superior returns of stocks.

[5] The interpretation of the Brinson study's conclusions has come under fire for being erroneous (as have the conclusions themselves). But those leading this attack nevertheless admit that asset allocation is an important determinant of variance in investment returns. Yet even if it was concluded after further study that asset allocation is actually less important, the fact remains that stock picking and market timing would *still remain relatively unimportant* as determinants. The reason why, in the words of one investment educator who has faulted the Brinson study, is that "for many individual investors, cost is the most important determinant of portfolio performance, not asset allocation policy, market timing or [stock picking]." In fact, "[o]ver an investor's investment life cycle, excessive costs can reduce wealth accumulation by 50 percent!" "The Asset Allocation Hoax" by William W. Jahnke, *Journal of Financial Planning*, February 1997, pages 109-113. It is vital to understand that *excessive investment costs are a product of stock picking and market timing, not indexing*. So regardless of whether asset allocation is im-

portant as a determinant of variance in investment returns, stock picking and market timing will always remain relatively unimportant in terms of achieving superior returns because of their high costs (and taxes).

[6] Rex A. Sinquefield in "Active or Passive: The Debate about Investment Management Styles," a speech at the International Association for Financial Planning Success Forum, Boston, Massachusetts, September 12, 1994.

[7] *Ibid.*

[8] Though it is not well known, the prospectuses of many active stock mutual funds permit investments in bonds.

[9] I wish to thank Bruce J. Temkin for stimulating my thinking in this area.

[10] This is far more entertaining than learning from some drone on television how to set up an appropriate asset allocation policy. Yet if the investment media made a true effort to inform investors that almost 95% of the variation in performance is determined by a portfolio's asset allocation policy and less than 5% is due to stock picking, it is highly problematic that there would be as many financial magazines and newspapers to sell and TV and radio investment programs. In this light, it is no surprise that there is an overwhelming bias in favor of stock picking and market timing in the investment media despite its favorable references to the general conclusion of the Brinson study.

[11] Philip S. Wilson of Wilson Associates International in "Active and Passive Dimensions of the Asset Allocation Process," an audio tape from the International Association for Financial Planning national conference, Anaheim, California, September 23, 1992.

ELEVEN

INDEX FUNDS REDUCE INVESTMENT RISK

Diversification is your buddy.
 - Merton H. Miller (1923-   )
   Co-Recipient, 1990 Nobel Prize in Economic Science

Risk is risk.
 - Harry M. Markowitz (1927-   )
   Co-Recipient, 1990 Nobel Prize in Economic Science

Overview

The control of risk is central to the whole investment process. By holding all the investments or a representative sample of those that comprise an asset class, index funds are able to come closer to the complete elimination of diversifiable risk from an investment portfolio than actively-managed mutual funds. Thus, the most efficient and effective way to diversify a portfolio of investments and thus control risk is to invest in index funds.

An Important Caveat About Investment Risk

The quotations at the beginning of this chapter attributed to two eminent financial economists represent both good news and bad news for investors who hold portfolios of index funds. The good news is that "diversification is your buddy." An investor who holds a properly diversified portfolio of index funds can eliminate more investment risk from his portfolio than any active investor. The bad news is that "risk is risk." In spite of the excellent diversification of risk achieved by an index portfolio, a good amount of investment risk will always remain in it.

Therefore, it is important for investors to understand that *investing in index funds is no panacea for escaping investment risk. Although the use of index funds is the best way to rid a portfolio of as much risk as possible (and the only way of eliminating the risk of underperforming a given financial market), it can never do away with the risk of losing money.*

The Diversification Of Investment Risk

"Diversification" is the process of selecting appropriate investments and then combining them in a "portfolio" (a collection of investments) to reduce risk and/or increase return. Diversification of investment risk appears to boil down to a simple warning: "Do not put all your eggs in one basket." (How diversification can increase return is described later in this chapter.)

An example of why this warning is given can be found in the situation where an investor invests in only one stock. Even though it is possible that his stock may enrich him some day, it also has the potential to take him to the poorhouse. The essential problem is that there is no way for the investor to know which of these two scenarios (or any number of other less extreme ones) will come true. Because he cannot predict the future, he must add different investments to his one stock in order to reduce the risk of being financially ruined if the stock takes a dive in value.

However, diversification of investment risk is far more sophisticated than merely adding different investments to a portfolio. It actually requires an investor to add the *right kinds* of different investments. For example, if five mutual funds held in a portfolio are invested in the same asset class, the average return of the five funds is a simple weighted average of their individual returns. Likewise, the average risk of the funds is a weighted average of their individual risks.

But there is a different result if the mutual funds are invested in dissimilar asset classes. By combining these different mutual funds in a portfolio, the portfolio's risk becomes something *less* than the weighted average risk of the five individual funds that comprise it. Some of the risky uncertainty of the expected return of each mutual fund is diversified away because the other funds in the portfolio rise and fall in price at different times in different amounts. Thus, the whole (portfolio) becomes less risky than the sum of its parts (the dissimilar mutual funds that comprise the portfolio).

Yet the portfolio's expected return remains exactly the *same* as the simple weighted average return of the five individual funds that comprise it. There is no loss in the average expected return of the different funds when they are combined in a portfolio. Does this mean that a well diversified investor has earned a "free lunch" by reducing his portfolio's risk at the same time that he avoids a sacrifice of return? Not at all - there is no free lunch in investing!

In fact, the price that an investor pays in exchange for a reduction of risk and no loss of return in his portfolio is that he must give up the possibility of earning a return potentially *greater* than the expected return of the portfolio. In our example, this greater return could have been earned by the portfolio holding the single asset class - if the prevailing market environment happened to favor the performance of that particular asset class.

The Revolutionary Insight Of Modern Portfolio Theory

In the early 1950s, Modern Portfolio Theory introduced the revolutionary insight that a properly diversified investment portfolio can reduce risk and/or increase return. This investment theory, one of the most important of the century, was formulated by economist Harry M. Markowitz, a co-recipient of the 1990 Nobel Prize in Economic Science.

Markowitz's research is important because it shows how an investor can improve his investment performance by optimizing tradeoffs between risk and return. Applying the principles of Modern Portfolio Theory allows an investor to tailor a portfolio suitable to his unique investment goals and risk tolerance. A more aggressive investor can build a portfolio that provides a higher expected return given a certain level of risk. A less aggressive investor can build a portfolio that bears lower risk given a certain level of return. According to Markowitz, it makes much more sense to reduce investment risk and/or increase return than attempt to pick investment winners.

Today, it is hard to see why Modern Portfolio Theory was so revolutionary for its time. After all, just about every piece of investment advice is now accompanied by this warning: "Always diversify your investments." However, until Markowitz's theory was conceived, no one had tried to understand the connection between investment risk and return in a systematic way. Prior to then, if an investor thought that an investment contained some arbitrary or undefined notion of risk, it wasn't included in his portfolio. By the 1960s, the principles of Modern Portfolio Theory began to be taught in the elite business schools of America. These principles found their earliest practical application in the institutional investment world in the early 1970s and it was not long before individual investors also began to benefit from them.

Because of Markowitz's insight that investors should be concerned with risk as well as return, the issue of how best to control investment risk has become central to the whole process of investing. As we will see, the most efficient and effective way for individual investors to profit from this insight is to invest in a properly diversified portfolio of index funds.[1] Sound and time-tested indexing strategies, which govern the management of hundreds of billions of dollars throughout the world, attest to the wide-ranging influence that Modern Portfolio Theory has had on the indexing revolution.

Total Investment Risk: Diversifiable Risk And Nondiversifiable Risk

While Markowitz demonstrated the importance of optimizing the tradeoffs between investment risk and return in a portfolio, economist William F. Sharpe defined the nature of investment risk and how it affects investment return. Sharpe, who shared a Nobel Prize with Markowitz, identified the two kinds of risk that comprise the total risk found in any individual stock or bond. The "diversifiable" risk in an individual stock or bond constitutes about 60-70% of total risk while "nondiversifiable" risk comprises about 30-40% of total risk.

The diversifiable risk in a stock or bond arises from those factors that uniquely affect the market price of that *particular* stock or bond. For example, a few years ago IBM experienced employee layoffs, lower profitability and deteriorating market share.[2] These particular problems were unique to IBM and got reflected in the market price of its stock. As a result, the stock declined in value.

Sharpe recognized that investors can do something about reducing the diversifiable risk in their portfolios - that's why it is called diversifiable. In our example, investors who wanted to reduce the diversifiable risk of a decline in value of their IBM stock could have held other stock and/or bond investments in their portfolios. Investors who don't do everything that they can to reduce diversifiable risk may receive lower returns or, at a minimum, fail to earn higher returns. (As we know, it is also possible that they may earn higher returns.)

Nondiversifiable risk (unlike diversifiable risk) has nothing to do with the factors that can affect the price of a particular stock or bond. Rather, nondiversifiable risk is inherent in *all* stocks and bonds. If, in our example, IBM had instead displayed strong financial indicators, it could still have gone down in value during a plunging stock market just like any other stock - even those with even stronger financial indicators. Living with the ever present risk of seeing their portfolios decrease in value during plunging markets is the "price of admission" that investors must pay in exchange for gaining entrance to the stock and bond markets to earn the returns offered by investments in these markets. This price must be paid *even by investors who hold portfolios of "conservative" stocks and/or bonds.*

Sharpe found that investors have no power to reduce nondiversifiable risk in their portfolios - that's why it is called nondiversifiable. The best way that investors can totally rid a portfolio of nondiversifiable risk - that is, to avoid paying the price of seeing their portfolios go down in value during plunging stock or bond markets - is not to own stocks and bonds.

The rest of this section examines an underdiversified and a well diversified portfolio to see how a stock's rise and fall in value impacts each portfolio.

An Underdiversified Portfolio

About 30-40% of the total investment risk carried by a poorly diversified actively-managed portfolio is diversifiable risk. Since 60-70% of the total risk in an individual stock is diversifiable, we can see that even a poorly diversified portfolio cuts diversifiable risk by about half. Yet even an actively-managed portfolio that reduces diversifiable risk even more than this is still inherently underdiversified.

In the IBM example, suppose that the stock rose in value because of factors that were *unique* to it. If there was sustained good news about IBM over a long time period and this resulted in the steady rise in price of its stock, some investors who had portfolios consisting solely of IBM stock could have gotten rich if they had held enough of it. The cause of this windfall would have been diversifiable risk.

This kind of scenario is the good side of diversifiable risk. That is, when an underdiversified investor invests in any stock or bond (or a stock or bond mutual fund) there is always the possibility that he will hit an investment "home run." In fact, underdiversified portfolios that outperform the market do so because they made "risky" bets on a relatively few investments or sectors of the market that turned out to be big winners. In such scenarios, maximum exposure to diversifiable risk is desirable *if* investors bet right.[3]

But if they bet wrong and wind up on the bad side of diversifiable risk, then they not only lose their chance to hit a home run, but they can "strike out" and may even have to leave the game altogether. In our example, many employees of IBM held only one investment - IBM stock. When its value subsequently deteriorated because of factors unique to it, investors who chose to bear the diversifiable risk of holding only IBM stock were penalized with lower returns. Yet there can be a penalty even worse than this. An investor who holds only one or a relatively few stocks in his portfolio must always be prepared for the possibility that they can become completely *worthless*. That's investment risk!

But what about rises and falls in stock values that are caused by factors *not unique* to these stocks? In the IBM example, one such factor causing a surge in the value of all computer stocks (including IBM stock) could be a new invention that made all computers much more efficient. A factor causing a crash in the value of all stocks (including IBM stock) could be an increase in interest rates. In both scenarios, nondiversifiable risk is involved. Yet as we know, there is nothing that an underdiversified (or even a well diversified) investor can do about reducing this kind of risk.

A Well Diversified Portfolio

A well diversified portfolio largely eliminates diversifiable risk, but like the typical underdiversified portfolio it cannot eliminate · nondiversifiable risk.

In our IBM example, well diversified investors who held IBM stock could have lessened the impact of its decline in value by holding more of the right kinds of stock and/or bond investments in their portfolios. For such investors, this is the good side of diversifiable risk. The bad side is that when they largely eliminate diversifiable risk, they give up the possibility of hitting an investment home run with one or a few stocks or mutual funds.

Because a well diversified portfolio has largely eliminated diversifiable risk, it can only be nondiversifiable risk that could cause the portfolio to rise or fall in value. Again, there is nothing that a well diversified investor can do about reducing this kind of risk. Thus, a well diversified portfolio (even one that is impossible to achieve in an absolute, if not a practical, sense - i.e., a portfolio that completely eliminates diversifiable risk) can sharply plunge in value because it always retains nondiversifiable risk. (In a practical sense, the Vanguard Total Stock Market index fund[4] eliminates virtually all (about 99.5%) of the diversifiable risk contained in the American stock market.)

SIMON SAYS: *The Role Of Human Nature In Assessing Investment Risk*

In looking at investment performance from the past, we can see that riskier investments have outperformed less risky ones. But how do we know that this will be true in the *future*? The answer to this question comes from Roger C. Gibson:[5] "While today's world is different than the nineteenth century or the 1930s or even the 1980s, human nature is the same in its preference for stability over uncertainty."

This means that, assuming the return is the same in each case, investors will naturally prefer to invest in stable (and less risky) investments such as Treasury bills rather than uncertain (and riskier) investments such as small company stocks. Because *all* investments must be held by someone, though, investors have to be enticed to invest in riskier investments. The pricing system that is the heart of any financial market ensures this by pricing riskier investments such as small company stocks low enough so that their expected returns are high enough to compensate investors for the higher risk of holding these uncertain and volatile investments.[6] In this process, some investors will respond to the attraction of potentially higher-returning investments by taking on added risk while others will calculate that the attraction of higher returns is not worth the risk. If this pricing system did not exist, all investors would simply hold Treasury bills.

Thus, in a world where investors prefer stability to uncertainty and where they can select from a variety of investments (which bear different expected returns because of different amounts of risk), it must follow that riskier investments will outperform less risky ones. In this way, the future will be like the past because human nature is constant in assessing the full spectrum of investment risk.

Index Funds Are The Best Way To Reduce Investment Risk

As noted in Chapter Three, The Prudent Investor Rule was adopted by the American Law Institute in 1992. The Rule serves as a guide for trust attorneys and trustees when investing and managing a trust's assets. One of the most important duties normally required of a trustee in making and implementing investment decisions for a trust is to prudently diversify its investments.[7]

A Comment to the Rule succinctly states diversification Nirvana:[8] "The ultimate goal of diversification would be to achieve a portfolio with only the rewarded [nondiversifiable] or 'market' element of risk." This means that, in a perfect world, diversifiable risk would not exist in an investment portfolio; it would only contain nondiversifiable risk.

Realistically, it is not possible to completely eliminate diversifiable risk from a portfolio. However, a properly diversified portfolio of index funds can come closer to this goal than *any* actively-managed portfolio - *even one holding hundreds of individual stocks and/or bonds or one holding mutual funds containing hundreds of stocks and/or bonds.*

A "properly" diversified portfolio of index funds reduces risk at two levels: *within each* asset class comprising the portfolio and *among all* the portfolio's asset classes. First, proper diversification of risk within each asset class is ensured when an index fund manager holds all the investments or a representative sample of those that comprise the asset class invested in by the fund. Second, an investor (or his investment advisor) can ensure proper diversification among all the portfolio's asset classes by including index funds that suitably offset each other's performance under different market conditions.

Index Funds Can Simultaneously Reduce Investment Risk And Increase Return

A properly diversified portfolio of index funds not only largely eliminates diversifiable risk but can also increase investment return at the *same time*. But if "high risk brings high return," how is it possible that an indexer can reduce his portfolio's risk and increase its return at the same time? Because this investment maxim applies only to the *nondiversifiable* risk in a portfolio, not to its diversifiable risk. Thus, the virtual elimination of diversifiable risk from an index portfolio does not harm investment performance because it has nothing to do with bringing about higher returns.

In fact, by largely excluding diversifiable risk from an index portfolio, an investor may *increase* his return since diversifiable risk can produce lower return. (Earlier, we saw diversifiable risk produce a lower return in the case of the IBM investor who failed to hold other investments in his portfolio. Yet there is always the possibility, however remote, that by retaining diversifiable risk, an investor can hit a home run.) Thus, a properly diversified portfolio of index funds is one in which *minimal diversifiable risk is allowed and nondiversifiable risk is appropriately rewarded.*

Actively-Managed Portfolios Are Always More Underdiversified

Actively-managed portfolios are always more underdiversified than properly diversified index portfolios because they carry more diversifiable risk. Different reasons account for this. One reason is that active portfolios can include too many mutual funds that use the same investment style. Another reason is that active portfolios can be too heavily concentrated in one industry or market sector. Yet another reason is that relatively too few individual stocks are included in a portfolio. (Sanford Bernstein & Co., a well known active money manager, holds 40-60 stocks in its portfolio of large company "value" stocks while portfolio managers at Goldman, Sachs & Co. typically invest in only 20-30 stocks for their high net worth clients.)

Though many active investors may think that they have well diversified portfolios, none of them measure up to the standard of diversification set by a properly diversified portfolio of index funds. For example, the fact that the performance of a portfolio of 50 'carefully' selected stocks will correlate 90-95% with the market's performance does not mean that 90-95% of its diversifiable risk has been eliminated.[9]

The reason for this is that in any given year, the expected return of the 50-stock portfolio will not be the same as the expected return of the overall market. Rather, it will be within a large potential range of returns falling around the market return. If the market produces, say, an annual 10% return, statistically there is a very good chance that the portfolio's return will fairly often differ as much as 4.5 percentage points above or below this return. So the 50-stock portfolio could yield as little as 5.5% or as much as 15.5% in any given year. Since the range of potential returns on either side of the market return substantially varies from year to year, a portfolio of even 50 carefully selected stocks does not do much to reduce diversifiable risk.

Even a portfolio of two hundred stocks only reduces an active portfolio's expected return to about one percentage point on either side of the market's expected return. This generates a return substantially greater or lesser than the reliable market return achieved by a portfolio of index funds. (While a one percentage point differential is certainly not substantial in any one year, it can represent enormous differences in accumulated wealth when compounded over extended periods of time.) Investors holding portfolios of actively-managed mutual funds investing in hundreds and hundreds of stocks can be better diversified than investors invested in portfolios of individual stocks. But even such mutual fund portfolios fall short of the standard of diversification set by a properly diversified portfolio of index funds.

SIMON SAYS: *Staying In The Closet - Active Investors Who Index*

Sometimes an actively-managed investment portfolio can become "overdiversified" especially if it includes numerous mutual funds with distinctly different investment objectives. This can give rise to a condition known as "closet indexing" where an actively-managed portfolio can *look* very much like an index portfolio because of its relatively good diversification. The only problem is that it doesn't *perform* like an index portfolio because of its high costs and taxes. Thus, the closet indexer has the worst of both worlds: he can be accused by his active brethren of looking like an indexer, yet fail to get an indexer's performance.

Even if an active investor were to have all the time and money in the world to research and pick stocks for his portfolio, he could *never* hold enough of the right kinds of mutual funds (or individual stocks and bonds) to create a portfolio that would reduce diversifiable risk as completely as a properly diversified index portfolio. So active investors who think that they are as well diversified as indexers are wrong.

They pay for this mistake by unnecessarily incurring more total investment risk than indexers. As a result, they fail to obtain higher returns and often must settle for lower returns. (But as we know, it is also possible for active investors to obtain higher returns by assuming more investment risk. However, even assuming that such superior returns will actually be earned, the periods of time that they are earned as well as the identities of those who will earn them cannot be known until after the fact.) Thus, the typical actively-managed portfolio is one in which *diversifiable risk is allowed which often leads to lower returns*.

SIMON SAYS: *Even Morningstar Cannot Help An Active Investor Avoid Underdiversification*

An active investor cannot avoid underdiversification even when he uses a mutual fund ratings guide such as Morningstar to help him build what he believes to be a well diversified portfolio. Since Morningstar evaluates each mutual fund as an individual investment, an active investor has no way of knowing how the mutual funds that he selects for his portfolio will affect each other and how that will impact overall portfolio performance. As a result, an active investor can run into problems when he picks individual mutual funds from Morningstar's ratings guide, combines them in his portfolio and then finds out as performance returns roll in that he has an underdiversified portfolio.

Diversification With Index Funds Does Not Reduce Nondiversifiable Risk

It is important to understand that *even properly diversified portfolios of index funds will not protect investors from experiencing serious declines in their values during downturns in the stock and bond markets*. But aren't such portfolios supposed to help investors avoid this very risk? No! The diversification provided by index fund portfolios shields investors from diversifiable risk better than active fund portfolios. Yet no amount of diversification can reduce the nondiversifiable risk - the risk that a person's investments, however conservative, will decline in value because of a market downturn - that is inherent in *all* investment portfolios, whether active or indexed.

Even though this is true, the investment information system widely disseminates the belief that because index funds remain fully invested in the market at all times they go down *more* in value during market downturns than active funds. The validity of the reasoning that supports this notion has never really been seriously explored even though it is generally accepted by the investing public.

The claim that index funds will go down more in value during market downturns than active funds is based on the idea that active fund managers have the option of using their cash reserves to meet shareholder redemptions.[10] By first utilizing cash for this purpose, they can avoid (or at least delay) the forced sale of fund holdings at fire sale prices in declining markets. According to this thinking, though, index funds do not have the option of paying off their departing shareholders with cash because they carry no cash reserves. Instead, they are forced to immediately sell off their fund holdings at reduced prices in declining markets in order to meet shareholder redemptions. As a result, the thinking goes, index funds go down more in value during market downturns than active funds.

Initially, such reasoning seems to make a lot of sense but under closer scrutiny it just doesn't hold up. In fact, there are a number of reasons for believing that investors who go through market downturns invested in index funds are probably in a better position than investors who do so holding actively-managed mutual funds (or individual stocks).

First, there is no way to accurately predict the occurrence of declining markets. That being the case, active funds are always caught in these markets the same as index funds. To hear active mutual fund managers tell it, though, their funds aren't invested in the same declining markets that can reduce the value of index funds! But obviously they are and they can decline in value just as much. Indeed, some active funds (theoretically 50%, but whatever the actual percentages, a good number) will go down even *more* in value than index funds during these downturns because they happened to concentrate their investments in market sectors that were particularly hard hit.[11]

Even when the market (and index funds that track it) declines and underperforms the average stock mutual fund, the underperformance is *not anywhere near* the wide margin that active fund managers warn investors about. For example, the S&P 500 underperformed the average stock mutual fund by 1.5 percentage points (-29.6% vs. -28.1%) during the period of September through November 1987 while the

Wilshire 5000 underperformed the Lipper average "general equity" mutual fund by 2.09 percentage points from August 27 through December 3, 1987.

Second, as we know, active managers claim that their mutual funds will go down less in value in declining markets because of the "cushion" provided by their cash reserves - typically 10-12% of fund assets.[12] (Although this partially offsets the cost advantages of index funds, it does so only in down markets.) But idle cash reserves held by cash-rich active funds will not help their investors take advantage of up markets nearly as well as cashless indexers. Cash that cushions the shock of down markets becomes a *deadweight loss* in up markets.[13]

We also know that active fund managers claim that they hold cash during market downturns because it allows them to pay off departing shareholders without having to sell off fund holdings at fire sale prices. They say that this helps them reduce losses in declining markets better than index funds. Despite this, studies show that active fund managers *steadily maintain* their cash reserves *even in market downturns*. It seems that they keep cash on hand so they can take advantage of any stock picking or market timing investment "opportunities" to beat the market.[14] Since active fund managers do not use cash reserves to pay off departing shareholders, they are forced to sell off fund holdings to raise the necessary cash. In declining markets, this can generate losses as great or greater than those experienced by index funds.

There is also a widely held perception among investors that index funds will incur capital gains taxes to a greater degree in a serious market downturn than active funds. This is unlikely. For example, an internal study conducted by Vanguard shows that if there was a 20% downturn in the stock market, its S&P 500 index fund could sell off about 30% of its assets without realizing and distributing any capital gains that would negatively impact performance because of taxes. The reasoning behind this finding, which is based on market conditions as they existed in mid-1997, follows.

During a market downturn, short term losing positions held by the S&P 500 index fund would increase as the stocks represented in the S&P 500 declined in value. Any departing shareholders would be paid off by the fund with money that it received for selling these losing stocks. Up to this point, the index fund would not be forced to incur any capital gains taxes. If more than 30% of the fund's asset base had to be sold off, stocks with high cost bases would be liquidated first to minimize any impact on performance caused by capital gains taxes. Thus, the index fund would have to experience massive shareholder redemptions before taxes could begin to even minimally impact its performance. (Stocks with lower cost bases would be the last to be sold since they would trigger the largest amounts of capital gains taxes.)

Third, although the typical active investor may avoid some of the decrease in portfolio value experienced by an indexer in a declining market, this usually doesn't give him a clear-cut advantage over the *long run*. For example, an active investor who holds cash reserves of 10% in a 20% down market avoids two percentage points of loss. While this is advantageous, an indexer saves about the same amount every year (not just when a down market comes along) because the costs and expenses of running his portfolio are about two percentage points less than the typical actively-managed portfolio.[15] So in this example, the active investor gains no advantage over the indexer.

Even during extreme market downturns of 40% or more, those active investors who experience less decrease in their portfolio values than indexers enjoy only a relatively short term advantage. The reason why is that indexers almost always outperform them by significantly greater margins in the up markets (which are typically longer in duration) that inevitably follow down markets (which are typically shorter in duration).

Fourth, evidence gathered over a long period of time shows that index funds actually perform better than active funds even during a period which included the second most severe market downturn of the century. For the 25-year period of 1971-1995, about 65% of all active mutual funds underperformed the S&P 500.[16] This is true even though the S&P 500 lost nearly 50% of its value in the market downturn of 1973-1974. In addition, from January 1973 through September 1974, the average stock mutual fund[17] underperformed the S&P 500 by over five percentage points - -47.9% vs. -42.5%. So even over a long period that included a prolonged declining stock market (when index funds supposedly underperform the market by a wide margin), the funds that actually underperformed the market were active funds.

For all these reasons, investors who are fully invested in portfolios of index funds in declining markets are not any worse off (and are probably better off) than investors holding portfolios of actively-managed funds. Thus, active money managers are wrong when they engage in simplistic assertions that index funds will decline more in value during market downturns than active funds.

In spite of this, it bears repeating that "risk is risk" and that there is no guaranteed safe way to reap the rewards of investing in stocks. In addition, investors should understand that there is always the possibility that the variability of future stock returns will be worse than the past. This warning applies to indexers as well as to active investors. (It is important to note that this is not an admonishment to avoid the risk of stock investing. Quite clearly, inflation is also a risk and, for many investors with long investment time horizons, it represents an even bigger risk than investing in stocks. Consequently, "doing nothing" about inflation (i.e., failing to buy stocks as an inflation hedge) is not a prudent investment alternative either.[18])

Peter Lynch: An Investment Guru Who Dismisses The Importance Of Diversification

Although diversification of risk has become central to the whole process of investing, there are investment gurus such as Peter Lynch who dismiss its importance.[19] (Yet Nobel Laureate Harry M. Markowitz, the father of Modern Portfolio Theory, observed almost fifty years ago:[20] *"Diversification is both observed and sensible; a rule of behavior which does not imply the superiority of diversification must be rejected both as a hypothesis and as a maxim."*)

In his book, *Beating the Street*, Lynch advises the individual investor to keep his eyes open for 8-12 products that particularly appeal to him and then follow the stocks of the companies that produce these products. From this group, he suggests that an investor hold no more than *five* stocks in his portfolio. Lynch warns: "By owning too many stocks you lose the advantage of concentrating on a few good stocks." He adds: "It only takes a handful of winners to make a lifetime of investing worthwhile."

The problem with Lynch's advice is that if an investor holds only five stocks in his portfolio, it only takes a *handful of losers* to make a lifetime of investing a *nightmare*. When an investor invests in only five stocks, he has potentially disastrous underdiversification since even one stock that takes a permanent dive in value can be a major disaster. Although none of us ever expects such a total loss to occur, it might, so we must protect ourselves from that possibility. The need to diversify investment risk arises precisely from this fact.

Furthermore, how can part-time amateur investors expect to find a handful of winners among five stocks? That's a batting average that even Lynch could not match in 13 years as a full-time professional stock picker. He needed to hold hundreds, even thousands, of stocks to produce a handful of winners, not just five stocks.[21] Instead of gambling on a few stocks to produce a handful of winners, the smarter investment move is to make a diversified bet on a portfolio of index funds.

This chapter has explained that the best way to control investment risk is to invest in index funds. The next chapter shows why it is understandably more satisfying for investors to see how index funds boost performance by reducing investment costs.

Chapter Notes

[1] Although the principles underlying Modern Portfolio Theory can be applied to portfolios of individual stocks and actively-managed mutual funds, the *best* way to benefit from them is to invest in properly diversified portfolios of index funds.

[2] By the time that this book went to print, IBM stock had come roaring back. However, depending on the times when investors read the book, the stock may have plunged in value again, posted even higher returns or remained unchanged in its performance. That's the nature of entirely normal fluctuations in the values of stocks in complex financial markets.

[3] Hitting a home run with one stock (or relatively few stocks) is rare. What is much more typical is that, over the long run, to the extent that an investor is invested in stocks he will be compensated by the stock market with returns consistent with stocks. Likewise, to the extent that he is invested in bonds he will be compensated by the bond market with returns consistent with bonds.

[4] This fund tracks the Wilshire 5000 index which represents virtually 100% of the market value of all the stocks that are listed and traded in the stock markets of the United States. The index was created in 1971 with 5,000 stocks by Wilshire Associates, an investment consulting firm. As of December 31, 1996, it represented 7,368 stocks. The Vanguard Total Stock Market index fund samples about 2,900 of these stocks.

[5] Roger C. Gibson has thoroughly explored the role played by human nature in the investment process. *See* his book *Asset Allocation: Balancing Financial Risk*, second edition (Burr Ridge, Illinois: Irwin Professional Publishing, 1996).

[6] *The Portable MBA In Investment* edited by Peter L. Bernstein (New York: John Wiley & Sons, Inc., 1995), page 167.

[7] A trustee's general duty to prudently diversify a trust's investments is absolute "unless, under the circumstances, it is prudent not to do so." *Restatement (Third) of Trusts (Prudent Investor Rule)* (Washington D.C.: The American Law Institute, 1992), page 8. The most common situation where it may be imprudent to diversify a trust is when a family-owned business constitutes most or all of a trust's assets. Another situation is when efforts to improve diversification generate excessive costs and capital gains taxes. For example, upon first assuming the duties of managing a trust a new trustee may immediately determine that it is woefully underdiversified. His first thought might be to sell off some or all of the trust's investments and buy new ones in order to improve its diversification. However, any benefits that may be achieved by improved diversification of a trust must always be balanced against the excessive costs and capital gains taxes that could result from the sale of the trust's existing investments.

[8] *Restatement (Third) of Trusts (Prudent Investor Rule)* (Washington D.C.: The American Law Institute, 1992), comment g, page 27. Italics added.

[9] "The Revolution in Trust Investment Law" by John H. Langbein and Richard A.

Posner, *American Bar Association Journal*, Volume 62, July 1976, pages 887-891. *See* "Diversification: Old and New" by James H. Lorie, *The Journal of Portfolio Management*, Winter 1975, pages 25-28.

[10] This claim is also based on the fact that active fund managers always have the option (denied to index fund managers) to sell off all their holdings and go into cash 100% in order to ride out any market downturns. However, this is rarely exercised because active fund managers are afraid (and rightly so) that if they hold a heavy percentage of cash they will have less ability to take advantage of advancing stock prices in any ensuing market recoveries.

[11] On the day of the October 1987 Crash, the average mutual fund fell 22% in value while the S&P 500 fell 21%. When the market (the S&P 500) was down for the period of June through October 1990, it outperformed the average stock mutual fund by 3.2 percentage points (-14.7% vs. -17.9%) and when it was down for the period of all of 1994 it outperformed it by 2.7 percentage points (+1.3% vs. -1.4%). "Don't Fret: Here's Why Passive Still Pays" by John Wyatt, *Fortune*, February 17, 1997, pages 150-152.

[12] Since cash is not invested in the stock market, it is not exposed to the risk of earning stock market returns when they are less than money market returns. On the other hand, cash does not earn the reward of stock market returns when they are greater than money market returns.

[13] For example, in the year after the 1987 Crash the S&P 500 outperformed the average mutual fund by 3.4 percentage points. "Don't Fret: Here's Why Passive Still Pays" by John Wyatt, *Fortune*, February 17, 1997, pages 150-152.

[14] This usually involves purchasing stocks that have gone down in price in declining markets.

[15] George U. Sauter, who runs Vanguard's index funds, notes: "To have a 2% head start [in a market that averages a 10% return] is a tremendous advantage. It's like starting a 100-yard dash on the 20-yard line." *The Wall Street Journal*, April 4, 1996, page R11.

[16] John C. Bogle in "Be Not the First, Nor Yet the Last," a speech at the annual conference of the Association for Investment Management and Research, Atlanta, Georgia, May 8, 1996. It is likely that this percentage is understated because it is based on mutual fund data that doesn't account for the higher taxes and commission loads generated by most active funds. It is also probable that survivorship bias (examined in Chapter Eight) would further increase this figure. Whatever the actual percentage, though, it is clear that a heavy majority of active mutual funds underperformed the S&P 500 over the last quarter century.

[17] The Lipper general equity average.

[18] Investors have been told by the investment information system that inflation in the 2-3% range is not a threat to their long term financial security. This is patently false. An annual 3% inflation rate compounded over 20 years results in a 45% loss of purchasing power while a rate even as low as 2% results in a 33% loss. It is clear

that many investors understand the "miracle" of compounding when it runs in their favor such as when their investments grow in value. But not many appreciate the reverse: when the "curse" of negative compounding (discussed in Chapter Twelve) works against them. Inflation and investment costs and taxes are examples of this phenomenon and each, separately or in concert with the others, can vastly slow down the accumulation of wealth in a portfolio. Of course, there is nothing that an investor can do about the adverse impact of inflation on the accumulating wealth in his portfolio. *But there is one major step that he can take to minimize the impact of investment costs and taxes - become an indexer.*

[19] *Beating the Street* by Peter Lynch with John Rothchild (New York: Fireside/ Simon & Schuster, 1993), page 306.

[20] "Portfolio Selection" by Harry M. Markowitz, *The Journal of Finance*, Volume 7, No. 1, March 1952, pages 77-91. Italics added.

[21] A year before Lynch left as the manager of Fidelity Magellan, it held over 1,400 stocks. *Forbes*, April 3, 1989, page 176.

TWELVE

INDEX FUNDS MINIMIZE INVESTMENT COSTS

Once in the dear dead days beyond recall, an out-of-town visitor was being shown the wonders of the New York financial district. When the party arrived at the Battery, one of his guides indicated some handsome ships riding at anchor. He said, "Look, those are the bankers' and brokers' yachts."
"Where are the customers' yachts?" asked the naive visitor.[1]
- Fred Schwed, Jr., 1940
  Where Are The Customers' Yachts?

Costs do not regress to the mean.[2]
- John C. Bogle (1929-   )

Costs are controllable but performance isn't.
- Anonymous

Overview

Index funds generate minimal investment costs. They do not have the high annual operating expenses, trading costs or commission loads that characterize many actively-managed mutual funds. This makes it likely that index funds will outperform most active funds on an after-cost basis over the long run.

The Cost Advantages Of Index Funds

An understanding of the investment process is not complete unless an investor grasps the fact that any financial market is a zero sum game. In this kind of game, all investors in the aggregate achieve the same gross investment performance. But once investment expenses, costs and commission loads and their negative compounding effect on accumulating wealth are taken into account, it is likely that most actively-managed mutual funds will be inferior in performance to index funds on a *net* basis over the long run. Thus, the overriding reality of any financial market is that investment costs (and taxes) matter tremendously. (This is true in *both* efficient and inefficient markets.) All the slick mutual fund advertising and confusing investment presentations in the world will not change this basic fact of arithmetic. There are three principal reasons why index funds are likely to outperform most active funds.

First, index funds do not have the high annual operating expenses that typify many active mutual funds. These expenses chiefly consist of investment advisory fees that compensate the active fund for its manager's efforts at stock picking and 12b-1 fees that reimburse it for its sales and marketing costs. Second, index funds do not have the high trading costs characteristic of many active funds. Most of these costs are due to the efforts of active fund managers to implement their stock picking ideas to beat the market. Third, index funds do not charge commission loads while most active funds carry some type of load.

SIMON SAYS: *The Cost Advantages Of Bond Index Funds*

Stock index funds offer investors significant investment advantages in comparison to actively-managed stock funds. But the superiority of bond index funds when compared to active bond funds is even greater, particularly in the area of taxable bonds.

A manager of an active stock mutual fund has, at least in theory, various ways to beat the stock market. In contrast, the manager of an active bond fund really has only one way to beat the bond market: he must accurately forecast changes in interest rates.[3] But a bond fund manager has small chance of achieving this since there is so much competition in the bond market. That's why active bond funds that have similar standards of credit quality and maturity are pretty much alike in their performances. For example, the returns of the top ten government bond funds over the last five years have only varied by about one percentage point.[4]

Net differences in investment performance among comparable bond funds really come down to differences in costs.[5] Since the costs of bond index funds are much lower than active bond funds, it is not hard to see why they are superior. Quite simply, it is very hard to beat the performance of taxable bond index funds. So even though managers of active bond funds say that they can get superior performances through their well-timed buying, selling and hedging of positions, they really have little ability to deliver on these promises.

The Total Investment Costs Of The Average Actively-Managed Stock Mutual Fund

Illustration 10 on page 181 shows the total investment costs of the average actively-managed stock mutual fund.[6] A manager of a stock mutual fund who attempts to beat the market must overcome each of these costly hurdles if he is to be successful in his attempts. The rest of the chapter shows the great difficulty of this and why, as a result, index funds are likely to be superior in performance on an after-cost basis in comparison to most active funds over the long run.

Illustration 10

Total Investment Costs Of The Average Actively-Managed Stock Mutual Fund

Annual Operating Expenses (1.50% of net asset value [NAV] which is the published market value of a mutual fund share. Annual operating expenses are incurred on a yearly basis.)
    a. investment advisory fees (.50 to 1.00% of NAV)
    b. administrative fees (.20 to .40% of NAV)
        1. record-keeping expenses (shareholder statements and annual reports)
        2. transaction expenses
    c. miscellaneous fees (.10 to .30% of NAV)
        1. custodial fees
        2. legal and accounting expenses
        3. directors' fees
    d. 12b-1 fees (.25 to 1.00% of NAV) (marketing and sales expenses)
(Annual operating expenses are itemized in a mutual fund prospectus but are actually reflected in the NAV of a mutual fund share.)

Trading Costs (About .90 to 1.00% of NAV. Trading costs are incurred on a yearly basis.)
    a. brokerage commissions (the costs of buying and selling stocks for a mutual
       fund)
    b. market impact costs
    c. bid-ask spread costs
(Trading costs are not reflected in annual operating expenses, but in the NAV of a mutual fund share.)

Commission Load (3.00 to 8.75% of the offer price of a mutual fund share. A commission load is incurred on every purchase of mutual fund shares.)
(The commission load is not reflected in *either* a fund's annual operating expenses or in the NAV of a mutual fund share.)

Source: *Bogle on Mutual Funds* by John C. Bogle.

Annual Operating Expenses

A mutual fund's annual operating expenses are made up of investment advisory fees, administrative fees, miscellaneous fees and 12b-1 fees. While annual operating expenses are itemized in a mutual fund prospectus, their actual effect is reflected in the net asset value (NAV) (or published market value) of a mutual fund share.

Investment advisory fees are paid to a mutual fund's investment advisor and range from .50% to 1.00% of the NAV of a mutual fund share. These fees are typically greater in active funds because they employ highly compensated fund managers as well as legions of securities analysts. Administrative fees, which range from .20% to .40% of a share's NAV, include record keeping and transaction expenses. Miscellaneous fees consist of custodial fees, legal and accounting expenses and directors' fees and range from .10% to .30% of NAV. Thus, before adding in 12b-1 fees, an actively-managed stock mutual fund's annual expenses can run from .80% to 1.70%.[7] (All these expenses are deducted 'painlessly' from an investor's mutual fund account by the fund itself.)

12b-1 Fees

A 12b-1 fee is separately itemized in a mutual fund prospectus as part of the fund's annual operating expenses. The 12b-1 fee, imposed by most active mutual funds, pays for marketing costs and the commissions of salespeople.[8] Few index funds charge 12b-1 fees.[9]

SIMON SAYS: *Salespeople Generally Fail To Educate Investors About Costs*

Investment salespeople generally fail to properly educate investors about the harm caused by investment costs. They simply do not have the time, training or the interest to do so. After all, investment salespeople are part of a highly motivated sales force that is compensated by the money that comes from the pockets of the very investors that they target. A sale is much more difficult for them if they educate investors too much about the real meaning of investment costs.

An annual 12b-1 fee of 1% has a surprisingly large impact on an investor's accumulating wealth over a 20-year period. This is apparent when comparing two no load mutual funds - one carrying a 1% 12b-1 fee and the other not carrying this fee. Both funds earn a 10% gross return.

A $100,000 investment compounded on a monthly basis at a 10% annual rate yields $732,807 in the mutual fund without the 12b-1 fee. The same investment compounded at a 9% annual rate yields $600,915 for the fund with the fee. The difference of $131,892 is due to the effect of a deceptively small 1% annual 12b-1 fee negatively compounding against wealth over a 20-year period. This fee consumes 18% of the wealth that would otherwise be accumulated without the fee.

Trading Costs

The trading costs of a mutual fund consist of both *visible* brokerage commission costs and *invisible* market impact and bid-ask spread costs. As we know, trading costs are generated by portfolio turnover which is the rate at which a mutual fund manager buys or sells stocks or bonds for the fund during the course of a year. A mutual fund's portfolio turnover rate equals the lower of these purchases or sales divided by the average net assets of the fund.[10]

The "visible" trading costs of a mutual fund are the brokerage commissions that it incurs when the fund manager buys and sells stocks. (Visible trading costs aren't separately itemized in a mutual fund's prospectus but are reflected in the NAV of a mutual fund share.) In an active fund, these costs are typically high because they are the result of implementing the many ideas that the fund manager has to beat the market.[11]

The brokerage commission costs generated by an index fund remain low (typically about one-third those of active funds) because its manager doesn't try to beat the market. An index fund generates these visible trading costs only when its investors buy and sell fund shares, they reinvest income or the fund manager buys and sells stocks to match any changes in the composition of the index tracked by the fund.[12] The cost of brokerage commissions does not significantly impact the performance of an index fund.

The "invisible" trading costs of a mutual fund are market impact costs and bid-ask spread costs. Market impact costs are impossible to measure in a precise way and bid-ask spread costs are very difficult to measure so they are not separately itemized in a mutual fund prospectus.

"Market impact costs" are the difference between a stock's price when bought or sold and its price in the absence of such purchase or sale. For example, the manager of an active mutual fund may want to immediately purchase a stock that he believes will outperform the market. Placing an order for a large block of a single stock indicates to the market that a professional such as a mutual fund manager or a corporate pension plan manager is behind the purchase. Since the market 'assumes' that such professionals possess superior information about any given stock, it 'thinks' that whenever they purchase a stock they must know something favorable about it - hence, it must be a good buy. So other investors, after seeing the large order for the stock, rush to place their own orders to purchase it. This surge in demand eats up the available supply of the stock which "impacts" its price by pushing it upward.

The increase in price happens nearly instantaneously after the order is placed and before the active fund manager can buy the stock. So by the time that he and others place orders to buy the stock at a price of, say, $10 a share they may end up paying, say, $12 for it. This transaction thus generated market impact costs of $2 which is the difference between the stock's price before the large order set in motion a change in its price and its subsequent price afterward. Even though the institutional investor that placed the large order for the stock was the initial cause of its jump in price, all those that purchase it must pay the higher price.

The stock's price can also be impacted upward by the *immediate* need of a purchaser to buy a large block of the stock. The purchaser must pay for the accommodation of his need by paying a price for the stock that is higher than it was before the order.

What happens when an active mutual fund manager wants to immediately sell a stock that he believes will underperform the market? In that situation, the market 'thinks' that the stock is a bad buy because a large seller is getting rid of it. The size of an order like this to sell a large block of stock can immediately impact the price by pushing it downward. As a result, the active fund will receive a price for the stock that will be lower than its price before the sale. Again, the difference between these two prices constitutes market impact costs.

The performances of index funds are not affected by market impact costs nearly to the extent of active funds. (The market impact costs incurred by an index fund are about one-fourth those of the typical active fund.) Unlike an active fund manager who may order the purchase or sale of one million shares of a single stock, an index fund manager places a single order for a relatively small number of shares for each of many stocks. For example, one such order may involve 5,000 shares for each of 200 stocks. Because the order for each stock is so small, there is no upward or downward impact on its price. Thus, the index fund incurs no market impact costs when placing orders for any of the 200 stocks.

"Bid-ask spread costs" are created by the difference ("spread") between the bid price of a stock and its ask price.[13] The bid price is what a buyer is willing to purchase a stock for and the ask price is what a seller is willing to sell a stock for. The investment performances of both active funds and index funds are affected the same by bid-ask spread costs.[14]

In sum, the only trading costs that can have a significant affect on the performances of index funds are bid-ask spread costs. These costs can also be harmful to the performances of actively-managed funds. The performances of active funds are impaired by market impact costs and brokerage commissions, while these two costs do not seriously affect the performances of index funds. The net result of this is that when trading stocks, index funds tend to receive higher sale prices and pay lower purchase prices than active funds.

While it is difficult to precisely calculate the amount of a mutual fund's investment performance that is lost to trading costs each year, it is possible to make a rough estimate. John C. Bogle suggests to take a mutual fund's portfolio turnover rate, double it and then multiply that number by .60%.[15] For example, today's average stock mutual fund bears an 85% annual portfolio turnover rate. Doubling .85% equals 1.70% and multiplying 1.70% by .60% equals 1.02%. Thus, the amount of return lost to trading costs (both visible and invisible) every year by the average actively-managed mutual fund is about 1.00%.[16]

Even an index fund with a high (for an index fund) 40% portfolio turnover rate would lose less than half (.48%) the annual 1.00% return lost to trading costs by the average active stock fund. An index fund with a 5% portfolio turnover rate would suffer a .06% loss in annual return which is only about *one-twentieth* the trading costs of the average active stock fund.

SIMON SAYS: *Why Expenses And Costs Buried In Mutual Fund Ratings Matter*

Investors perusing the list of Morningstar's 5-star mutual funds usually do not concern themselves with annual expenses and trading costs because they are *already* incorporated into these ratings. This is particularly the case when the market is up and mutual funds are earning double digit returns. But what happens when the market goes down and those fabulous returns go into single digits or even turn negative? The high expenses and costs of actively-managed mutual funds will stick out like a sore thumb. Thus, the very *uncertainty* of future investment performance should cause investors in active funds to be seriously concerned about the continuing *certainty* of the high expenses and costs that are buried in mutual fund ratings.

Commission Loads

The shares of most actively-managed mutual funds are sold to investors at their net asset value plus a commission "load" (a sales charge).[17] Sometimes an active fund offers different classes of commission loads. Many active funds that carry commissions only offer class A and class B loads. A class A designation signifies a front load commission and a class B designation usually signifies a back load. Ultimately, though, investors pay the same amount of money whatever the class of commission load.[18]

SIMON SAYS: *Some Are Created More Equal Than Others*

Mutual fund ratings that appear in the investment media do not take into account the effect that commission loads have on their performances. Thus, all mutual funds, including high load active funds and no load index funds, are unfairly created equal in that they *all* seem to be no loads.

The impact of a commission load on a mutual fund's performance is always *understated* by the investment information system. For example, language such as the following often appears in the media: "A high front load commission will put a big dent in a mutual fund's return if an investor holds it for only a short time. But the adverse impact of the load is *averaged out and increasingly reduced* the longer the investor remains invested in the fund."

This is not true. In fact, we will see in the next section that the impact of a commission load on the accumulating wealth in a mutual fund *increases* over time.

SIMON SAYS: *When A No Load Actively-Managed Mutual Fund Is Not No Load*

Investors should be aware that even *no load* actively-managed mutual funds can carry commission loads.[19] The Yacktman Fund is a good example of this. Since 1993, all new investors in this mutual fund have had the privilege of helping pay trail commissions to stockbrokers - on behalf of *other* investors who bought shares in the fund years ago! (Ongoing "trail" commissions - often .25% annually - are paid to stockbrokers in addition to the front load or back load commissions that they previously earned.)

This situation was created when Yacktman offered to pay trail commissions to certain stockbrokers for bringing in new money to the fund during the second half of 1992. The brokers were promised that they would continue to receive these commissions on any money invested during this six-month period - even *after* the end of the period. This means that investors who bought the fund shares carrying the trail commissions must continue to pay these commissions until they sell the shares.

Over the last several years, the Yacktman Fund's assets have grown at a healthy rate. As a result, its annual expenses in percentage terms have decreased because they are spread over a larger amount of invested money. But the trail commissions have not decreased - they have fluctuated from .14% in 1994 to .07% in 1995 to .09% in 1996. While these sums *are* trivial when compared to the Yacktman Fund's annual expenses of .94%, they are not so insignificant when compared to the annual expenses of a low cost index fund where they would constitute 35-70% of total expenses.

The Negative Compounding Effect Of "Lost Money" On Accumulating Wealth

Many investors understand that annual operating expenses, trading costs and commission loads can be damaging to the accumulating wealth in a mutual fund. But few are aware of the *additional and invisible* damage that is caused by the negative compounding effect of money used to pay for these expenses, costs and loads.

This money must be thought of as "lost money" because it is immediately gone forever and thus can never be used to compound future wealth. For example, Illustration 11 on page 188 compares the differences in accumulated wealth held in a no load and a front load fund for different time periods. The $100,000 beginning wealth of a no load investor compounds on a monthly basis at a 10% annual rate to yield $732,807 at the end of 20 years. But an investor in a 5% front load fund invests only $95,000 which yields $696,157 - a $36,650 (plus $5,000) disadvantage for the load investor. (When the investment time period is increased to 30 years, the load fund's disadvantage balloons to $99,200 (plus $5,000).)

The investment information system only focuses on how the impact of the visible $5,000 outlay for the load will affect the mutual fund's performance. When a simple averaging method is used, naturally the impact of a load in any given year is increasingly reduced as the number of years in the averaging period becomes greater. But what is not acknowledged is the invisible damage to future compounded wealth caused by the $5,000 outlay. In this example, that damage caused by the negative compounding effect of the $5,000 lost money used to pay for the load amounts to $36,650 over 20 years and $99,200 over 30 years.

Thus, the total adverse impact of a front load commission on investment performance consists not only of the immediate visible blow of the load itself but also the invisible loss of future compounded wealth.[20] When these visible and invisible costs combine, the total adverse dollar impact of a front load commission on the accumulating wealth in a mutual fund *absolutely increases* with the passage of time. (This isn't true just for front load funds (class A shares) but also for back load funds (class B shares).[21]) As a result, the difference in the amount of money held by a no load investor in an index fund and that held by an investor in a front load active fund will grow increasingly in favor of the no load indexer the longer the compounding period.[22]

Illustration 11

A Commission Load's Adverse Impact Becomes Greater, Not Lesser, Over Time

	Today's Investment	5 Years	10 years	20 Years	30 Years
Load Mutual Fund (5%)	$95,000	$156,304	$257,154	$696,157	$1,884,540
No load Mutual Fund	100,000	164,531	270,704	732,807	1,983,740
No load Advantage	**5,000**	**8,227**	**13,550**	**36,650**	**99,200**

Assumptions: Lump sum investment compounded on a monthly basis at a 10% annual rate.

We have just seen how the total impact of a commission load can cause it to more negatively impact accumulating wealth with time. However, the total impact made by the annual operating expenses of a mutual fund rapidly surpasses that of a commission load because these expenses are imposed every year, not just on a one-time basis as is the case with a load.

This means that with the passage of time, annual expenses (in comparison to a load) account for an *increasingly greater* amount of the damage to a fund's performance. For example, a 5% commission load causes a $1,355 decrease in the value of a $10,000 front load mutual fund over a 10-year period and a $9,920 decrease over a 30-year period. In comparison, annual operating expenses of 1% cause a $2,557 decrease in value over a 10-year period, but a $51,068 decrease over a 30-year period. (While it might appear so, the $10,000 lump sum is not swallowed up by the $51,068 in annual expenses. The reason why is that the lump sum's value is compounding at a *greater positive* rate than the negative compounding rate of the annual expenses. Thus, $10,000 compounded on a monthly basis at a 10% annual rate generates a gross amount of $198,374 at the end of 30 years and a net amount, reduced by the $51,068 in annual expenses, of $147,306.)

Illustration 12 on page 190 shows how the performance of a lump sum investment is affected more adversely the longer the investment time period by the *combination* of a front load commission, annual operating expenses and their respective negative compounding effects. For example, assume that an investor invests a lump sum of $10,000 in a mutual fund at a 10% annual rate (compounded on a monthly basis) for a period of 20 years. The mutual fund bears a 5% front end commission load and carries annual operating expenses of 1.50%.

Over this period, the investor would see his investment grow in value to $73,281. However, the boxed number in Illustration 12 shows that this gross figure would be reduced by $22,533 as a result of a commission load, annual operating expenses and their respective negative compounding effects. This leaves the investor with $50,748, or a 31% reduction in future wealth. But when the investment period is increased to 30 years, the resulting gross wealth of $198,374 is reduced by loads and expenses of $81,369 (shown in the other boxed number), or a reduction of 41%.

It is important to understand that the dollar amounts in Illustration 12 are valid only when investing *one* lump sum of money.[23] But if an investor systematically invests his money by dollar-cost averaging[24] he would see an exponential increase in the adverse impact of a front load commission on his investment performance. The reason for this is that there would be many individual investments of money (not just one lump sum) and thus many commission loads to pay when he dollar-cost averages. The greater number of loads vastly increases the amount of times that lost money negatively compounds against accumulating wealth. The answer to this problem is not to stop dollar-cost averaging, but to purchase no load index funds.

Comparing The Investment Costs Of An Active Mutual Fund And An Index Fund

Illustration 13 on page 191 shows that the commission load, annual expenses and their respective negative compounding effects generated by an active mutual fund much more significantly impact accumulating wealth than the annual expenses (and their negative compounding effect) of a no load index fund. In fact, the impact on an active fund is *nearly three times* greater than on an index fund over a 30-year period. As a result, an indexer can accumulate approximately 40% more wealth than an active investor in this example. A more dramatic difference in the accumulation of wealth can be achieved by an indexer if he invests in an even lower cost index fund.

Illustration 12

The Negative Compounding Effect Of Mutual Fund Commission Loads And Annual Operating Expenses On Accumulating Wealth
(One $10,000 Lump Sum Invested At A 10% Annual Rate Compounded Monthly)

Commission Loads	No Load			3%			5%			7%		
Years	10	20	30	10	20	30	10	20	30	10	20	30
Annual Operating Expenses												
.00	$0	$0	$0	-$813	-$2,199	-$5,952	-$1,355	-$3,665	-$9,920	-$1,897	-$5,131	-$13,888
.25	-662	-3,545	-14,221	-1,475	-5,744	-20,173	-2,017	-7,210	-24,141	-2,559	-8,676	-28,109
.50	-1,315	-6,920	-27,425	-2,128	-9,119	-33,377	-2,670	-10,585	-37,345	-3,212	-12,051	-41,313
.75	-1,941	-10,132	-39,685	-2,754	-12,331	-45,637	-3,296	-13,797	-49,605	-3,838	-15,263	-53,573
1.00	-2,557	-13,189	-51,068	-3,370	-15,388	-57,020	-3,912	-16,854	-60,988	-4,454	-18,320	-64,956
1.25	-3,158	-16,099	-61,637	-3,971	-18,298	-67,589	-4,513	19,764	-71,557	-5,055	-21,230	-75,525
1.50	-3,744	-18,868	-71,449	-4,557	-21,067	-77,401	-5,099	**-22,533**	**-81,369**	-5,641	-23,999	-85,337
1.75	-4,316	-21,504	-80,559	-5,129	-23,703	-86,511	-5,671	-25,169	-90,479	-6,213	-26,635	-94,447
2.00	-4,874	-24,013	-89,017	-5,687	-26,212	-94,969	-6,229	-27,678	-98,937	-6,771	-29,144	-102,905
2.25	-5,419	-26,400	-96,869	-6,232	-28,599	-102,821	-6,774	-30,065	-106,789	-7,316	-31,531	-110,757
2.50	-5,950	-28,763	-104,159	-6,763	-30,962	-110,111	-7,305	-32,428	-114,079	-7,847	-33,894	-118,047

Assumptions: Commission loads and annual operating expenses negatively compounded on a monthly basis.
CAUTION: These dollar amounts apply *only* when investing a lump sum of money at the beginning of a period.
Source: This illustration is based on a matrix developed by Gregory N. Hight of Hight Capital Management, Brainerd, Minnesota.

SIMON SAYS: *But Is The Performance Seven Times Better?*

Today's average actively-managed stock mutual fund not only bears annual operating expenses of 1.42%,[25] but also usually carries a hefty commission load. In contrast, a "plain vanilla" index fund tracking the performance of the S&P 500 has annual operating expenses of 0.20% (1/5 of 1%) and no commission load. Thus, the annual expenses of the average active fund alone can be *seven times more* than a low cost index fund.

Illustration 13

The Effect Of Commission Loads, Annual Operating Expenses And Their Respective Negative Compounding Effects On The Wealth Of A Load Active Fund Compared To A No Load Index Fund

Load Active Fund	10 years	20 years	30 years
$100,000 Investment	$270,704	$732,807	$1,983,740
Load (3%)	-8,130	-21,990	-59,520
Annual Expenses (1.50%)	-37,440	-188,680	-714,490
Total Loads and Annual Expenses	-45,570	-210,670	-774,010
Net Accumulated Wealth	**225,134**	**522,137**	**1,209,730**
Percentage of Gross Wealth Consumed by Loads and Expenses	16.8%	28.7%	39.0%

No Load Index Fund	10 years	20 years	30 years
$100,000 Investment	270,704	732,807	1,983,740
Load (0%)	0	0	0
Annual Expenses (.50%)	-13,150	-69,200	-274,250
Total Loads and Annual Expenses	-13,150	-69,200	-274,250
Net Accumulated Wealth	**257,554**	**663,607**	**1,709,490**
Percentage of Gross Wealth Consumed by Loads and Expenses	4.9%	9.4%	13.8%

Assumptions: $100,000 lump sum investment compounded on a monthly basis at a 10% annual rate. Commission loads and annual operating expenses negatively compounded on a monthly basis. CAUTION: These dollar amounts apply *only* when investing one lump sum of money.

Investors should be aware that Illustration 13 does not take into account the effect of trading costs. The higher trading costs incurred by the average actively-managed mutual fund may add another fifteen percentage points to the 39% of gross wealth consumed by a commission load, annual expenses and their respective negative compounding effects over a 30-year period. Thus, even without accounting for the significantly higher taxes typical of active funds, the investment costs of the average active mutual fund can consume nearly 55% of its gross wealth in this example.

SIMON SAYS: *Justifying The Use Of Costly Active Investment Strategies Under The Prudent Investor Rule*

One of the objectives of the individuals who drafted the Prudent Investor Rule was to make it more flexible by permitting a wider range of investment strategies. So when investing and managing the assets of a trust, the Rule permits attorneys, trustees and investment advisors to use active investment strategies, indexing investment strategies or a combination of both. However, the Rule is very clear in cautioning these individuals that *they must carefully justify the use of costly active investment strategies*.

Edward C. Halbach, Jr., the Reporter for the Restatement (Third) of Trusts (which incorporates the Prudent Investor Rule) and former dean of Boalt Hall, the law school at the University of California, explains:[26] ". . . [active investment] management activities . . . present practical concerns that a cautious investor should not disregard." "[M]ost obviously, active management involves new or increased expenses of investigation and analysis and transaction costs, including capital gains taxation, plus . . . additional risks." "Prudent fund managers should carefully consider . . . cost and risk concerns in deciding whether to undertake an active investment strategy and then in deciding how to implement it. In particular, they should evaluate increased return expectations, cautiously and realistically, before concluding that these expectations justify the extra costs that typically result from active investment programs. Market efficiency information is especially relevant in assessing these expectations; *the greater the departure from sound [indexing] strategies, the greater the manager's burdens* not only of justification [for recommending a costly active investment strategy in the first place] but of continuous monitoring [and ongoing use of it] as well."

This chapter has shown that the primary reason why index funds achieve better investment performance than most high cost active funds is because they incur low investment costs. In the following chapter, we will see that index funds generate lower taxes than most active funds which also helps them achieve better investment performance.

Chapter Notes

[1] *Where Are The Customers' Yachts?* by Fred Schwed, Jr. (New York: Simon & Schuster, 1940).

[2] *Bogle on Mutual Funds* by John C. Bogle (Burr Ridge, Illinois: Irwin Professional Publishing, 1994), page 115.

[3] U.S. Treasury and federal agency obligations comprise about 50% of the taxable investment-grade bond market in the United States. The values of these bonds are determined entirely by changes in interest rates. Mortgage securities backed by federal agencies make up about 30% of the taxable investment-grade bond market. Their returns could be said to be even more unpredictable because they involve the behavior of homeowners who take advantage of any interest rate declines to refinance their homes. *See* "Why Bond Indexing Is Catching On" by Randall W. Forsyth, *Barron's*, February 3, 1997, pages 41-42.

[4] *Money*, August 1995, page 72.

[5] "When bond funds have closely specified quality and maturity standards, they tend to earn similar gross yields. Their net return is differentiated simply by their expenses relative to other comparable funds. Since net income is the overwhelming component of bond fund returns, the advantage of a low-cost fund is potent. Further, there is no evidence that particular portfolio managers can provide substantial and sustainable capital appreciation over a full interest-rate cycle. Thus capital returns differ only modestly and tend to regress to the mean. It is *net* income return that drives the equation, and net income is heavily influenced by costs. Since costs do not regress to the mean, a powerful correlation exists between bond fund returns and bond fund costs." *Bogle on Mutual Funds* by John C. Bogle (Burr Ridge, Illinois: Irwin Professional Publishing, 1993), page 115.

[6] The 2.4% "annual costs" of the average actively-managed common stock mutual fund consist of (a) 1.5% "annual operating expenses" (excluding commission loads) and (b) .9% "turnover costs" (i.e., trading costs). *Ibid.*, page 178.

[7] *Ibid.*, page 198.

[8] Originally, the SEC allowed imposition of 12b-1 fees to help true no load funds finance their sales and distribution costs since, unlike load funds, they didn't have a sales force to market them. But load funds also saw this as an opportunity to increase revenue so they, too, adopted 12b-1 plans. A 12b-1 fee ("12b-1" refers to the Securities and Exchange Commission Rule that allows the fee) normally ranges from .25% to 1.00% per year. The SEC has mandated that a mutual fund cannot bill itself as a "no load" unless its 12b-1 fee is .25% or less. In addition, mutual funds are restricted from charging more than 1.00% per year for a 12b-1 fee or .75% for a 12b-1 fee plus a .25% service fee. Of course, the underlying reason for the existence of 12b-1 fees is to help increase the amount of assets held by a mutual fund so that it can earn a greater amount of investment management fees. So when existing investors in a mutual fund pay a 12b-1 fee, they acquire the dubious

privilege of paying for some of the advertising and sales commissions incurred by the fund to persuade people to become investors in it. Because they have nothing to do with enhancing returns, 12b-1 fees therefore represent a deadweight loss of return for investors. Mutual funds charged investors $4.19 billion in 12b-1 fees in 1996, according to Lipper Analytical Services, Inc.

[9] The typical index fund is a "pure" no load fund (no front load, spread load, back load or 12b-1 fees). The index funds that aren't pure no load are low load and have small 12b-1 fees. However, indexers should avoid index funds that carry any load or 12b-1 fee.

[10] Most investors don't care about the effect of high portfolio turnover on the performance of actively-managed mutual funds when they hold them in their tax-deferred retirement plans or annuities. Why? Because they know that they won't be *taxed* on any gains generated by this turnover. However, investors forget about the *trading costs* generated by turnover. These costs can have a significant impact on the investment performance of even tax-deferred investments.

[11] To a lesser extent, trading costs are generated by investors who trade in and out of a mutual fund. But trading costs must be shared by *everyone* in a mutual fund, not just those who trade shares. Since it is unfair to impose these costs on non-trading investors, index funds sometimes charge short term investors redemption fees to discourage them from excessive trading. While these fees typically comprise 1-2% of a trade's value, they do not benefit the mutual fund company. Instead, they are added back to the fund's assets to compensate non-trading fund investors who involuntarily share these trading costs. Vanguard is an example of a mutual fund company that has sought to limit in and out trading by its investors. In mid-1996, a long-time Vanguard client wanted to "park" $40 million in a short term Treasury debt fund for two months. To the consternation of this client, Vanguard refused to do so because the trading costs involved in buying and selling the required securities would have increased fund expenses by about $50,000, thus hurting existing shareholders. In taking this stance, Vanguard gave up about $30,000 in management fees. *See* "Vanguard Puts Up 'No Parking' Sign" by Ellen E. Schultz, *The Wall Street Journal*, July 2, 1996, page C1.

[12] Sometimes index funds can even make money on a stock trade. A specific example of a passive fund (which, as we know, is a first cousin to an index fund) that did this is the DFA 9-10 fund run by Dimensional Fund Advisors Inc. In April 1994, this passive fund sought to acquire a stock, Southern Energy Homes, to rebalance its holdings of small company stocks. A block of 225,000 shares became available in the market at a bid price of $12^{3/4}$. The ask price was $13^{1/2}$, but DFA offered $12^{1/4}$ - $^{1/2}$ point below even the bid price. What was the reason for accepting DFA's below-market offer? The average daily trading volume for this stock was 32,400 shares and it could have taken more than a week for the seller to get rid of the whole block of shares. This could have easily driven the market price substantially below the bid price - even to a price lower than that offered by DFA. In order

to avoid this possibility, the seller unloaded the entire block of shares at DFA's lower-than-market price. This passive fund was thus able to actually make money on the transaction since the net trading cost, including the discount from the last sale and all commissions, incurred by DFA was a *negative* 2.8%. *See* "The Brave New World of Indexing" by Robert N. Veres, *Fee Advisor*, January 1995, page 19.
[13] One of the reasons for a wide spread between the bid and ask prices of a stock is that neither side has much information about it.
[14] Some sophisticated traders believe that they can exploit index funds with a stock trading tactic called the "Paris March." "Knowing that most indexers have to buy the same stocks at the very end of each trading day, the pros start buying up the stocks in great quantities - like the German Army marching through Paris in 1940, grabbing everything it can - and driving prices up shortly before the market's close. If the traders' timing is right, the indexers will have to buy the shares at the higher prices at the 4 p.m. closing bell." *See* "The S&P's Surprising Fangs" by Steven D. Kaye, *U.S. News & World Report*, August 5, 1996, page 63. For numerous reasons, though, the Paris March is not a tactic that can be successfully used to exploit index funds. First, index fund managers invest in the market *throughout* the day, so they can buy at a variety of prices other than the allegedly higher prices that appear just before the closing bell. Even after the market closes, they can still place trades in "crossing networks" which are markets that accommodate large high volume traders around the clock. Second, while it is true that at times there is a slight "bounce" toward the ask price of a stock just before the closing bell, studies have not found a way for stock traders to actually profit from this at the expense of index funds. Any stock listed in a financial market is quoted at a bid price and an ask price. The difference between these two prices is known as the "spread." The quoted spread for any given stock can be thought of as a "sandwich." The top layer of the sandwich is the stock's ask price, the bottom layer is its bid price and the market price at which the stock trades on average is the layer in the middle between these two prices. The continuous stream of bid and ask prices quoted by a financial market for any given stock "bounces around" within its sandwich of ask, average market and bid prices. But contrary to what most investors think, there is no actual change in the average market price of a stock when these bounces occur. A change in price occurs only when the *entire sandwich* "moves" up or down. Thus, the bounces in the price of a stock toward its ask side just before the market closes do not represent opportunities to "trap" index funds into paying a higher price for the stock. Third, if the Paris March actually was a rewarding tactic, index funds could *also* play the same game. That is, their managers could buy stocks at 3:45 p.m. (or 1 p.m. or at any other time) at lower prices and profitably unload them just before the closing bell at higher prices just like the pros attempting to exploit them.
[15] *Bogle on Mutual Funds* by John C. Bogle (Burr Ridge, Illinois: Irwin Professional Publishing, 1993), page 204.

[16] Only visible trading costs - brokerage commissions - are reflected in the published performance of a mutual fund. Specifically, they are deducted from the NAV of a fund share.

[17] The effect of a commission load is not included either in a mutual fund's annual operating expenses or in the net asset value of a share in the fund. Thus, published mutual fund returns do not reflect the impact of commission loads.

[18] Whenever an investor buys an actively-managed mutual fund from a salesperson such as a stockbroker, insurance salesperson or commissioned financial planner, it *always* has a commission load in it somewhere. In addition, whatever the type of load carried by a mutual fund, the salesperson still receives the same commission (sometimes more with a back load) at the same time (immediately after the sale). See page 196, Chapter Note 21 for an explanation of why investors end up paying the same for a front load and a back load commission.

[19] "Yacktman Investors Still Pay Commissions" by Ellen E. Schultz, *The Wall Street Journal*, October 14, 1996, page C21.

[20] "Calculating Costs" by Gregory N. Hight, *Barron's*, October 11, 1993, page 44.

[21] Some investors want to avoid paying a class A front load commission when they purchase mutual fund shares. So they buy shares carrying a class B back load thinking that by holding them long enough, they won't have to pay a commission when they cash out. In fact, an investor pays virtually the *same* whether he buys a mutual fund with a front load or a back load. With the introduction of back load funds, mutual fund companies have simply *replaced* front loads with a combination of back loads and *increased* 12b-1 fees. (One result of this is that, all other things being equal, the published performances of class B shareholders are usually lower than for class A shareholders in the same fund because class B shares typically have higher annual 12b-1 fees than A shares.) Illustrations by mutual fund companies usually show a back load being reduced one percentage point for each year that an investor continues to hold a mutual fund. What they don't show is that this reduction is usually negated by the imposition of an annual 1% 12b-1 fee. This is apparent from an example where an investor has invested in a mutual fund with a 6% back load. If he decides to cash out after just one year, he will be charged a 5% back load (otherwise known as a "surrender charge") plus a 1% 12b-1 fee. If he decides to remain invested in the fund for six years and then cashes out, the back load would zero out but he would have still paid a 6% load (six years of an annual 1% 12b-1 fee). If the investor holds the mutual fund for longer than six years, he *continues* to incur an annual 1% 12b-1 fee. Thus, investors shouldn't be fooled into thinking that they are getting something for nothing when they buy a back load fund. In fact, the back load/12b-1 fee usually has a slightly *worse* impact on accumulating wealth than a front load/12b-1 fee. Although it would seem that a back load's effect on performance would be slightly less than that of a front load because of the additional negative compounding period of the front load, it usually isn't because a back load often comes with a 12b-1 fee that is larger than the one

accompanying a front load. Thus, the combined impact of the larger 12b-1 fee back load and its shorter negative compounding effect damages investment performance to a greater extent over the long run than the combined impact of the smaller 12b-1 fee front load and its longer negative compounding effect.

[22] Published mutual fund returns almost never reflect the impact of commission loads. Even when they rarely do take loads into account, they don't show the increasingly negative compounding effect caused by lost money.

[23] "Calculating Costs" by Gregory N. Hight, *Barron's*, October 11, 1993, page 44.

[24] Dollar-cost averaging is a method of buying individual stocks or bonds or mutual funds at regular intervals with a fixed amount of money. This produces an average *cost* per share that is lower than the average *price* at which the purchases were made. Thus, investors will buy fewer shares when their prices are high and more shares when their prices are low. However, dollar-cost averaging doesn't ensure that investors can avoid a loss or make a profit.

[25] According to Lipper Analytical Services, Inc., as of September 1996. In comparison, the annual expenses of the average S&P 500 index fund were .45%.

[26] "Trust Investment Law in the Third Restatement" by Edward C. Halbach, Jr., 27 *Real Property, Probate and Trust Journal*, Fall 1992, pages 432-433. Italics added.

THIRTEEN

INDEX FUNDS MINIMIZE TAXES

If you can eliminate the government as a 39.6% partner, then you will be much better off.
- Warren E. Buffett (1930-   )
  Chairman, Berkshire Hathaway and noted multibillionaire investor

Overview

Index funds generate minimal taxes. By maintaining low portfolio turnover, they minimize realized capital gains which keeps capital gains taxes low. Thus, the best way for a taxable-basis investor to minimize taxes and thus more efficiently compound investment wealth is to assemble a portfolio of index funds and keep it for life.

Managers Of Actively-Managed Mutual Funds Manage Money As If "Taxes Don't Matter"

Managers of actively-managed mutual funds usually give little thought to the excessive amount of taxation generated by their stock picking and market timing and its adverse effect on fund performance. Robert D. Arnott, a strong proponent of tax-sensitive investing, observes:[1] "Most people managing taxable money manage it as if taxes don't matter. They ignore the tax consequences of active trading. I think it's shocking."

The belief that "taxes don't matter" when managing an active mutual fund is found in the reasoning of an executive at a mutual fund company:[2] "To force portfolio managers to think about the tax consequences of their actions would shackle their investment styles." What this really means is that active fund managers don't worry about these consequences because the capital gains taxes generated by their "actions" to beat the market are not reflected in mutual fund performance ratings.[3] Since there is little incentive for such managers to minimize these actions, it is no wonder they manage money as if taxes don't matter.

Portfolio turnover usually creates an immediate hurdle that must be overcome with smart stock picking and/or astute market timing. For example, after an active fund manager has sold an appreciated stock, he must achieve a return on the new stock that is greater than the sum of the return on the old stock *plus any capital gains taxes paid and dividends lost* as a result of its sale.

SIMON SAYS: *The Difference Between "Good" And "Bad" Portfolio Turnover*

From the standpoint of *taxation*, high portfolio turnover is not necessarily always bad. (In terms of *costs*, though, high turnover is always bad.[4]) It must be considered within the context of a mutual fund's investment strategy. For example, an active stock mutual fund manager who generates high portfolio turnover may still manage to keep capital gains taxes to a minimum. How? By holding winners and selling off only losing stocks, he can offset future capital gains. So while his turnover may be high, he can still minimize capital gains taxes. It should be noted, however, that hanging onto winners and selling losers is, by definition, a *temporary* game for an active fund manager. Eventually all that will be left are winners that must be taxed when sold.

On the other hand, an active fund manager with the same or an even lower portfolio turnover rate who sells off only winners (and no losers to offset the gains) can generate a greater amount of capital gains taxes.

Since managers of active mutual funds typically manage money as if taxes don't matter, it is difficult to separate out the relatively few active fund managers who manage their funds as if taxes do matter. Investors would be wise to avoid this guesswork and invest in a portfolio of index funds. This guarantees that they will *always* invest with managers who manage their funds as if taxes *do* matter.

Because most active mutual fund managers manage their funds as if taxes don't matter, they ignore the significance of this hurdle. Robert H. Jeffrey, another champion of tax-sensitive investing, notes:[5] "To replace a highly appreciated stock without considering how long it will take the new stock to 'make back' the tax expense of the trade, which can be as much as 25 percent to 40 percent, is being irresponsible."

Compounding this problem is that many investors in actively-managed mutual funds are unaware about the excessive amount of taxation generated by these funds. As a result, little pressure is brought on active fund managers to reduce their tax-generating stock picking activities. But at least investors have an excuse - they either haven't been told about the nature of the tax problem or just don't understand it. Active money managers are well aware of the problem but either will not or cannot do anything about it.

The Value Of Unrealized Capital Gains

"Unrealized" capital gains are valuable because investors do not have to pay taxes on them.[6] They are that portion of the appreciated value of a mutual fund share that aren't distributed to an investor, but instead remain embedded or "locked up" in the net asset value of the share. Unrealized capital gains are simply "paper profits" - profits that haven't yet been realized for tax purposes.

By minimizing portfolio turnover, an index fund manager maximizes unrealized capital gains which thereby defers (or even completely avoids) the payment of taxes and enhances the long term compounding growth of wealth.[7] More precisely, an index fund manager must minimize the fund's "capital gains realization rate."[8] This is the portion of the total unrealized capital gains that the fund begins with each year that is realized by the end of the year.

In contrast, "realized" capital gains must be distributed to investors who are then required to pay taxes on them. (The negative compounding effect of the money that is used to pay for these taxes further slows down the accumulation of wealth in a mutual fund.[9]) This happens, for example, when stocks in an actively-managed mutual fund increase in value and are sold for a profit by the fund's manager. When the sale takes place, what were previously unrealized paper profits (unrealized capital gains) that had remained untaxed become realized actual profits (realized capital gains) that are currently taxed.[10]

The value of the strategy followed by index funds in maximizing unrealized capital gains can be seen in the following example. Suppose three mutual funds - "Index Fund," "Less Active Fund" and "More Active Fund" - each generate a pre-tax return of 10% (3% from dividends and 7% from capital appreciation). Index Fund realizes no capital gains, Less Active Fund realizes and distributes 50% of its capital gains and More Active Fund realizes and distributes 100% of its capital gains. After-tax returns are computed for an investor who pays a 36% tax rate on dividends and 28% on capital gains.

The results? Index Fund achieves an after-tax return of 8.92%, Less Active Fund earns a 7.94% return and More Active Fund gets a 6.96% return. Thus, Index Fund beats Less Active Fund by one percentage point and More Active Fund by two percentage points even though all three mutual funds earned a 10% pre-tax return.

Another way of looking at this is to calculate the pre-tax returns needed by Less Active Fund and More Active Fund in order to offer the same after-tax return as Index Fund - 8.92%. This calculation shows that Less Active Fund must generate a pre-tax return of 11.42% and More Active Fund needs a pre-tax return of 13.06% to match Index Fund's after-tax return. Thus, Less Active Fund must add two and a half percentage points and More Active Fund over four percentage points of performance just to keep up with Index Fund. But to be in a position to achieve the goal of earning higher returns, both mutual funds would have to invest in riskier investments than those held by Index Fund.

The Benefits Of Deferring Capital Gains Taxes

Any investor, whether invested in mutual funds or in individual stocks or bonds, can obtain two benefits from deferring capital gains taxes.[11] (A taxable-basis investor can't do much about controlling taxes on dividends and interest.) The first benefit is that an investor has more money available to compound wealth.[12] The second benefit, often overlooked, is that the liability for deferred capital gains taxes does not compound against an investor. While these benefits are available to both indexers and active investors, indexers are in a better position to actually obtain them. This is true for two reasons.

First, an indexer can defer capital gains taxes at the *personal* level as long as he wants (even to death[13]) by not selling appreciating mutual fund shares.[14] This maximizes the compounding of wealth. Although an active investor can also defer capital gains taxes, he is unlikely to do so because he believes that he can beat the market. His attempts to do this generate high portfolio turnover which maximizes capital gains and thus capital gains taxes. On average, this reduces an active investor's opportunities to maximally compound wealth.

Second, an indexer can defer capital gains taxes at the *mutual fund* level. Although it is true that he must delegate to index fund managers his option to defer or avoid the payment of capital gains taxes, an indexer does so with the knowledge that they manage money as if taxes do matter. Index fund managers *rarely* give away to Uncle Sam an indexer's option to defer or avoid taxes. But as we know, an active investor invests with fund managers who typically manage money as if taxes don't matter. They *often* give away to Uncle Sam the option to defer or avoid taxes delegated to them by an active investor.

Taxes Significantly Affect The Performance Of Active Mutual Funds

A landmark study released in 1993 details the significant impact that taxes have on the performance of actively-managed mutual funds.[15] This study, conducted by two scholars at Stanford University, examined the difference between the median pre-tax and after-tax performance of 62 actively-managed stock mutual funds for the 30-year period from 1963 through 1992.[16]

"Pre-tax" performance reflects a *fantasy world*. It assumes that any distributions which a mutual fund investor would actually receive and on which he would have to pay tax in the real world are, instead, reinvested 100% to buy more shares of the fund. Thus, pre-tax performance includes the effect of reinvesting *all* distributions free of tax.

"After-tax" performance reflects the *real world*. It assumes that only money left over after payment of taxes on taxable distributions is reinvested in more mutual fund shares. Thus, after-tax performance includes the effect of reinvesting only *after-tax* distributions.

The study also measured "liquidation value." This is the net amount that an investor would receive after deducting any taxes due on previously unrealized capital gains and then selling all his mutual fund shares. Finally, the study calculated after-tax returns and liquidation values by determining the necessary payment of taxes in three different tax brackets.[17]

The Stanford study made two principal findings. First, the high-tax bracket active investor achieved after-tax accumulated wealth per dollar invested equal to *less than half* (45% or $9.87 of $21.89) of the pre-tax performance. An active investor in a medium-tax bracket wound up with 59% ($12.52 of $21.89) and a low-tax bracket active investor accumulated 75% ($16.45 of $21.89) of pre-tax performance. Second, in terms of liquidation values, the high-tax bracket active investor accumulated only 42% ($9.17 of $21.89) of pre-tax performance after cashing out. The medium-tax bracket investor saw his $1 grow to $12.06 (55% of $21.89) and the low-tax bracket investor saw his $1 accumulate to a value of $15.95 (73% of $21.89) after cashing out.

In summary, the high-tax bracket active investor saw 55% of his accumulated wealth wiped out by taxes on an after-tax basis and 58% of it eliminated by taxes on a liquidation value basis. But even the medium-tax bracket investor (facing ordinary income tax rates ranging from 25% to 43% over this 30-year period) lost 41% of his wealth on an after-tax basis and 45% of it was lost to taxes on a liquidation value basis. These truly staggering numbers and others are shown in Illustration 14, below.

Illustration 14

Stanford University Study
(62 Mutual Funds Studied Over The 30-Year Period Of 1963-1992)

PRE-TAX VALUE
(investing tax-deferred money in a 401k or an IRA,
so 100% of distributions are reinvested)

$1.00 invested in 1963 grew into
this amount by 1992

S&P 500 Index	$22.13
Median Mutual Fund (31 funds grew in value more than this and 31 funds grew less)	$21.89

AFTER-TAX VALUE
(reinvesting only money that's left after paying taxes on distributions)

High-Tax Bracket (45% of the median fund's value of $21.89)	$9.87
Medium-Tax Bracket (59% of the median fund's value of $21.89)	$12.52
Low-Tax Bracket (75% of the median fund's value of $21.89)	$16.45

LIQUIDATION VALUE
(selling out completely and paying all taxes)

High-Tax Bracket (42% of the median fund's value of $21.89)	$9.17
Medium-Tax Bracket (55% of the median fund's value of $21.89)	$12.06
Low-Tax Bracket (73% of the median fund's value of $21.89)	$15.95

Source: "Ranking Mutual Funds on an After-Tax Basis" by John B. Shoven and Joel M. Dickson, Stanford University Center for Economic Policy Research Discussion Paper No. 344, April 1993.

SIMON SAYS: *Real Life Confirmation That The Market Is A Zero Sum Game*

We saw in Chapter Three that a rare certainty in the investment world is that the stock market (as well as all other financial markets) is a zero sum game. In this kind of game, all investors who attempt to beat the market will, in the aggregate, achieve the market return. One of the expectations that arises from this is that the average actively-managed mutual fund portfolio will, like the index fund portfolio, achieve about the same pre-tax return - the market return.

The Stanford study of actual market behavior confirms this expectation. $1 invested in the S&P 500 in 1963 grew into $22.13 on a pre-tax basis by 1992,[18] while the median mutual fund of the 62 funds studied accumulated $21.89 on a pre-tax basis over this 30-year period.[19] The fact that these two performances wound up being *nearly identical* at the end of a long investment time period validates not only the theory, but also the reality, that the stock market is a zero sum game.

The Stanford study shows how investors can be misled when they rely on pre-tax returns as an accurate gauge of investment performance. Yet these returns are the only kind featured in mutual fund advertisements and prospectuses and published mutual fund ratings.[20] They fail to capture the significant impact that taxes can have on the investment performances of many actively-managed mutual funds. Another problem with pre-tax returns is that they fail to convey how superior index funds are on an after-tax basis.

SIMON SAYS: *Just Another Thirty Years Of Market Performance*

The 30-year period (1963-1992) covered by the Stanford study typifies the past long term behavior of the market. It included such events as the long and deep bear market of 1973-1974 and the short and relatively shallow bear market following the Crash of 1987. Yet this period also encompassed major bull markets such as the one in the 1980s. Most importantly, however, the 1963-1992 stock market was up, on average, about two out of every three years with the up years being much more beneficial than the down years were harmful. This period matches the long term behavior of the market.

The Tax Efficiency Of Index Mutual Funds

The minimization of capital gains taxes by an index fund results in a comparatively small difference between its pre-tax and after-tax performance. This makes an index fund a tax "efficient" investment. In contrast, the maximization of capital gains taxes by the typical actively-managed mutual fund creates a relatively large difference between its pre-tax and after-tax performance. This makes it a tax "inefficient" investment.

> **SIMON SAYS:** *Measuring The Tax Efficiency Of A Mutual Fund*
>
> The "ratio of net investment income to average net assets" that appears in the front of all mutual fund prospectuses is an important indicator of a fund's tax efficiency. This ratio will usually be lower for index funds than for actively-managed funds. Furthermore, a small company stock index fund will have a lower ratio than an S&P 500 index fund that holds large company stocks. The reason why is that the large company stocks of the S&P 500 generate more dividends and thus a greater amount of taxes in comparison to small company stocks. This makes a small company stock index fund even more tax efficient than an already tax efficient S&P 500 index fund.

A 1993 study conducted by Robert H. Jeffrey and Robert D. Arnott compared the pre-tax and after-tax performance of all 72 of the Morningstar-classified large "growth" and "growth and income" mutual funds in existence over the 10-year period from 1982 through 1991.[21] This group of mutual funds included the Vanguard Index 500, an index fund that tracks the performance of the S&P 500. Illustration 15 on page 207 summarizes the results of the study.

On a *pre*-tax basis, the index fund outperformed 79% (56 of 71) of the actively-managed mutual funds. This alone demonstrates, over a relatively short period of time, the superiority of an index fund following a simple investment strategy when it is matched against 71 active funds employing highly paid stock pickers and market timers.

This study also shows the superiority of an index fund when compared to active funds on an *after*-tax basis. On an "after capital gains taxes" basis, the index fund beat 86% (61 of 71) of the active funds. It also outperformed 87% (62 of 71) of the active funds on an "after capital gains and dividend taxes" basis.

Even when "all taxes including deferred taxes" were paid and after *cashing out* every mutual fund share, the index fund still beat 82% (58 of 71) of the active funds.[22] This finding may be surprising to many investors. After all, it is expected that an indexer would incur heavy taxation after cashing out all his shares since an index fund maximally defers capital gains. Once this occurs, the tax efficient edge of an index fund would seem to largely disappear. But according to the Jeffrey-Arnott study, this may not necessarily be true. The reason why is that by maximally deferring taxes, an index fund maximizes long term compounding of wealth. This gives it the extra "cushion" needed to achieve better after-tax accumulation of wealth (even after cashing out completely) than most active funds.

Despite the high turnover that usually leads to high capital gains taxes, on an "after capital gains and dividend taxes" basis, 13% (9 of 71) of the active funds did generate greater returns than the index fund. However, seven of these nine active funds barely statistically beat the index fund and when commission loads were taken into account, none of the seven outperformed the index fund. So the bottom line is that *only 3%* (2 of 71) of the active funds outperformed the index fund over this ten-year period on an after-tax and after-commission load basis.

SIMON SAYS: *The Correlation Between Portfolio Turnover And After-Tax Investment Performance*

The Jeffrey-Arnott study was the first to reveal that the tax impact produced by portfolio turnover is not proportionate to the amount of turnover. That is, increasing turnover from 0% to 25% generates a great deal more tax damage than increasing it from 25% to 100%. "At just 5% turnover, about 40% of the maximum capital gains at 100% turnover has already been incurred. The impact increases to 65% of the maximum at 10% turnover, and to 95% at 25% turnover."[23] Thus, the adverse tax impact of turnover is most severe at its lower levels. Thereafter, the impact of turnover declines rapidly to a point - about 25% - "where the tax damage is virtually complete."

The portfolio turnover of most actively-managed mutual funds falls within a range of 25% to 100% or more. Most index funds have turnover rates below 25% and there are many below 10%. This is why index funds post superior long term after-tax investment performance and why they are so tax-efficient in comparison to active funds.

Illustration 15

Jeffrey-Arnott Study
(Numbers And Percentages Of 71 Large Actively-Managed Mutual Funds Beaten By The Vanguard Index 500 Index Fund - 1982-1991)

Total Return	Number of 71 Mutual Funds Beaten	Percentage of 71 Mutual Funds Beaten
Pre-Tax	56	79
After Capital Gains Taxes	61	86
After Capital Gains and Dividend Taxes	62	87
After all Taxes Including Deferred Taxes	58	82
After all Taxes, Commission Loads and Fees	69	97

Source: "Is Your Alpha Big Enough to Cover its Taxes?" by Robert H. Jeffrey and Robert D. Arnott, *The Journal of Portfolio Management*, Spring 1993.

SIMON SAYS: *Capital Gains Taxes Have To Be Paid "In The End" Anyway - Or Do They?*

Even the most ardent "I can beat the market" advocates cannot argue with the fact that index funds generate lower taxes than active funds. However, they point out that "in the end" capital gains taxes must be paid anyway when an indexer sells his mutual fund shares and uses the money for retirement or other purposes.[24] So they claim that there is no advantage to indexing tax-wise since their belief is that there is little difference between paying capital gains taxes now or in the future.

But these advocates are wrong - there is a big difference. First, the deferral of any expense is advantageous (assuming that there are no penalties such as interest charges) because it leaves more money to currently save and compound or spend. In effect, deferring the payment of capital gains taxes is a zero-interest free loan from Uncle Sam. Second, these advocates ignore the fact that a critical assumption underlying the statement that "in the end capital gains taxes will have to be paid anyway" is almost never true.[25] This assumption is that the *entire* portfolio will have to be liquidated *at once*. What is a much more likely scenario is that the portfolio will be liquidated over a long period of time to meet the spending requirements of its owner.

Another more realistic scenario than the immediate and total liquidation of a portfolio is that an investor can make smaller liquidations and supplement them with after-tax income from the portfolio. In either scenario, by maximizing unrealized capital gains, a portfolio of index funds defers capital gains taxes and compounds wealth more efficiently than an active portfolio.

The Jeffrey-Arnott study came to two conclusions. First, an index fund is very difficult to beat on an after-tax basis.[26] To really appreciate this, however, it is necessary to compare an index fund and an *appropriate* actively-managed fund on the basis of after-tax returns. This ensures an apples to apples comparison when weighing performances. Second, almost without exception, the performances of the 71 active mutual funds gave no indication that their high turnover efforts to beat the market added enough return to outweigh the capital gains taxes generated by the turnover.

The study only examined an investment period of ten years. But had it covered a longer period, it is expected that the active funds would have continued to generate more taxes in comparison to the index fund. Since this would leave more net wealth for an indexer (all other things being equal), the compounding growth of the additional wealth would create an increasingly larger gap in favor of the indexer in comparison to an active investor. So generally, with the passage of time an index fund portfolio becomes more tax efficient while an active fund portfolio becomes more tax inefficient.

The Jeffrey-Arnott study shows that the chances of being a winner at the end of 1991 depended entirely on an investor's ability to correctly pick, *a decade earlier* at the beginning of 1982, the two active mutual funds (out of a lineup of 71) that beat the index fund. This raises an obvious question. Can an investor (or someone that he hires) skillfully invest in a mutual fund now to ensure himself a winning performance over some future period of time? (Peter L. Bernstein discussed this issue in connection with Fidelity Magellan investors in Chapter Six.) All evidence, including this study, indicates that the odds in succeeding at this are essentially nil. However, the odds of being a winner with an indexing investment strategy are excellent.

SIMON SAYS: *First The Good News And Then The Bad News*

The misleading difference between the pre-tax and after-tax investment performances of actively-managed mutual funds is highlighted in a study that compares the impact of taxes on the performances of Fidelity's Magellan Fund and the S&P 500 from mid-1985 to mid-1995.[27] Magellan achieved a very impressive average annual compound return of 18.3% which put it in the top 3% of mutual funds for that decade. In the same period, the S&P 500 had a return of 14.7%. However, after adjusting for Magellan's 3% front load commission and taxes, its performance fell to 12.7%. In comparison, the S&P 500 pre-tax return of 14.7% was reduced to an after-tax return of 11.5%.

The good news put out by the marketing department at Fidelity (other mutual funds also do the same thing) and picked up by the investment media goes something like this: "Fidelity Magellan outperformed 97% of the other mutual funds over the decade ending in mid-1995. Magellan's net 1.2 percentage point edge over an index fund tracking the S&P 500 compounded over this ten-year period represents a healthy amount of additional wealth for a Magellan investor."

But Fidelity fails to tell investors the bad news. The winner that will be King of the Hill at the end of the next ten years must be correctly identified today. Investors who are invested in index funds don't have to make impossibly crazy predictions about which mutual funds will be future winners in order to achieve excellent investment performance.[28]

Tax-Managed Index Mutual Funds

Some stock index funds are specifically designed to minimize the impact of taxes on investment performance.[29] Much of the practical reasoning that supports the notion of tax-managed index funds came from the Jeffrey-Arnott study discussed earlier and another study conducted at Stanford University.[30] The latter study sought to "consider the feasibility of creating and implementing a tax-conscious 'index' fund which eliminates all realized capital gains distributions for long horizons."

To achieve this goal, the authors of the Stanford study assembled a tax-managed index fund designed to replicate the S&P 500 index for the 15-year plus period from August 1976 through December 1991. The results were impressive. By eliminating all realizations of capital gains, the tax-managed index fund not only matched the pre-tax return of Vanguard's S&P 500 index fund but also outperformed its annual after-tax return by about one percentage point on an annual basis.

A subsequent study that was published in mid-1997 shows how investing in a tax-managed index mutual fund can significantly increase the returns that are otherwise eaten up by the taxes and fees typical of actively-managed funds. It examined the performance of an S&P 500 portfolio for the 25-year period of 1971-1995.[31]

The study made these principal findings: (1) $100 invested in the portfolio at the start of this period grew into $1,721 by the end of it ("the base portfolio"). This assumed that the portfolio had no turnover, taxes or fees. (2) Introducing turnover of 80%, a capital gains tax rate of 28%, a dividends tax rate of 36% and fees of 1.00% brought the ending value of the portfolio down to $706 from $1,721. This was only 41% of the value of the base portfolio.[32] (3) A non tax-managed index fund with reduced turnover of 6%, the preceding tax rates and reduced fees of .30% increased the ending value of the portfolio to $1,101, or 64% of the value of the base portfolio. (4) A tax-managed index fund that lowered its turnover to 1% but maintained the same tax rates and fees increased the ending value of the portfolio even more to $1,247, or 73% of the value of the base portfolio. Obviously, there is a big difference between the wealth accumulated in the tax-managed index fund ($1,247) and the typical active fund ($706) examined by the study.

This study also showed that the only way that an active fund manager could have outperformed the tax-managed index fund over this period was for him to have generated an average annual pre-tax and pre-fee excess return of 2.63%. This figure assumes that the portfolio was fully cashed out at the end of the 25-year period. Had there been no liquidation, the excess return required of the active fund manager would have risen to 4.24%. The fact that we can count the number of mutual fund managers *on one hand* over the last 40 years who are even in the ballpark in matching such performances over such periods of time plus the fact that there is no way to find these wonders before they become famous proves the essential impossibility of beating the market on an after-tax (and after-cost) basis.

Thus, tax-managed index funds are yet another way for an indexer to increase investment performance without needing to beat the market. As the author of the study observes:[33] "It's not brains or brawn that matter in taxable investing; it's efficiency. *Taxable investing is a loser's game. Those who lose the least - to taxes and fees - stand to win the most when the game's all over.*" The mutual funds that lose the least to taxes and fees are index funds, not active funds.

Up to now in Section II, we have seen the many tangible advantages of index funds that allow their investors to achieve better net investment performance than investors in active funds. The next chapter shows why index funds are emotionally easier on investors than active funds. This may be one of their most important advantages.

Chapter Notes

[1] "Be A Tax-Savvy Investor" by Susan E. Kuhn, *Fortune*, March 18, 1996, pages 88-91.
[2] "Magellan and Taxes," a commentary by John A. Rekenthaler in *Morningstar Mutual Funds*, Volume 24, Issue 1, December 23, 1994. Unfortunately, active investors cannot occupy the same Olympian heights as active fund managers. Instead, they must remain earthbound and pay needless taxes because such managers don't think about the damage that they do to the investment performance of the mutual funds that they manage.
[3] This is because capital gains taxes are not reflected in *either* a mutual fund's annual operating expenses or in the NAV of a mutual fund share.
[4] *See* page 194, Chapter Note 10 for more about how the costs associated with portfolio turnover can adversely affect the performance of tax-deferred retirement plans and annuities.
[5] *The Portable MBA In Investment* edited by Peter L. Bernstein (New York: John Wiley & Sons, Inc., 1995), page 353.
[6] Other than this exception, an investor must pay taxes on all mutual fund distributions such as realized capital gains (both long term and short term), dividends and interest (from bond mutual funds or money market funds). This is true whether he takes distributions in cash or reinvests them in more mutual fund shares. Any distributions that an investor reinvests to obtain more mutual fund shares are added to his cost basis. These distributions include the taxes that he has already paid "along the way" on capital gains, dividends and interest. Thus, whenever an investor decides to cash out mutual fund shares, their cost basis includes both the amount of any distributions and the taxes paid on them. Even transfers or exchanges between mutual funds can generate capital gains taxes.
[7] *The Portable MBA In Investment* edited by Peter L. Bernstein (New York: John Wiley & Sons, Inc., 1995), page 359.
[8] "The Attraction of Tax-Managed Index Funds" by James P. Garland, *The Journal of Investing*, Spring 1997, pages 13-20, endnote 1.
[9] "Capital gains taxes not only result in an immediate reduction of wealth, but also create opportunity costs as assets paid to the government [in the form of taxes] can no longer earn [an investment return]. Over time, the cumulative loss [in wealth] can be significant." "Tax-Aware Equity Investing" by Roberto Apelfeld, Gordon B. Fowler, Jr. and James P. Gordon, Jr., *The Journal of Portfolio Management*, Winter 1996, pages 18-28. *See* pages 187-189 for a discussion of the negative compounding effect of "lost money" on accumulating wealth in a mutual fund.
[10] The total investment return from the share of a stock mutual fund upon which an investor must pay taxes is composed of (1) net investment income and (2) realized capital gains. "Net investment income" is the amount of income left over after annual operating expenses (mutual fund management fees, 12b-1 fees and other

fees) and trading costs (brokerage commissions, bid-ask spread costs, market impact costs and all other non-tax costs of portfolio turnover) have been removed from the mutual fund's gross investment income. Net investment income is taxed to a shareholder as "dividends." "Realized capital gains" are profits distributed to an investor that are derived from sales of stocks by a mutual fund. Realized capital gains can either be "long term" which are taxed as "long term capital gains" or "short term" which are taxed as "dividends." Breaking down total investment return this way is important because the form of the money distributed to an investor - long term capital gains or dividends - is taxed at different rates. The federal tax code provides that long term capital gains (capital gains distributions held 18 months or longer) are taxed at the lower, more favorable long term capital gains tax rate (currently a maximum of 20%). But dividends and short term capital gains (realized capital gains distributions from mutual funds held less than 18 months) are taxed at the higher, less favorable ordinary income tax rate (currently a maximum of 39.6%). Every mutual fund must distribute substantially all its net investment income and realized capital gains to its investors every year or it will lose its favorable tax status.

[11] If an investor holds mutual fund investments in an annuity, an IRA, a 401(k) or any other tax-deferred vehicle, he will owe no taxes on capital gains, dividends or interest under any of these circumstances. However, investments held within any of these tax-deferred vehicles do not get a "stepped-up" basis when the investor dies, so the heirs must pay *estate* taxes on any gains generated by them. (Investors should consult their estate planning advisors for expert advice in this area.)

[12] Taxes paid on capital gains, dividends and interest can be significant and immediately reduce wealth. But as noted in the previous chapter, there is also the negative compounding effect of "lost money" on accumulating wealth. Thus, the payment of taxes alone deceives investors because it understates the *total* tax impact on accumulating wealth.

[13] An investor may permanently defer the liability of capital gains taxes by not selling his appreciating mutual fund shares during his lifetime. However, while an investor's estate will not owe any capital gains taxes to the government in this situation, it may still be liable for estate taxes. *See* page 213, Chapter Note 11.

[14] The goal of maximizing the deferral of capital gains taxes can conflict at times with an investor's asset allocation policy which, under certain circumstances, may require him to sell off some of his portfolio to rebalance it back to its original asset allocation. In this situation, the ideal rebalancing strategy for an investor who regularly saves and invests money (or who has a portfolio that generates excess income that can be reinvested) is to buy more shares in the asset classes that have decreased in value rather than sell those that have increased in value. This avoids the problem of incurring taxable capital gains. Unfortunately, most investors are not in this ideal situation. The more common situation is either one in which investors have no excess savings or reinvestable income or one in which they (1) first use

excess savings and/or reinvestable income to purchase more of those asset classes that have decreased in value and, to the extent that this falls short in rebalancing the portfolio back to its original asset allocation, (2) then sell off any asset classes that have increased in value (possibly incurring net taxable capital gains).

[15] "Ranking Mutual Funds on an After-Tax Basis" by John B. Shoven and Joel M. Dickson, Stanford University Center for Economic Policy Research Discussion Paper No. 344, April 1993.

[16] One of the assumptions of the Stanford study was that all the mutual funds remained fully invested in the market - none engaged in any market timing. So all capital gains taxes generated were *entirely* due to the stock picking attempts of active mutual fund managers to beat the market.

[17] During the 30-year period (1963-1992) covered by the study, ordinary income marginal tax rates for high-tax bracket investors ranged from 31% to 64% and capital gains marginal tax rates ranged from 19.6% to 28%. For medium-tax bracket investors, ordinary income tax rates ranged from 25% to 43% and capital gains tax rates ranged from 12.5% to 28%. Low-tax bracket investors encountered ordinary income tax rates from 15% to 20% and capital gains tax rates ranged from 6% to 15%.

[18] The capacity of $1 to grow into a value of nearly $22 over a 30-year period demonstrates the awesome power of the stock market to create wealth for long term investors. However, taxable investors could not have fully benefited from this growth in wealth.

[19] "Median" means that 31 of the 62 funds had a value greater than $21.89 in 1992 and 31 funds grew to a value in 1992 that was smaller than $21.89.

[20] Generally, the investment media doesn't accurately inform taxable-basis investors about the bite of taxes. There are two notable exceptions to this. Since 1991, *Fortune* has published an annual list of the best-performing mutual funds after fees, expenses and taxes are subtracted from their gross returns. In addition, *Morningstar Mutual Funds* began reporting tax-adjusted mutual fund returns in 1993. "Morningstar reduces the historical pretax returns by the taxes on the fund's income and capital gains dividends (using assumed rates), and then reports the percentage of the after-tax to the pre-tax return. In addition, the 'potential capital gains tax exposure' is calculated, which is basically the deferred capital gains taxes on the unrealized gains expressed as a percentage of the total assets." *See The Portable MBA In Investment* edited by Peter L. Bernstein (New York: John Wiley & Sons, Inc., 1995), page 372. But even these two sources of information don't take into account the negative compounding effect which creates a *largely ignored but growing category* of lost wealth caused by the payment of taxes.

[21] "Is Your Alpha Big Enough to Cover Its Taxes?" by Robert H. Jeffrey and Robert D. Arnott, *The Journal of Portfolio Management*, Spring 1993, pages 15-25.

[22] This assumes that the holdings of the mutual funds were sold at the end of 1991 and all taxes were paid at that time. *The Portable MBA In Investment* edited by Peter L. Bernstein (New York: John Wiley & Sons, Inc., 1995), page 362.

[23] *Ibid.*, page 357. *See* "Is Your Alpha Big Enough to Cover Its Taxes?" by Robert H. Jeffrey and Robert D. Arnott, *The Journal of Portfolio Management*, Spring 1993, pages 15-25.

[24] This argument is made in "Is Your Alpha Big Enough to Cover Its Taxes?: Comment" by Roger Hertog and Mark R. Gordon, *The Journal of Portfolio Management*, Summer 1994, pages 93-95.

[25] *The Portable MBA In Investment* edited by Peter L. Bernstein (New York: John Wiley & Sons, Inc., 1995), pages 360-361. All investors interested in how mutual fund taxation affects investment performance should thank Robert D. Arnott and Robert H. Jeffrey for the clarity and understanding that they have brought to this important area of the investment process.

[26] See *Wealth Management* by Harold Evensky (Chicago, Illinois: Irwin Professional Publishing, 1997), pages 58 and 68.

[27] "When Less is More: How to Increase Aftertax Returns by Doing Less" by Rex Macey, *AAII Journal*, January 1996, pages 12-14.

[28] It is interesting to note that had the time period in question been extended beyond the decade ending in mid-1995, Magellan's advantage would have *vanished* because of its subsequent underperformance of the market. *See* page 69 for another example of how flimsy an outstanding track record can be when its starting date or ending date is changed just slightly.

[29] Vanguard offers three such tax-managed index funds and Charles Schwab offers three others.

[30] "A Stock Index Mutual Fund Without Net Capital Gains Realizations" by Joel M. Dickson and John B. Shoven, National Bureau of Economic Research Working Paper No. 4717, April 1994.

[31] "The Attraction of Tax-Managed Index Funds" by James P. Garland, *The Journal of Investing*, Spring 1997, pages 13-20. Most investors are pursuing an illusion when they attempt to improve gross investment performance. The better way to improve their performance is to reduce taxes (and costs) by investing in a tax-managed index fund.

[32] Where did the other 59% of the portfolio's value go? About 47 percentage points went to taxes and about 12 percentage points were claimed by fees.

[33] Some active investors seek to take advantage of the spread between the maximum capital gains tax rate (20%) and the maximum ordinary income tax rate (39.6%). One investment strategy that they pursue is to buy zero-dividend stocks so that all their investments returns will be in the form of capital gains which will be taxed at a lower rate. But the study shows this strategy to be both ineffective and risky. It is ineffective because its use by an active investor only increases the ending value of the base portfolio from 41% to 43%. It is risky because the zero-dividend stocks in the S&P 500 are not only a poorly diversified lot but they also have below average returns in comparison to the other stocks in the S&P 500 that do pay dividends.

FOURTEEN

INDEX FUNDS ARE EMOTIONALLY EASIER ON INVESTORS

The fault, dear Brutus, is not in our stars, but in ourselves.
- William Shakespeare (1564-1616)
  Julius Caesar

We have met the enemy and he is us.
- Walt Kelly (1913-1973)
  American cartoonist, *Pogo*

Overview

Investors who adopt active investment strategies often subject themselves to a great deal of stress and anxiety because of the uncertainty as to when (if ever) they will beat the market. But investors who adopt indexing investment strategies give up efforts to beat the market. This allows indexers to free themselves from the stress and anxiety that characterize active investment strategies.

The Market Is Not The Problem - We Are The Problem

Many of us are our own worst enemies when it comes to investing money. What gets us into trouble is that we don't understand how to manage our own emotional reactions to fluctuations in the market.[1] In fact, the way in which an investor emotionally reacts to extreme (although entirely normal) market fluctuations can have far more of an impact on his investment performance than the performance of the market itself. Thus, it is important to recognize that it is often our inner emotional reactions to the outer realities of the market that affect our ability to be good investors.

The failure to understand this emotional dimension to investing is what really harms investment performance and forces many investors to accumulate less money than they could have done otherwise. This is why no investment strategy can be sound unless it protects us from *ourselves*.

Active Investment Strategies Create Stress

If we assume that "losing" (or even the possibility of losing) creates stress, then stress is inherent in active investment strategies. Since active investors attempt to beat the market, it is virtually guaranteed that all of them will at some point experience great stress. This comes from the disappointment and frustration of picking losing stocks, mistiming markets and the consequent failure to amass sufficient wealth to meet financial goals.

Despite the fact that active investors often experience stress, they continue to use stock picking and market timing investment strategies. This behavior is caused by the belief that there are sure-fire formulas for beating the market. The belief is particularly strong if reality, which is that *no particular individual who we can identify today can be expected to beat the market*, is too threatening to investors. Roger C. Gibson describes this threat:[2] "Once an investor admits not only that he cannot successfully pick stocks and time markets, but also that no one else can either, then he seemingly has no ground under his feet."

To avoid this threat, many investors remain emotionally hooked on the messages of active money managers. These messages, consisting of a myriad of stock picking and market timing investment strategies, all boil down to the one reassurance needed by active investors: "We can help you beat the market."

We saw in Chapter Two that even investors who are fortunate enough to be invested in wildly successful mutual funds experience extreme stress at times. In fact, they can be especially prone to it since they may come to believe that double digit returns year in and year out are their birthright. For example, during the mid-1980s investors in Fidelity Magellan got outstanding market-beating returns. Yet when the Crash of October 1987 came along, enough of them panicked to shrink Magellan's asset base by 35%. These departing shareholders were not the only ones who experienced extreme stress. The investors who chose to remain invested in Magellan probably included a fair number who prayed that they weren't going to face an even bigger financial meltdown.

However, none of this should be any surprise to active investors. After all, stress and anxiety for active investors are inherent in any zero sum financial market such as the stock market. This market, characterized by stock picking investment strategies, requires losers in order to produce winners.

Indexing Strategies Are Low Stress And Create Greater Emotional Commitment To Long Term Investing

An indexing investment strategy is generally less stressful and emotionally easier on an investor than an active investment strategy. One of the reasons for this is that an indexer has given up attempts to beat the market. (This also frees him from the heavy commitment of time necessary to plan and prepare such attempts.) As a result, he is not mesmerized by the daily winning and losing transactions that occur in the market and instead can concentrate on the big picture of the investment process. Indeed, an indexer never has to lose in the zero sum game of the market because he is always guaranteed the market return. This helps him to avoid the emotional rollercoaster that an active investor must ride as he worries about losing (or the possibility of losing).

This is not to say that an indexer never experiences greed and fear in his investment life. But an investor who really understands why he invests in index funds is usually able to better manage these emotions. For example, an indexer is apt to be more emotionally detached than an active investor in making the decisions needed to manage and monitor his portfolio's asset allocation over time through changing market conditions. Since he bases these decisions on the cut and dried written guidelines of his portfolio's asset allocation policy, he can remove some of the emotional dimension when making them. (Despite this, indexers must always remain on guard against letting emotional reactions to normal fluctuations in the market control their investment decision-making.)

The benefit of relying on written policy guidelines to make asset allocation decisions is seen in the situation where an indexer's asset allocation policy calls for his portfolio to be invested, say, 70% in stocks.[3] The policy's guidelines state that should this allocation increase or decrease by ten percentage points or more then it must be rebalanced back to the 70% allocation. So if a soaring stock market increases the allocation to 80%, an indexer can with little emotion rebalance his portfolio back to its original allocation according to its policy guidelines.

An investor who implements his chosen asset allocation by investing, via index funds, in the stocks and/or bonds that comprise distinct asset classes can therefore more efficiently and effectively earn the expected return of his portfolio. This, and the fact that an indexer can rather mechanically manage and monitor his portfolio's asset allocation over time through changing market conditions, make it more likely that he will achieve his investment goals than an active investor.

An active investor generally finds it more difficult to manage and monitor his portfolio's asset allocation primarily because he is so emotionally attached to the idea that he can beat the market. To continue the previous example, an active investor is less likely than an indexer to rebalance his portfolio if his asset allocation policy calls for a 70% allocation of stocks and a soaring stock market increases it to 80%. The reason why is that he will often "let the winners run" because of his desire to outperform the market. This results in overexposure to stocks at market highs (and underexposure at market lows).

Overexposure such as this can lead to emotional meltdown for an active investor when a plunging market inevitably comes along and, because of an overallocation of stocks, takes a larger portion of the portfolio's value with it. Thus, an investor is generally in better shape emotionally if he uses index funds rather than active funds to manage and monitor his portfolio's asset allocation.

In summary, because indexers have given up attempts to beat the market and are more likely to be emotionally detached in making their asset allocation decisions, they should experience less stress and anxiety and therefore enjoy a more calm and civilized life than active investors. They can also spend less time managing their investments. This is why investors who place their money on the reliable tortoise of indexing investment strategies will usually be more emotionally committed to long term investing than those who bet on the unpredictable hare of active investment strategies.

———————————

This chapter has shown that an investor who gives up the attempt to beat the market and adopts an indexing investment strategy can save himself a lot of emotional problems. The last section of this book briefly sums up why investors should invest in index funds.

Chapter Notes

[1] But with the passage of time, the net effect of fluctuating gains and losses "smooths out" a portfolio's average annual percentage return.

[2] "Asset Allocation Short Course," a presentation by Roger C. Gibson for the College for Financial Planning, Denver, Colorado, 1990.

[3] Some proponents of "life cycle investing" suggest that young investors should be invested 100% in stocks. But institutional investors, which have far longer (actually infinite) investment time horizons than the relatively short life expectancies of individual investors, only invest about 60-65% of their money in stocks. The reason why is that they do not want to be maximally exposed to the risk of experiencing a prolonged down market. This is why investors of any age should think twice about investing a high percentage of their portfolios in stocks. It is important to understand that this statement is *not* made to advise investors to avoid investing in stocks. Instead, it is only offered to warn them that if they are heavily invested in stocks *and if* they have a tendency to emotionally react to sharp and/or prolonged fluctuations in the stock market, they can get themselves into real trouble.

SECTION III

JOINING THE INDEXING REVOLUTION

THEME OF THE SECTION:

*A SUMMARY OF WHY INVESTORS SHOULD INVEST IN
INDEX MUTUAL FUNDS*

FIFTEEN

WHY INVESTORS SHOULD INVEST IN INDEX FUNDS

You create a pool of assets that mimics the market. You don't try to pick stocks. You don't try to beat the market. You just harness the market's long term upward climb and the power of compounding returns. By doing so, you minimize portfolio management costs and taxes and thereby beat most stock pickers.[1]
- *Forbes*, 1996

Ignore market timers, Wall Street strategists, technical analysts, and bozo journalists who make market predictions . . . Admit to your therapist that you can't beat the market.[2]
- A financial columnist

Overview

Investors who use index funds (and thus do not beat the market) are more likely to be successful investors than most of those who attempt to beat the market. The reason why is that index funds provide a better investment return after expenses, costs, commissions and taxes with a minimum amount of stress. This is the goal of many long term investors and the most efficient and effective way to achieve it is to invest in a portfolio of index funds.

An Indexer Does Not Need To Predict The Future Or Beat The Market To Be Successful

An investor who uses index funds does not need to predict the future in order to be a successful investor. Nevertheless, an indexer believes in three general predictions about the future of financial markets.

First, an indexer believes that it is not possible to identify anyone today who can accurately predict in a consistently profitable way the magnitude of future movements in stock or bond prices. This is true whether such fluctuations occur tomorrow, much less over the next 90 days or twenty years. After all, the 53 stock market declines of 10% or more in this century have occurred in entirely unpredictable ways. So how is it possible to have any degree of confidence that we can name those today who will successfully identify future declines in financial markets? It is for this reason that an indexer ignores those in the investment information system who make forecasts about the performance of mutual funds (or individual stocks and bonds) or who predict the future specific course of markets.

Second, an indexer believes that riskier asset classes will outperform less risky ones over the long run. This conviction that the historical risk/return relationships among asset classes in financial markets will be maintained isn't based on any crude guesses about the future. Instead, it rests on the permanency of human nature in how it assesses the full spectrum of investment risk. Furthermore, an indexer does not attempt to predict the specific "spread" between the returns of asset classes because this would only amount to guesses about the future.

The third belief about the future of financial markets held by an indexer is that, despite their entirely normal but unpredictable ups and downs, the value of stock asset classes that comprise stock markets will increase over the long run. This growth, which is efficiently captured by index funds, is a reflection of the enormous vitality of an ever expanding capitalist economy.

Nor does an indexer need to beat the market in order to be a successful investor. In fact, an indexer (who doesn't need to predict the future because he doesn't try to beat the market) is likely to be a more successful investor than most active investors (who must accurately predict the future in order to beat the market).

A Summary Of Reasons Why Investors Should Invest In Index Funds

An investor who participates in the second wave of the indexing revolution obtains the many advantages offered by index funds. The principal advantage is straightforward. Over the long run, an investor using index funds will likely obtain greater net investment performance with less stress than most investors who invest in portfolios of actively-managed mutual funds or individual stocks and/or bonds. The principal reason for this is that financial markets are zero sum games where the average indexed dollar will always outperform the average actively-managed dollar, after costs and taxes. (We know from Chapter Three that this is a mathematical certainty.)

The following is a brief summary of the reasons why investors should invest in index funds. They clearly show why indexing investment strategies are the best choices for most investors.

The Best Way Of Implementing An Asset Allocation Policy

Investment experts widely agree that asset allocation is the overwhelmingly most important determinant of variance in investment performance. The best way for an investor to implement his portfolio's asset allocation policy is to use index funds.

The manager of an index fund keeps it invested solely in the investments that comprise a particular asset class. As a result, the index fund efficiently and effectively captures the investment performance of the entire asset class. This ensures that an investor can more reliably implement an asset allocation policy with index funds. It also makes it easier to rebalance a portfolio and thus manage and maintain its asset allocation over time through changing market conditions.

An actively-managed mutual fund does not remain constantly invested in the same asset class and thus cannot reliably capture the performance of any particular asset class. Instead, its manager invests in unpredictably different asset classes in unpredictably different proportions because of attempts at outperforming the market. The most spectacular recent example of this is Jeffrey Vinik who was the manager of Fidelity Magellan. He made the wrong bet in attempting to beat the market when he increased the fund's investments in bond asset classes. Examples such as this are why investors who invest in active funds are hard-pressed to formulate and maintain reliable long term asset allocation policies.

Reduction Of Investment Risk

Investors who hold properly diversified portfolios of index funds can reduce investment risk in two ways. The first way is at the *individual fund* level. An index fund manager achieves this by holding all (or a representative sample) of the stocks or bonds that comprise an asset class. The second way that indexers can reduce investment risk is at the *portfolio* level. Proper diversification among the different asset classes held in an index portfolio reduces the risk of the entire portfolio.

In comparison, portfolios of actively-managed funds are relatively underdiversified at *both* the individual fund and portfolio levels. Managers of active funds often concentrate their investments in certain sectors of the market. This, by definition, makes them underdiversified. But even active funds that are more broadly invested do not reduce the risk of a portfolio as well as index funds. As a result, active mutual fund portfolios and portfolios of individual stocks and/or bonds are inherently riskier than index fund portfolios.

Minimization Of Investment Costs

Once the high costs (and taxes) of active investing are taken into consideration, most investors (whether amateur or professional) are not likely to outperform the market return. In fact, it is much more likely over the long run that they will underperform the market return (and indexers who earn that return). It is important to remember that this is true whether the market in question is a zero sum *efficient* market or a zero sum *inefficient* market.

The annual management fees of index funds are significantly lower than those of active funds. Since index fund managers do not attempt to beat the market, such fees are minimized as computers and mathematical formulas take the place of highly paid stock pickers and market timers that are employed by active funds.

The sales costs of index funds are much lower than those of active funds. Index funds are sold directly to the public so they don't carry commission loads. But approximately 50-60% of active stock funds charge loads of 3% to 8.5% of the value of any fund shares purchased by investors.[3] The money generated by the loads is used to reimburse vast numbers of salespeople that have successfully convinced investors to buy shares in active funds.

Apart from their expense, the commission loads that active funds charge are confusing to many investors. Active funds frequently offer a number of classes of shares that differ only in the kind of load that they carry. For example, an active fund may offer one class of shares that carries a front load and another that carries a back load. Many investors are led to believe that they will pay a smaller commission load if they purchase shares with a back load (class B shares) instead of shares with a front load (class A shares). But there is virtually no difference in the amount of commission paid. Different classes of shares only represent different ways to pay the same amount of load. Since index funds do not carry commission loads, indexers do not have to decipher this alphabet soup.

Index funds do not impose 12b-1 fees on their shareholders. But active investors annually fork over billion of dollars in such fees for the sole purpose of paying for the advertising and marketing costs of active funds. Even certain active mutual funds that are permitted to designate themselves as "no load" may impose an annual .25% 12b-1 fee on their shareholders.

The trading costs of index funds are also significantly lower than active funds. A low turnover index fund may incur trading costs of only .05% (5/100ths of one percent). An index fund manager trades stocks only when he buys them for, or sells them from, the fund to match the changes that are made in the fund's underlying index. Index funds also trade stocks when fund investors invest and reinvest in fund shares and (more rarely) cash out of them. In contrast, managers of active funds often run up excessive trading costs in their stock picking attempts to beat the market. The investors in active funds also typically engage in heavy stock trading which further increases trading costs. The average active stock fund incurs annual trading costs of about 1.00% - or twenty times more than that of a low turnover index fund.

It is important for investors to understand that the advantages of low investment costs (as well as taxes) enjoyed by index funds do not depend on the fleeting nature of investment skill (or luck). They are not even sensitive to a particular time period. In fact, they are working *for* indexers *all* the time. But the high management fees, commission loads and trading costs burdening many active funds are *constantly* working *against* the investment returns of their shareholders.

Minimization Of Taxes

In general, index funds are tax efficient and active funds are tax inefficient. The best clue in determining a mutual fund's tax efficiency is its portfolio turnover. Since the correlation between portfolio turnover and after-tax investment performance is not proportionate, though, it is far from a perfect indicator of tax efficiency. In spite of this, low turnover index funds post superior after-tax performance in comparison to active funds that incur high turnover.

An index fund's portfolio turnover is typically low because its manager does not try to beat the market. He buys and sells relatively few stocks which means less capital gains and thus a lower tax bill for the fund's investors. But the manager of an active mutual fund attempts to beat the market. This heavy stock picking typically produces capital gains which generate taxes. The result can seriously impact an active fund's investment performance when it is held outside a tax-deferred retirement plan or annuity.

It is true that some active funds have low portfolio turnover which makes them more tax efficient than others. However, the low turnover of these funds is often deceptive because it is not consistent. Active funds that feature low turnover in some years may have relatively high turnover in other years. Indexers do not face this problem. They will always be invested in mutual funds that feature low turnover and are sensitive to the adverse impact of taxes on investment performance.

It is also true that there are active funds that have high turnover yet are still tax efficient. This is made possible by the fact that these funds offset their realized gains with realized losses which produces a low tax bill for their investors. Unfortunately, such activity often requires active fund managers to make a large number of trades which sharply drives up both visible (brokerage commissions) and invisible (market impact costs and bid-ask spread costs) trading costs. This problem, which can even severely impair the investment performance of mutual funds held in *tax-deferred retirement plans and annuities*, is often overlooked by active investors.

Reliable Investment Performance

An investor who holds a portfolio of index funds is assured of the reliable investment performance of the market. An index fund invested in the investments that comprise an asset class will reliably earn the returns of that asset class. Thus, indexing *delivers what it promises* to investors.

In comparison, returns of active funds are more erratic and thus riskier than index funds - sometimes outperforming the market and sometimes underperforming it. These variations in performance are caused by the market unpredictably favoring or disfavoring for unpredictable periods of time the particular stocks held by an active fund. They can also result from changes in the management personnel of an active fund or in its investment strategy (i.e., modifying the asset class mix of the fund or altering its overall investment strategy). Stock picking and market timing fund managers unpredictably beaten by the market must explain to their shareholders the *broken promises* of their "I can beat the market" investment strategies.

Less Stress

Indexing investment strategies generally cause less stress for investors than active investment strategies. Indexers can maintain their investment strategies with more peace of mind since they are always assured that they will earn the market return. The fact that indexing has proven itself to be an investment winner over the *past* also helps reduce the stress of indexers. The emotional well-being of indexers is further enhanced by the fact that indexing will remain an excellent investment strategy in the *future*. This is primarily true because of the mathematical certainty that indexers will always outperform active investors as a group, after costs and taxes.

In contrast, active investors often undergo the emotional roller-coaster of getting beaten by the market as they pick losing mutual funds (and individual stocks and bonds) and mistime markets. Efforts to overcome such losses usually involve trading out of these investments and into others. (This is why active investors are generally not buy and hold investors. One study has found that the average length of time that an active investor remains invested in a mutual fund is only 2-4 years.[4]) The problem with such efforts is that they can severely impact investment performance because trading is costly.

Even a good number of persons invested in *winning* active funds may experience stress. They are often left wondering whether they should be invested in other active funds (or should follow other hot fund managers) that are achieving even higher returns. This insecurity is constantly fed by the investment information system which will *always* be able to show these investors that they could have been better off in different active mutual funds. For many active investors, winning can often be just as stressful as losing!

A Simple And Understandable Investment Strategy

Indexing is a relatively simple and readily understandable investment strategy. Since indexers have given up the pretense that they can beat the market, they can concentrate on assembling and maintaining portfolios that efficiently build long term wealth. In comparison, active investors often go from one active investment strategy to another in their quest to beat the market. They are usually too frustrated from trying to pick the top winning strategy to ever focus on a truly understandable long term investment strategy. In addition, active investment strategies often require investors to spend a large part of their waking hours reading corporate annual reports, analyzing price/earnings ratios and worrying about the direction of interest rates.

An Easier Way To Track Investment Performance

It is easier to track the performances of index funds (each of which invests in the investments that comprise a specific asset class) against their respective underlying indexes. Since each of these indexes reflects the performance of the investments that comprise a specific asset class, the return earned by an index fund usually ends up being virtually the same as the fund's index. This makes it simple for indexers to see how their portfolios are performing.

The performances of active funds are difficult to track against *any* index. The reason for this is that active funds invest in multiple asset classes at different times. But an index such as the S&P 500 reflects the performance of only one asset class. Since comparing the performances of many active funds against this index (or any other) is therefore like comparing apples to oranges, active investors have a hard time keeping track of how their portfolios are performing. (Despite this, the performances of most active funds are compared to the S&P 500.)

Increased Leveraging And Compounding Of Investment Wealth

Investors who invest in index funds can maximally leverage their investments and thus more efficiently compound investment wealth. Since index funds carry no cash reserves, indexers are invested 100% in the market at all times. (This is not to say that cash should not be part of any investment strategy. But it is better for investors themselves to keep cash reserves and not look to mutual funds to do it for them. After all, investors invest in stock mutual funds because they want to invest in the stock market, not in cash.) Indexers are also better able to leverage their investments because they can invest the money that they would otherwise need to pay the commissions and high annual expenses and taxes associated with active mutual funds.

These two factors that characterize index funds - no cash reserves and low costs and expenses - mean that more of their hard-earned dollars immediately go to work for indexers. These small additional amounts of money compound through the years and, when added to the reliable long term performance of the market, help to accelerate the accumulation of wealth.

Investing The Same Way As Some Of The Largest And Most Sophisticated Investors In The World

We have seen that large and sophisticated institutional investors such as corporate pension plans and educational endowment funds made up the vanguard of the indexing revolution a quarter century ago. Having many billions of dollars under management, they can certainly afford to hire any money manager in the world. Yet they continue to index a substantial amount of their investments. With the introduction of increasingly greater numbers and kinds of index mutual funds, individual investors can follow the lead of these giant institutions and enjoy the same investment advantages.

A Statement By A Well Known Investment Authority Can Be Understood To Make The Case For Indexing

Don Phillips, a well known investment authority, is the president of Morningstar. He often cautions investors about Morningstar's 5-star method of rating mutual funds. Phillips warns that these ratings, which measure past performance, should not be used by themselves to attempt to find mutual funds that will beat the market in the future. Why? Because as Phillips puts it:[5] *"Funds aren't static, managers come and go, strategies evolve, you can expect regression to the mean."* Upon closer examination, this short and notably revealing statement can also be understood to make the case as to why investors should invest in index funds.

"Funds aren't static." This is certainly true of actively-managed mutual funds. After all, those who manage these funds do not want to be perceived as "static" investment managers. If they were, they wouldn't be able to justify their high management fees and other investment costs. That's why they must remain "in motion" and constantly scramble to think up and implement new investment strategies to try to beat the market. These many efforts increase investment costs as well as taxes.

But index funds *are* static for the simple reason that their goal is not to beat the market. Instead, they remain invested in the investments that are represented in indexes so that they can provide the performance of these indexes. This saves investment costs and minimizes taxes which enhances the bottom line investment performance of index funds.

"Managers come and go, strategies evolve." This is a weakness common to many actively-managed mutual funds. Every time a new fund manager takes the place of an old one, there is the chance that he will modify the fund's asset class mix or change its investment strategy. This can further increase the uncertainty of whether the investors in an active fund will beat the market and meet their investment goals. As a result, active investors can experience a lot of stress precisely *because* "managers come and go, strategies evolve."

Since indexers focus on matching the market's return, they do not experience the stress created by the uncertainty of whether or not they will beat the market. It makes no difference to them whether the managers of an index fund "come and go" because the fund's strategy never "evolves." It always remains the same - to provide the performance of the investments represented in the index tracked by the fund.

"You can expect regression to the mean." "Regression to the mean" is really just another way of saying that "things eventually return to normal." In the investment field, this means that superior-performing active mutual funds (as well as individual stocks) tend to become average performers. (We saw in Chapter Six that even a superstar stock picker such as Peter Lynch was already regressing to the mean (average) *well before* he left as manager of Fidelity Magellan.) Actually, once their excessive costs and taxes are taken into account, the performances of most active funds regress to *less* than the mean performance of the market.

However, since index funds bear low costs and taxes, they stay virtually *at* the mean performance of the market. This makes them superior to most active funds.

SIMON SAYS: *Investors - Choose Your Weapons!*

In the investment world there are basically two kinds of investors. The first kind consists of active investors who believe that they can beat the market by stock picking and/or market timing. The second kind consists of indexers who believe that no one who can be identified today can be expected to beat the market.

Active investors attempt to score investment bull's-eyes by earning returns that beat the market. The weapons that they use in these attempts are active mutual funds. Indexers attempt to score investment bull's-eyes by earning the market return. The weapons that they use are index funds.

While active investors sometimes score bull's-eyes, it is virtually guaranteed that indexers will always score bull's-eyes. So over time, it is likely that indexers will shoot cumulatively higher scores than most active investors. Yet the media focuses on the temporarily winning active funds that score the more spectacular bull's-eyes, not index funds that score every year and accumulate less flashy, but ultimately winning, scores.

So investors, choose your weapons! *Will they be active mutual funds that sometimes score bull's-eyes but rarely meet their target of beating the market over the long run? Or index funds that not only nearly always score bull's-eyes and meet their target of earning the long term market return, but also are likely to outperform most active mutual funds?*

Nine Myths About Index Mutual Funds

Myth 1: Indexing Guarantees Investment Mediocrity

On the contrary, indexing is not a mediocre investment strategy. Its superior performance has been proven beyond doubt during the last quarter century by the inferior investment returns turned in by active investment strategies. For example, over the ten-year period from 1986 through 1995, 80% of actively-managed diversified stock mutual funds underperformed the S&P 500 index (and index funds tracking it).[6] (As noted in Chapter One, this percentage is probably far higher since it does not account for taxes and commission loads.) Other periods of longer duration produce similar results.

The *future* superiority of indexing is also guaranteed since financial markets are zero sum games. This destines active investors in the aggregate to the mathematical certainty of a net investment return less than the average market return earned by indexers.

Myth 2: Index Funds Are Riskier In Market Downturns

Not true. In fact, index funds are probably better investments to be in during market downturns than active funds. There are numerous reasons for this.

First, the lower costs and taxes of index funds make it likely that they will outperform most active funds over the long run. This is the principal reason why investors should be (and remain) invested in index funds - regardless of whether the market is soaring or falling. Thus, any margin by which active funds outperform index funds in market downturns become rather transitory, particularly from the perspective of an investor who has a long investment time horizon.

Second, the actual historical record is mixed as to whether index funds go down more in value during market downturns than active funds. In some declining markets index funds do go down more in value but in other such markets active funds go down more in value. Yet even when index funds go down more in value, the amount is not anywhere near what the investing public is led to believe.

Third, because market downturns are wholly unpredictable, active funds will be caught in them the same as index funds. While active fund managers admit this, they note that they have greater flexibility in getting out of a declining market in order to limit their losses than index fund managers who must always remain fully invested. They maintain that they can pay off departing shareholders with cash and thus avoid the need to sell off fund holdings at fire sale prices. But in reality, active fund managers don't reduce their cash reserves. As a result, they have to sell off fund holdings at reduced prices which increases their losses in market downturns.

Fourth, even though the cash cushion held by active funds helps them to limit losses in declining markets, it becomes a deadweight loss in ensuing market recoveries.

Myth 3: Indexing Is Just A Fad

If indexing is a fad, it must be the investment world's longest-running fad. Indexing has proven itself as not only a viable, but a superior, investment strategy over a long period of time. Institutional investors index about one-third of the money that they invest in stocks. S&P 500 index funds alone have increased their assets six-fold to $105 billion in less than four years.[7] It is obvious that indexing is not only here to stay, but will continue to take an increasing amount of market share from active investment strategies.

Even Fidelity Investments, that bastion of actively-managed mutual funds, has jumped on the indexing bandwagon. Ten years ago, a spokesman for Fidelity said that "indexing guarantees long term mediocrity." In response to the groundswell for indexing, Fidelity has added three more of those funds that guarantee long term mediocrity to the three index funds that it already offers.

Myth 4: Index Funds Are Inappropriate For Investing In Foreign And Other Less Researched And Inefficiently Priced Stocks

Active money managers maintain that many stocks such as certain foreign stocks, emerging markets stocks and small company stocks are not efficiently priced by the market. They say that this allows smart stock pickers to beat the market and outperform indexing strategies. But index funds often prove to be superior even when they are invested in foreign and other less researched and inefficiently priced stocks.

The reason for this has to do with investment costs. Active money managers face high costs when trading foreign and other less researched and inefficiently priced stocks. The amount of these costs usually cancels out the margin by which a skillful (or lucky) stock picker outperforms the market. Such costs are much lower for index funds invested in these kinds of stocks. This often translates into better net performance in comparison to active funds. In addition, the broad diversification of index funds invested in less researched and inefficiently priced stocks reduces the impact of poor performance that may be turned in by any one group of these stocks.

Because financial markets are zero sum games in which the average indexed dollar will always outperform the averaged actively-managed dollar after costs and taxes, index funds are the best choice for investing in *all* stocks (or bonds), whether they are priced efficiently or inefficiently.

Myth 5: The Investment Options Offered By Index Funds Are Limited

The investment options offered by index funds may have been limited two decades ago. But today, indexers have many investment options in addition to the blue chip stocks represented in the S&P 500. For example, two index funds track the Wilshire 5000 index which represents virtually the entire market value of all stocks traded in the United States. Indexing has also been extended to specific market sectors such as small company stocks and mid-size company stocks.

In addition, there are index funds that provide the investment performance of specific "styles" of investing such as "value" and "growth." There are even index funds that invest overseas in emerging markets stocks and other foreign stocks. Indexing is not just limited to stocks either. There are also numerous fixed-income index funds that satisfy the need for different indexing investment options. An increasing number of index fund options will be offered in the future as indexing continues to grow in popularity.

Myth 6: Index Mutual Funds Create A "Self-Fulfilling Prophecy" Of Success

Some critics of indexing warn that its growing popularity creates a "self-fulfilling prophecy" of success. In effect, they say that "too much money" chases the stocks in the S&P 500 index for no other reason than the fact that they are represented in this index. This favorable "pricing effect," critics maintain, causes the value of the S&P 500 to rise which in turn reinforces the motivation to invest more money in an index fund tracking the index. As more money continues to pour into an S&P 500 index fund it rises in value, which will cause it to 'unnaturally' outperform actively-managed mutual funds. According to this view, this fund is sure to fall like a house of cards once the market turns sour and investors stop investing in the stocks represented in the S&P 500.

Such thinking can be debunked by simple logic. The S&P 500 accounts for about 70-75% of the total capitalization of the stock markets in the United States. Thus, it should be no great surprise that the stocks in this index would attract a huge amount of available capital. It is also a fact (too often overlooked by those who know better) that the great bulk of money invested in the stocks of the S&P 500 - the index most commonly tracked by index funds - is not indexed money, but actively-managed money.

So if the stocks in the S&P 500 are affected by any unnaturally favorable pricing effects, they are caused by the much larger amounts of *actively-managed* money invested in the stocks of this index. For example, only 8% of the $200 billion of new money that flowed into stock mutual funds in 1996 was invested in S&P 500 index funds. So it is rather ludicrous to contend that index funds control the market when a large amount of the other 92% of the money went into actively-managed funds that are invested in the stocks of the S&P 500! Therefore, those seeking an explanation for the outstanding returns of the stocks represented in the S&P 500 index for 1995, 1996 and 1997 won't find it by pinning any "self-fulfilling prophecy" tag on indexing.

A specific example underscores the fact that it is not indexed money that affects the value of an index. In 1989, the S&P 500 soared 31.5%. That year, IBM had the largest market value of any stock in the S&P 500. Thus, index funds tracking the S&P 500 held more IBM stock than any other. If there was a pricing effect where a stock widely held by index funds inevitably goes up in price, IBM should have had a pretty good year - even outperforming the 31.5% return of the S&P 500. In fact, IBM was down 10% in value for 1989.

Two professors at the University of Chicago Graduate School of Business have published the only study that has specifically analyzed whether the stocks represented in the S&P 500 experience an increase in return just *because* they are in this index.[8] The 1993 study detected no evidence to support this idea.

In fact, the study found that a stock represented in the S&P 500 got there because of excellent investment performance *before* it was admitted to the index rather than after its admission. This finding directly contradicts the widespread but erroneous belief that increased investments in index funds create a self-fulfilling prophecy of success for stocks represented in an index such as the S&P 500.[9]

Myth 7: Index Mutual Funds "Unbalance" The Market

Another erroneous belief held by some investors is that because index funds only invest in stocks that make up an index, they somehow unbalance the market. If "unbalanced" is defined as being invested in too few stocks, it is *active* investors that are guilty of unbalancing the market, not indexers. For example, as noted before, far more money invested in the stocks of the S&P 500 is actively-managed money than indexed money. Indeed, many large institutional investors that actively manage money invest in fewer than 100 of the large blue chip stocks represented in the S&P 500.

In comparison, index funds *broaden* investments in financial markets and tend to be far less concentrated in a relatively few stocks as are active mutual funds. Sometimes fund managers purchase as many as 2,000 stocks for a really broad-based index fund. These include many small, less-capitalized stocks that are never touched by most active investors because they are perceived to be too "risky."

Just as Claude Rains tells his underlings to "round up the usual suspects" at the end of the movie, *Casablanca*, so, too, active money managers "round up the usual excuses." They periodically recycle these excuses to try to explain away their own underperformance of the market and the success of index funds. The notion that indexing somehow unbalances the market is just another one of those excuses.

Myth 8: Active Investors Have Greater "Bragging Rights" Than Indexers

When the market is up, it is understandable why many active investors brag at cocktail parties or on the golf course about their latest hot investments or colorful winning mutual fund managers. Because the subjects of all this bragging - unpredictable investment winners - never persist in their winning ways, active investors always run the risk of sounding foolish when these winners inevitably turn into losers.

Actually, it is indexing investment strategies that offer true bragging rights to investors since they are likely to beat most active strategies over the long run. Another reason for indexers' greater bragging rights is that they are among a relatively exclusive number of individual investors using the same successful investment strategies employed by most of the largest and most sophisticated institutional investors in the world. These two factors are *really* something that indexers can brag about to their friends and relatives.

Myth 9: Indexing Is A Boring Investment Strategy

This is not a myth, it is true! As Nobel Laureate Paul Samuelson puts it:[10] "Indexing is like watching paint dry or like kissing your sister. It's Dullsville. It just happens . . . " However, a boring investment strategy is not a bad thing. Actually, it should be as boring as, say, the state of one's own personal health. After all, when a person's doctor gives him the results of his annual physical exam, all that he wants to hear is the same old boring news that there's not a thing wrong with him. In the same way, an indexing investment strategy produces the same old boring news year in and year out that an indexer is efficiently earning the market return. But this news is welcome to an indexer because it portends that he will likely outperform most active investors over the long run.

Becoming An Indexer Is Only The First Step In Achieving Long Term Investment Success

An investor's decision to join the indexing revolution and invest in a portfolio of index funds is a major one. But it is only the first step on the road to achieving long term investment success. An indexer must also understand how to fashion an asset allocation policy that will accurately reflect his own unique tolerance for investment risk and best accomplish his financial goals. Once he has decided on an appropriate asset allocation policy, he must implement it with the right kinds of index funds. An indexer is further required to know when to rebalance his portfolio to ensure that his asset allocation is competently managed and monitored over time through changing market conditions. Mastering this process includes the need to properly handle any negative emotional reactions to the despair of down markets as well as any positive emotional reactions to the euphoria of up markets.

There are a number of other important issues that an indexer must be concerned about when investing his money. These include: (1) transitioning from actively-managed mutual funds to index funds, (2) balancing the need for better portfolio diversification against the potential consequences of increased costs and taxes, (3) deciding whether retirement plan investments and personal investments should be invested in different ways and, if so, how, (4) understanding the long term impact of inflation on investment performance, (5) determining the possibility of paying for children's educational costs while simultaneously saving for retirement and (6) handling cash flow issues.

Joining The Indexing Revolution

This book has explored the historical reasons for the indexing revolution. You learned that sophisticated institutional investors have long been committed to the indexing revolution. You read testimonials from leading investment experts about the superiority of indexing. You saw that index funds are increasing their market share and that indexing has spread to other parts of the world. You were shown the many inherent shortcomings of active investing - the traditional system of investing followed by most investors today. You were introduced to the many advantages of indexing and why it delivers what it promises.

So take action and join the second wave of the indexing revolution *now*. A knowledgeable investor using index funds to implement his asset allocation policy is likely to outperform most active investors over the long run with a minimum amount of stress.

Chapter Notes

[1] "Some Like It Hot, Some Like It Cheap" by Thomas Easton, *Forbes*, February 12, 1996, page 118. This quotation has been slightly edited.

[2] "Follow All These Money Resolutions, And You Might Not Need My Column" by Jonathan Clements, *The Wall Street Journal*, December 31, 1996, page 13.

[3] Most mutual funds that charge a front load maximize it at 5.75%. But as noted, some charge 8.5% and one, the Templeton Capital Accumulator, offered by the Templeton Group, charged investors a front load of 9.0% as of mid-1997.

[4] "1993 Quantitative Analysis of Investor Behavior" by Fund RATE Services of DALBAR Financial Services, Inc., January, 1995.

[5] "Are Five-Star Funds Black Holes?" by Eric J. Savitz, *Barron's*, June 6, 1994, page 35, quoting Don Phillips.

[6] According to Lipper Analytical Services, Inc.

[7] According to Vanguard as of mid-1997.

[8] "Survivorship Bias" by C.B. Garcia and F.J. Gould, *The Journal of Portfolio Management*, Spring 1993, pages 52-56.

[9] Yet the investment media remains intent on spreading this story. "The index funds buy, well, stocks in the indexes, and that makes the indexes go up and the index funds with them; that attracts more investors into the index funds, which gives the funds more money with which to buy stocks in the indexes, etc., etc., etc." "Hello, Dolly" by Alan Abelson, *Barron's*, March 3, 1997, pages 5-6. *The media's mindless repetition of this will not make it come true.*

[10] *John Bogle and the Vanguard Experiment* by Robert Slater (Chicago, Illinois: Irwin Professional Publishing, 1997), page 167.

APPENDIX

Stock and Bond Indexes

U.S. Total Market Indexes

Russell 3000 Index[1] This index is composed of 3,000 large U.S. stocks. It represents about 98% of the market value of publicly traded stocks in the U.S. It is value-weighted but is based on price changes only; it does not reflect dividends and other income. The eligibility of particular stocks for inclusion in the Russell 3000 is based on stock market value. Only common stocks representing companies domiciled in the U.S. and its territories are eligible for inclusion in the Russell 3000. Stocks traded on U.S. stock exchanges but domiciled in other countries are excluded from this index. Preferred stock, convertible preferred stock, participating preferred stock, paired shares, warrants and rights are also excluded. Trust receipts, royalty trusts, limited liability companies, Over-The-Counter Bulletin Board companies, pink sheets, closed-end mutual funds, limited partnerships which are traded on any of the exchanges are also ineligible for inclusion in this index. However, Real Estate Investment Trusts (REITS) and beneficial trusts are eligible for inclusion.

Wilshire 5000 Index[2] This index measures the performance of all stocks with readily available price data that are headquartered in the U.S. The Wilshire 5000 originally contained 5,000 stocks when it was created in 1971 but since then it has grown to include 7,368 stocks as of December 31, 1996. Not all stocks contained in the S&P 500 are found in the Wilshire 5000 because some S&P 500 stocks represent companies that are not headquartered in the U.S. (There are only about a dozen stocks that fit this category.) The Wilshire 5000 is a value-weighted index which is composed of about 82% New York Stock Exchange stocks, 16% Over-The-Counter (OTC) stocks and 2% American Stock Exchange stocks.

U.S. Large Company Stock Indexes

Russell 1000 Index This index is composed of the largest 1,000 stocks in the Russell 3000, representing about 89% of its total market value. The Russell 1000 is very highly correlated with the S&P 500. The Russell 1000 is value-weighted but is based on price changes only; it does not reflect dividends and other income.

Russell Top 200 Index This index consists of the largest 200 stocks in the Russell 1000. It is a "blue chip" index which represents about 66% of the total market value of the Russell 1000. The Russell Top 200 and the Russell Midcap together comprise the Russell 1000. The Russell Top 200 is value-weighted but is based on price changes only; it does not reflect dividends and other income.

Schwab 1000 Index[3] This index is composed of the 1,000 largest publicly traded U.S. stocks. It is value-weighted and accounts for about 90% of the market value of the U.S. stock market. The Schwab 1000 Index Fund, a "tax-managed" index fund that tracks the Schwab 1000 index, is extra sensitive to the adverse effect of taxes on fund performance. Thus, it will not as closely track its underlying index in comparison to an index fund that is relatively less concerned with taxes. On the other hand, a tax-managed index fund may very well outperform an index fund that is less sensitive to the effect of taxes on its performance.

Standard & Poor's 500 Composite Stock Index[4] This index is usually what investors refer to when they speak of measuring "the market return." It is composed of 500 stocks broken down into approximately 400 industrial, 40 utility, 40 financial and 20 transportation stocks. (At year-end 1996, there were 381 industrial, 40 utility, 67 financial and 12 transportation stocks represented in the S&P 500.) Stocks from the New York Stock Exchange, the American Stock Exchange and the Over-The-Counter Market are represented in the S&P 500. The S&P 500 represents about 70-75% of the total market value of all publicly traded stocks in the U.S. It is value-weighted and is highly, but not perfectly, correlated with the Over-The-Counter (OTC) market.

U.S. Medium Company Stock Indexes

Russell Midcap Index This index is composed of the smallest 800 stocks in the Russell 1000. It represents about 34% of the total market value of the Russell 1000. This index is value-weighted but is based on price changes only; it does not reflect dividends and other income.

Russell 2500 Index This index consists of the bottom 500 stocks in the Russell 1000 in terms of market value and all 2,000 stocks in the Russell 2000. It represents about 23% of the total market value of the Russell 3000. This index is value-weighted but is based on price changes only; it does not reflect dividends and other income.

Standard & Poor's MidCap Index This index is made up of 400 medium-value U.S. common stocks. The stocks in this index are not included in the S&P 500. This index is value-weighted.

Wilshire 4500 Index This index is composed of the Wilshire 5000 less the S&P 500. About two-thirds of the value of this index is composed of medium company stocks and about one-third of small company stocks. Thirteen stocks in the S&P 500 represent companies that have foreign headquarters, so as of December 31, 1996, the Wilshire 4500 contained 6,855 stocks. The Wilshire 4500 is a value-weighted index which is composed of about 58% New York Stock Exchange stocks, 38% Over-The-Counter (OTC) stocks and 4% American Stock Exchange stocks.

U.S. Small Company Stock Indexes

CRSP 9-10 Index This index, compiled by the Center for Research in Security Prices at the University of Chicago, is composed of deciles 9 and 10 of the New York Stock Exchange for the period of January 1926 through June 1962 (rebalanced semi-annually) plus American Stock Exchange equivalents for the period of July 1962 through December 1972 (rebalanced quarterly) plus NASDAQ OTC equivalents for the period of January 1973 through September 1988 (rebalanced quarterly). Since October 1988, the CRSP 9-10 Index has been known as the DFA/ CRSP 9-10 Index which is comprised of size deciles 9 and 10 of the NYSE plus AMEX and NASDAQ OTC equivalents.

National Association of Securities Dealers Automated Quotation Over-The-Counter Market (NASDAQ OTC) This is an index composed of more than 4,000 small company stocks.

Russell 2000 Index This index consists of the smallest 2,000 stocks in the Russell 3000 and represents about 11% of its total market value. It is value-weighted but is based on price changes only; it does not reflect dividends and other income. The Russell 2000 is also segmented into two "style" indexes: the Russell 2000 Growth Index and the Russell 2000 Value Index.

Schwab Small Cap Index This index is made up of the second 1,000 largest publicly traded U.S. stocks. It is value-weighted. The Schwab Small Cap Index Fund, a "tax-managed" index fund that tracks the Schwab Small Cap index, is extra sensitive to the adverse effect of taxes on fund performance. Thus, it will not as closely track its underlying index in comparison to an index fund that is relatively less concerned with taxes. On the other hand, a tax-managed index fund may very well outperform an index fund that is less sensitive to the effect of taxes on its performance.

Standard & Poor's SmallCap 600 Index This index is comprised of 600 stocks with small market capitalizations. It represents the market value of over 2,000 small company stocks contained in the *Standard & Poor's Stock Guide* database.

"Style" U.S. Stock Indexes

Russell Top 200 Growth Index This index contains stocks from the Russell Top 200 Index with a greater-than-average growth orientation. The stocks in this index are also members of the Russell 1000 Growth Index.

Russell Top 200 Value Index This index contains stocks from the Russell Top 200 Index with a less-than-average growth orientation. The stocks in this index are also part of the Russell 1000 Value Index.

Russell 1000 Growth Index This index contains those Russell 1000 stocks with a greater-than-average growth orientation. Stocks in this index tend to have higher price-to-book and price-earnings ratios, lower dividend yields and higher forecasted growth values than the stocks in the Russell 1000 Value Index.

Russell 1000 Value Index This index contains those Russell 1000 stocks with a less-than-average growth orientation. Stocks in this index generally have low price-to-book and price-earnings ratios, higher dividend yields and lower forecasted growth values than more growth-oriented stocks in the Russell 1000 Growth Index.

Russell Midcap Growth Index This index contains stocks from the Russell Midcap Index with a greater-than-average growth orientation. The stocks in this index are also members of the Russell Growth Index.

Russell Midcap Value Index This index contains stocks from the Russell Midcap Index with a less-than-average growth orientation. The stocks in this index are also part of the Russell 1000 Value Index.

Russell 2000 Growth Index This index contains stocks from the Russell 2000 Index with a greater-than-average growth orientation. The stocks in this index tend to have higher price-to-book and price-earnings ratios than those in the Russell 2000 Value Index.

Russell 2000 Value Index This index contains stocks from the Russell 2000 Index with a less-than-average growth orientation. The stocks in this index generally have lower price-to-book and price-earnings ratios than those in the Russell 2000 Growth Index.

Standard & Poor's/BARRA Growth Index[5] The S&P 500/BARRA Growth Index and the S&P 500/BARRA Value Index were developed to track the two principal investment "styles" followed by many investors in the U.S. stock markets. The stocks in the S&P 500 are split into two mutually exclusive groups based on a single factor: price-to-book ratio. "Price" refers to the price of the company's stock. It is determined by the stock market. "Book" refers to the value of the company. This value, total assets (such as plant and equipment, inventories and receivables) minus liabilities, is fixed by the company itself. The Growth Index contains stocks with higher price-to-book ratios. This index, like the S&P 500, is market value-weighted.

Standard & Poor's/BARRA Value Index The Value Index contains stocks with lower price-to-book ratios. Like the S&P 500, this index is market value-weighted. The stocks are split into two groups so that about half of the market value of the S&P 500 is in the Value Index and half is in the Growth Index. However, a greater number of companies are classified as value than growth because growth companies tend to have larger market values.

U.S. Bond Indexes

Lehman Brothers Aggregate Bond Index[6] This index, composed of a wide spectrum of fixed-income investments, is made up of the intermediate and long term portions of the Lehman Brothers Government/Corporate Index and the Lehman Brothers Mortgage Backed Securities Index. It consists of more than 5,000 taxable government, investment-grade corporate and mortgage-backed securities. About 50% of the index is comprised of government Treasuries, 30% mortgage-backed securities and 20% corporate bonds. Many of these securities are not readily marketable. Because it is far too costly to exactly duplicate the holdings found in this index, index fund managers don't hold an exact cross-section of it. Instead, they seek to provide the performance of the index by using sophisticated computer programs that sample certain securities in the index based on maturity, credit quality and industrial sector.[7]

Lehman Brothers Long Treasury Bond Index This index consists of all outstanding U.S. Treasury bonds with maturities of 10 to 30 years. This index is value-weighted.

Lehman Brothers Government/Corporate Index This index consists of all publicly issued, fixed-rate, non-convertible domestic bonds. The bonds in this index must be rated at least BBB, have a maturity of at least a year and have certain minimum principal values.

Salomon Brothers Broad Investment Grade Bond Index[8] This index represents all U.S. Treasury, agency and mortgage bonds as well as corporate bonds traded by institutions. These bonds must carry a rating of at least BBB- or better, have remaining maturities of at least one year or longer and have certain minimum principal values. This index is value-weighted.

Salomon Brothers High Grade Bond Index This index is composed of about 800 industrial, financial and utility bonds. These bonds must carry a rating of at least AA or AAA and have maturities of at least 12 years. It is weighted by the remaining principal amount of each bond issue.

Foreign Large Company Stock Indexes

Financial Times All-Share Index Created in 1962, this index is the most widely quoted index in Great Britain. Published by the *Financial Times*, London's leading daily financial newspaper, it tracks the price movements of about 900 stocks listed on the London Stock Exchange (officially known as The International Stock Exchange of the United Kingdom and the Republic of Ireland (ISE)). The London Stock Exchange is positively correlated with the U.S. stock markets. More than 80% of the stocks in this index are not listed on any stock exchange in America.

Financial Times 100 Index This index, created by the *Financial Times*, is composed of the 100 largest capitalized stocks on the London Stock Exchange. Some index fund managers prefer to track this index rather than the All-Share Index because the stocks listed in it are more liquid and thus the costs to track it are lower.

Morgan Stanley Capital International EAFE Index[9] This index is made up of about 1,000 stocks traded on 20 stock exchanges in Europe, Australia, New Zealand and the Far East. This index also includes U.S. and Canadian stocks. The EAFE index overlaps the London and Tokyo indexes, but because it includes stocks representing companies from the major countries of Europe and the Far East, it is much broader. The EAFE is somewhat positively correlated with U.S. stock markets. It is value-weighted and is expressed in U.S. dollars.

Morgan Stanley Capital International Europe Index This index is composed of about 600 stocks traded on the stock exchanges of 14 European countries. It is value-weighted and is expressed in U.S. dollars.

Morgan Stanley Capital International Pacific Index This index is made up of about 350 stocks traded on stock exchanges in Japan, Hong Kong, Singapore and Malaysia. It also includes about 70 Australian and New Zealand stocks.

Morgan Stanley Capital International-Europe, Australia, Far East + Select Emerging Markets (Free) Index This index consists of stocks listed in twelve stock markets. Six of these markets are located in Southeast Asia (Hong Kong, Indonesia, Malaysia, the Philippines, Singapore and Thailand), three in Latin America (Argentina, Brazil and Mexico) and three in Europe (Greece, Portugal and Turkey). Currently, the value of this market-weighted index is allocated as follows: 44% to Southeast Asian stocks, 12% to Latin American stocks and 44% to European stocks.

Nikkei Stock Average This index, the most widely followed stock index in Japan, is composed of 225 stocks in the First Section of the Tokyo Stock Exchange (TSE). These particular stocks are extensively traded and thus highly liquid. They make up about 60% of the total market value of the 1,100 stocks listed in the First Section of the TSE. The Nikkei Stock Average is price-weighted like the Dow Jones Industrial Average, unlike the S&P 500 which is value-weighted.

Schwab International Index This index is composed of 350 of the largest publicly traded stocks from all over the world. The Schwab International Index Fund, a "tax-managed" index fund that tracks the Schwab International index, is extra sensitive to the adverse effect of taxes on fund performance. Thus, it will not as closely track its underlying index in comparison to an index fund that is relatively less concerned with taxes. On the other hand, a tax-managed index fund may very well outperform an index fund that is less sensitive to the effect of taxes on its performance.

Tokyo Stock Exchange Index (TSE) Stocks listed on the TSE are divided into the First Section, Second Section or Foreign Section. The First Section index of the TSE is made up of about 1,100 Japanese stocks, most of which are banking stocks and a few large industrial stocks. The Second Section index is composed of about 425 stocks. Both the First Section and the Second Section indexes of the TSE are value-weighted and calculated in similar fashion to the S&P 500. Most Japanese pension stock managers use this index to gauge their investment performance in much the same way that American money managers peg their performances to the S&P 500. All foreign stocks are listed in the Foreign Section and are thus not part of the TSE. The TSE is positively correlated with the U.S. stock markets.

Foreign Emerging Markets Indexes

Morgan Stanley Capital International Select Emerging Markets (Free) Index
This broadly diversified index represents stocks of over 450 companies located in Southeast Asia, Latin America and Europe.

Foreign Bond Indexes

J. P. Morgan Government Bond Index This index includes bonds issued by governments in fifteen countries. These countries include Australia, Belgium, Canada, Denmark, France, Germany, Ireland, Italy, Japan, the Netherlands, New Zealand, Spain, Sweden, the United Kingdom and the United States. The index tracks only those bond issues that are "investable," or readily available for purchase at actively quoted prices. Of all the non-U.S. fixed-income domestic government bonds in the world, about 60% are considered to be "investable." Introduced in 1989, this index is value-weighted. Inclusion of U.S. government bonds in this index does not strictly make it a "foreign" index.

Salomon Brothers World Government Bond Index This index tracks the performance of government bonds from fifteen countries. These countries include Australia, Austria, Belgium, Canada, Denmark, France, Germany, Italy, Japan, the Netherlands, Spain, Sweden, Switzerland, the United Kingdom and the United States. A country's eligibility for this index is based on market capitalization of the bond's issued by the governments and the ease by which institutional investors may transact in the government bond market. Introduced in 1984, this index is value-weighted. Inclusion of U.S. government bonds in this index does not strictly make it a "foreign" index.

Appendix Notes

[1] The following and all other information concerning the Russell Indexes has been provided courtesy of the Index Group at the Frank Russell Company. The Frank Russell Company is the owner of the following trademarks: "Russell Midcap," "Russell Top 200," "Russell Top 200 Value," "Russell Top 200 Growth," "Russell 1000," "Russell 1000 Value," "Russell 1000 Growth," "Russell 2000," "Russell 2000 Value," "Russell 2000 Growth," "Russell 2500," "Russell 3000," "Russell Midcap Growth," "Russell Growth" and "Russell Midcap Value."

[2] Wilshire Associates Incorporated is the owner of the following trademarks: "Wilshire 5000," "Wilshire 4000" and "Wilshire 2500."

[3] Charles Schwab Corporation is the owner of the following trademarks: "Schwab 1000 Index," "Schwab Small Cap Index" and "Schwab International Index."

[4] Standard & Poor's Corporation is the owner of the following trademarks: "Standard & Poor's 500 Composite Stock Index," "Standard & Poor's 500," "Standard & Poor's," "S&P 500," "S&P," "500," "Standard & Poor's MidCap Index," "Standard & Poor's SmallCap 600 Index," "S&P 500 Depositary Receipt," "SPDR," "S&P/BARRA Growth Index" and "S&P/BARRA Value Index."

[5] *S&P 500 1994 Directory* (New York: Standard & Poor's, 1994), page 31.

[6] Lehman Brothers, Inc., is the owner of the following trademarks: "Lehman Brothers Aggregate Bond Index," "Lehman Brothers Mortgage Backed Securities Index," "Lehman Brothers Long Treasury Bond Index" and "Lehman Brothers Government/Corporate Index."

[7] "Indexing Works With Bonds, Too" by Howard R. Gold, *Barron's*, September 4, 1995, pages 33-34.

[8] Salomon Brothers is the owner of the following trademarks: "Salomon Brothers Broad Investment Grade Bond Index," "Salomon Brothers High Grade Bond Index" and "Salomon Brothers World Government Bond Index."

[9] Morgan Stanley & Co., Inc. is the owner of the following trademarks: "Morgan Stanley Capital International Europe, Australia, Far East + Select Emerging Markets (Free) Index," "Morgan Stanley Capital International Select Emerging Markets (Free) Index," "MSCI EAFE," "EAFE Index," "EAFE," "Morgan Stanley Capital International Europe Index," "MSCI Europe Index," "Morgan Stanley Capital International Pacific Index" and "MSCI Pacific Index."

INDEX

- W -

- Y -

- Z -

ORDER FORM

- Telephone orders: Please call Toll Free at (888) 265-2732 (8-5 Central Standard Time, Monday-Friday) and have your Visa, MasterCard or AmEx credit card ready.

- Fax orders: (316) 442-9544 (24 hours a day, 7 days a week).

- Postal orders: Namborn Publishing Co., P.O. Box 3131, Camarillo, California 93011-3131, Telephone (805) 987-7161. Call this number for information on volume discounts.

- Internet orders: http://www.amazon.com

SHIP TO:

Name: _____

Company Name: _____

Address: _____

City: _____ , _____ State: _____ Zip: _____

Telephone: (   ) _____

Payment:
- Check _____ (please make payable to Namborn Publishing Co.)
- Credit card: VISA _____   MasterCard _____   AmEx _____

Card number: _____

Name on card: _____ Expiration Date: _____ / _____

Signature: _____

Please send me: *Index Mutual Funds: Profiting from an Investment Revolution*

Number of Books:	_____
x $26.95 per book:	$ _____
SUBTOTAL:	$ _____
SALES TAX:	$ _____
(For books shipped to a California address, please add 7.25% sales tax to subtotal)	
HANDLING CHARGES:	$ _____
($3.25 for the first book; add $1.00 for each additional book)	
SHIPPING COSTS:	$ _____
($3.00 per book sent USPS Priority Mail; please ask about other shipping alternatives)	
TOTAL ORDER:	$ _____